Industrial Strategy and Planning in Mexico and the United States

About the Book and Editor

The role of industrial planning in trade is one of the most important areas of dispute between Mexico and the United States. The official U.S. stance stresses the dominance of the marketplace, while official Mexican industrial policy demands a large and active government role. Although the United States espouses free trade in theory, in practice it responds to pressures from industry and labor by imposing uncoordinated restrictions on imports and often by providing government support. Mexico, usually more thorough and coordinated in its policy, has been forced by fiscal austerity and the noncompetitive posture of its industry to reconsider past programs. The contradictions faced by these two countries often result in policies that are indistinguishable in their effect on specific industries. Analyzing overall as well as industry-specific strategies in both countries, the authors explore ways to foster cooperation in the industrial arena and to reduce the damaging effects of existing policy.

Sidney Weintraub is Dean Rusk Professor in the Lyndon B. Johnson School of Public Affairs, University of Texas, Austin.

Industrial Strategy and Planning in Mexico and the United States

edited by Sidney Weintraub

Westview Press / Boulder and London

Westview Special Studies in International Economics and Business

----
This Westview softcover edition was manufactured on our own premises using
equipment and methods that allow us to keep even specialized books in stock.
It is printed on acid-free paper and bound in softcovers that carry the
highest rating of the National Association of State Textbook Administrators,
in consultation with the Association of American Publishers and the Book
Manufacturers' Institute.

Published in 1986 in the United States of America by Westview Press, Inc.;
Frederick A. Praeger, Publisher; 5500 Central Avenue, Boulder, Colorado 80301

Library of Congress Cataloging-in-Publication Data
Industrial strategy and planning in Mexico and the
   United States.
   (Westview special studies in international economics
and business)
   Includes index.
   1. Industry and state--United States. 2. Industry
and state--Mexico. 3. United States--Industries--Case
studies. 4. Mexico--Industries--Case studies.
5. Mexican-American Border Region--Industries.
I. Weintraub, Sidney. II. Series.
HD3616.U47I46   1986   338.972   86-18932
ISBN 0-8133-7268-2

Composition for this book was provided by the editor.
This book was produced without formal editing by the publisher.

Printed and bound in the United States of America

The paper used in this publication meets the requirements of the
American National Standard for Permanence of Paper for Printed
Library Materials Z39.48-1984.

6   5   4   3   2   1

Contents

PART 1
INDUSTRIAL STRATEGY

PART 2
INDUSTRY STUDIES

Tables and Figures

xii

Dedication:
To Stanley R. Ross

The *Norteamericano* who conceived this volume with me
died before the work could be completed. He brought
distinction to it as he had during his lifetime to the
study of the history of Mexico.

This volume grew out of Stanley Ross's conviction that
the Mexican-United States relationship, whether political,
economic, social, cultural, or the combination of all of
these, need not be conflictual. Contrasting histories,
unequal development, different social structures, and separate
ways of approaching the wonder and challenge of life are
often adduced as leading to inevitable strife between the
two countries. Stanley did not think so,and the collaboration that led to this book is testimony to that conviction.

Scholars and governments are often antagonists.
Scholars are critics, and government officials are defenders.
This venture seeks to reconcile the two stances in the
critical pursuit of knowledge to assist in the formulation
of policy in both countries. Industry was chosen as the
focus of the collaboration because it is a sector in which
jobs must be created--especially in Mexico--if development
and social aspirations are to be met.

Stanley was a much-honored scholar. As an undergraduate
at Queens College in New York City, he was named a Queens
College Scholar, an honor granted only to persons from the
upper two percent of the senior class. He graduated from
Queens *summa cum laude*. He later received his Ph.D. in
history from Columbia University. He once told me that his
passion for Mexican history was stimulated by the great
scholar of Mexican social and economic history then at
Columbia, Frank Tannenbaum.

I do not want this dedication to be a *curriculum vitae*, but I do wish to stress how much Stanley was respected by Mexicans. He was awarded the Order of the Aztec Eagle Medallion in 1983. This is the highest honor that the government of Mexico can give to a foreign national. Earlier in 1983 he was honored by his Mexican peers and was elected a corresponding member of the *Academia Mexicana de Historia*. The *Instituto de Investigaciones Historicas* of the National Autonomous University of Mexico nominated him to receive a *Doctorado Honoris Causa* shortly before he died.

This book is a fitting memorial to Stanley. It represents scholarship in the service of two countries. The legacy that a teacher leaves is in the works he published, the ideas he propounded, the students he inspired, the teachers he stimulated, and the scholarly institutions he helped create. Stanley's contribution was immense in each of these ways. We at The University of Texas at Austin miss him and so do his colleagues throughout the United States and Mexico.

Sidney Weintraub
Austin, Texas

PART ONE

Industrial Strategy

1

Introduction

Sidney Weintraub

The Mexico-United States economic relationship is a mixture of conflict and cooperation. As trade and economic interaction between the two countries grew, so too did the conflicts; but there is also cooperation across a broad spectrum of economic activities. There is ample evidence of the cooperation. The United States is by far Mexico's most important trading partner and in recent years Mexico has become the third largest trading partner for the United States after Canada and Japan. Hundreds of U.S. companies divide their industrial production between Mexico and the United States, producing segments of final output in the country which has a comparative advantage for that part of the production. This co-production first focused on simple manufactures, like doing the hand work on textile products or the assembly of integrated circuits in Mexico, but is now proceeding in more varied production involving automobile engines, machinery, and petrochemical products. The two countries are financially linked. The level of U.S. interest rates forces changes in Mexico's economic policy, and the concern that Mexican companies and government agencies cannot meet debt obligations on time has brought about a profound change in U.S. financial regulations. When the Mexican economy was forced to slow down after 1982, as part of the medicine to correct the economic crisis, hundreds of thousands of workers in the United States were affected because Mexico could no longer buy the goods they produced.

Conflict is inevitable when two countries are so interdependent. This conflict is sharpened because this interdependence is asymmetrical; Mexico depends more on the United States than the reverse. Basic U.S. industries that are declining in output or employment, like steel,

3

automobiles, trucks and parts, and textile products, are
precisely those which are growing in Mexico. Comparative
advantage is a dynamic phenomenon. The one immutable rule
of economics is that change takes place constantly and is
unsettling. Some gain by change, but others lose. It is
not accidental that the deepest trade conflicts between the
two countries are in those industries in which the change is
reciprocal, in which the U.S. industry is declining in
relative and even absolute importance and growing in
vitality in Mexico. Governments act to help or deter this
process, but the process itself is less a matter of what
governments dictate than what economic efficiency mandates.
    The two countries have different approaches to
determining policy toward their industrial sectors. The
Mexicans have been inclined toward centralized planning.
While each recent administration has formulated its own
industrial plan--and its own overall economic and financial
plan--there is a certain continuity in method and substance.
Industrial policy in Mexico has meant selecting industries
for special treatment. At first these were consumer
industries for production at home to replace imports. As
Mexico advanced economically, the chosen industries became
more complex, like automobiles--still largely in the
consumer field, but durables. An import substituting
industrial policy does not imply that imports will no longer
be needed, but rather that their composition will change.
Mexico changed from an importer of finished consumer goods
to bringing in the raw materials and intermediate products
for its home production. Except in years of economic crisis,
U.S. exports to Mexico grew, but their composition changed.
There were winners and losers among specific firms in the
United States growing out of this change in Mexico.
    Mexico is now at another stage in its development.
Future government stimulation is intended for more
sophisticated industries, those producing capital goods,
complex machinery for agriculture, and higher derivatives of
petrochemicals. Mexico wishes to develop a microelectronics
industry and make progress in biotechnology research.
Industrial policy in Mexico signifies that the chosen
industries will receive subsidies from and protection by the
government. Industrial policy in Mexico operates explicitly
at two levels, at the macroeconomic level setting the
framework for the entire economy, and at the industry level,
making choices on industries to encourage. When some
industries are supported, others are discriminated against.
The latter aspect is implicit, but nevertheless evident.
    The U.S. approach is explicit at the macroeconomic

level, but not at the industry level. The debate that has been taking place in the United States during the past five to ten years on what is called "industrial policy" revolves around this industry specification. Should the United States become more like Mexico and expressly discriminate in favor of certain industries; and, if so, how should these choices be made? Should the favored industries be high-tech, those involving a large input of research and which require a pool of skilled labor, or should the emphasis be on restoring basic industries to health? The issue is not resolved in the United States.

The United States does have an industrial policy, but it is haphazard, as papers in this volume make amply clear. Each tariff, import restriction, subsidy, regulation, industry bailout, preferential export finance, price support, to cite some of the measures, is part and parcel of a micropolicy involving choice among industries. The U.S. tax code favors certain types of activities and implicitly discourages others. The large defense buildup is an industrial policy for what President Dwight Eisenhower called the military-industrial complex.

There is a difference between Mexico and the United States, but it is not just that one has specific policies favoring certain industries and the other does not. The differences are more subtle. They are the differences of explicit choice versus less organized discrimination. The one is based on the thesis that specific choice and government encouragement stimulates economic and industrial development, and the other rests on the conviction that the government's role is to set the overall macroeconomic policy framework leaving the specific decisions to the marketplace. In each case there is inconsistency at the margin, but the core of industrial policy is different. It is the difference between a system that consciously protects fledgling industries and one that argues in favor of maximum freedom of trade among nations but in practice also protects some industries because of internal pressures.

The essays in this volume explore the elements of inherent conflict and desirable cooperation between two countries that approach their industrial sectors from different philosophic vantages. The essays are both general in outlook and precise by industry. Each of the two nations is questioning whether past policies toward industry have been adequate. This questioning is reflected in the U.S. debate on industrial policy which, in essence, asks if microindustrial decisions should be added to macroeconomic measures to promote industrial competitiveness. Mexican internal questioning asks the reverse question, whether fewer microindustrial decisions should be made. This would involve, according to Mexico's 1984-88 industrial development plan, more efficient import-substituting industrialization focusing on intermediate and capital goods industries and gradually liberalizing imports for industries which have long enjoyed protection. In each case, the internal discussion revolves around the relative distribution of economic strengths and the dynamics of comparative advantage.

The two countries must now ask themselves about their optimum production structures. Trade flows would reflect these decisions. It was this series of issues, the changing industrial structures in the two countries and the willingness on both sides to question the suitability of existing national policies, that made this such a propitious time for a bilateral conference on industrial policy and strategy.

This was the first such conference of this type between the two countries. Several speakers commented during the conference, both at the workshop in Austin, Texas, in April 1984, and the conference in Cuernavaca, Morelos, in August 1984, that a bilateral gathering asking these questions would have been inconceivable five or even two years earlier.

Several other elements came together to make this a suitable time for the project. A new government had recently come to power in Mexico. A new program was being formulated searching for a balance between industrial innovation and competitiveness in foreign trade. In the United States, there was concern over the loss of competitiveness in many basic industries and what this portended for the economic health of the nation. There was concern over growing protectionism.

The project was the product of cooperation between the Mexican Government and academic institutions in the two countries. The Office for Mexican Studies of The University of Texas at Austin joined forces with the Mexican authorities to make the conference a reality.

The agenda for the conference was defined jointly. Each paper was prepared primarily from a national perspective. In that way a Mexican could discuss his own country and an American his country. Each author was asked to analyze the effect of alternative national policies on the other country. The final editing was by Sidney Weintraub, but the organizers also included Francisco Javier Alejo, Stanley R. Ross, and Rene Villarreal Arrambide.

William Diebold focuses on industrial policy in the United States. He notes that a collection of interventions by the government does not constitute an industrial policy, but that the collection is quite comprehensive. Although the term "industrial policy" has had virtually no resonance in official U.S. circles, individual actions affecting the structure of the U.S. economy have been common. Rene Villarreal, focusing on the Mexican situation, notes that a review of earlier industrial policy was made necessary by the crisis of 1982. The new strategy will aim at a balance between the industrial structure and foreign trade. The policy will seek to link industrial innovation with developments in other economic sectors.

Sidney Weintraub's paper traces key themes in U.S. trade policy and the content of the current trade/structural policy debate. After examining issues that have emerged in a variety of industries--automotive, textiles and clothing, and steel--he examines the future trade/industrial policy options open to each of the two countries and their effects on the other. His conclusion is that the increasing interaction between them requires that each consider the effect on the other in formulating policies.

Francisco Barnés and Lars Christianson review the background of the Mexican petrochemical industry. They believe that there is considerable scope for complementarity between the two countries in this sector as Mexico becomes an important supplier to the U.S. market for petrochemical products for generalized uses.

The essay on the steel industry by Gerardo Bueno, Gustavo Cortés, and Rafael Rubio traces the development of this industry in Mexico. The authors recount the encouragement given to the industry by the Mexican Government, the high degree of actual governmental participation, and problems for the industry created by the economic crisis in Mexico and the growth of U.S. protectionism. They expect steel relations between the two countries to be both conflictive and complementary in the future. The nature and duration of the economic recovery in each nation will determine which aspect dominates, whether conflict or cooperation. Robert Crandall discusses the competitive advantages enjoyed by developing countries in this industry. He also traces the changing nature of the industry in the United States. He devotes attention to the actions of the U.S. industry to protect itself from import competition.

Neil Schuster develops the complementation theme further by noting the substantial investment in Mexico by

U.S. companies and reliance on Mexico as a source of vehicle components. He emphasizes the interdependence of the two industries.

José Luis Fernández and Jesús Tamayo argue that Mexico's industrial development, by its inward orientation, has not yet made a decisive attempt to incorporate its periphery. The border industries are a cash generator, but still inadequately incorporated into Mexico's overall industrial strategy. Jerry Ladman examines the impact of binational developments on different border regions of the United States. He argues that the U.S. government has not developed a policy to encourage border industrialization, but that this is occurring nevertheless.

Clark Reynolds discusses Mexican uneasiness about inevitable interdependence. His policy recommendation is that the two countries should move steadily toward joint production and market sharing. Economic convergence, he believes, can take place through migration, trade, investment, co-production, and technology transfer. If all channels are not exploited, then the main channel will be migration from Mexico. Francisco Javier Alejo refers to the unique, asymmetric relationship between the two countries. Their separate histories and unequal economic development have led to different national perceptions. These differences must be recognized as the basis for cooperation which has the potential for mutual enrichment. He argues that the only development road that Mexico can follow is that of a mixed economy. His conclusion is that each country must allow dynamic comparative advantage to operate; this implies less import protection by each, but not an equal dismantlement of protection because of Mexico's lesser degree of development.

The bilateral relationship with the United States is the most important such relationship for Mexico. The United States has not given the same prominence to this relationship, but this is changing. The impact on the United States of the Mexican economic crisis of 1982 and the growing human and cultural links have made it clear that developments in Mexico profoundly affect the United States. Their industrial and trade interaction is but one aspect of how the two countries come together, but it is a crucial one. Studying this was the motivation for the conference.

2

Industrial Policy in the United States

William Diebold

"Happy is the nation that has no history." Whether Beccaria linked this thought with the pursuit of "the greatest happiness of the greatest number," a expression for which he is given credit, I do not know. But there is a group in the United States who say that the country should be happy because it has no history of industrial policy, while another group holds that much of the contemporary economic unhappiness is a consequence of the lack of an industrial policy.

This argument is new for the United States. Until recently, well-educated Americans may never have heard the term "industrial policy." The exceptions were apt to be people who studied what was going on in certain other countries, or came up against foreign industrial policies either in the course of business or as government officials engaged in negotiations about trade and investment. The last two groups were likely to think poorly of foreign industrial policy. It was seen as an excuse to evade commitments to liberalize trade or as a source of unfair advantage for one's competitors. American economists, heavily oriented toward macroeconomic policy, disliked industrial policy for its politicization and lack of good theory. These views are still widely held and have a good bit of truth to them.

Another major source of dislike of the idea of industrial policy is the belief that it calls for measures that are alien to the American system and that, if undertaken, would be badly managed and woefully politicized. Again, while there is substance to the latter point, the subject can no longer be disposed of that easily. What is new is that there are many voices calling for some kind of American industrial policy.

This new thinking has a number of sources. The 1970s were a time of troubles. Fiscal and monetary policies that had worked well since the end of the second World War failed to produce the expected results. An accumulation of difficulties focused attention on problems and policies that were only partly identifiable as questions of trade, investment, the environment, productivity, adjustment to costly energy, and the like. The decline of American competitiveness in a number of fields and the gains made by other countries suggested that the United States should take a dose of the same medicine that had worked elsewhere; often the mixture was labelled "industrial policy."

The word "structural" came to be used more and more frequently (and in a variety of ways[1]) and it was clear that much industrial policy throughout the world was concerned with the structures of national economies and the changing structure of the world economy. Insofar as "structural" meant "sectoral," it seemed the right word to apply to questions of whether the loss of American competitiveness was in part the result of clinging too long to an outdated pattern of production. One thing that needed to be done, according to this argument, was to move labor and other resources out of older industries challenged by more efficient producers in other countries. It followed that it was also necessary to make sure--by means that were not always clear--that resources, including capital to apply new technologies and R&D to produce them, were plowed into activities in which the United States could not only be competitive but could continue to lead the world. That all this could not be achieved by the government alone was clear, but many people thought it could also not be achieved unless the government helped and probably took the lead. What exactly the government should do was the subject of much disagreement. As people began to look at the possibilities, they saw--as some had already pointed out-- that the United States was already engaged in quite a few activities that in other countries were called "industrial policy."

Against the background of these developments, it was natural enough that the Carter administration, about midway in its term, should appoint an interdepartmental committee to dig into these issues. The Reagan administration swept all this away and tried to rely on other sorts of measures. Soon it had to pay attention to the difficulties of key industries, international competitiveness, and a number of other "structural" matters. Meanwhile, work on industrial policy increased outside the federal government, in business groups, universities, and, to a degree, states and cities. A significant number of people became educated about the issues and new ideas and analyses were put forward. Naturally enough, disagreements also increased about objectives, methods, and even terminology. Part of the logomachy is symbolic; some is pure confusion. This paper hopes to clarify at least some of the salient points.

In what follows we start with a rough outline of what industrial policy is--rather, what industrial policies can be, stressing the plural. Two major sections follow. One concerns the de facto industrial policy of the United States and the other the major changes that have been proposed. These are followed by a relatively brief discussion of international measures--existing and under discussion-- bearing on American industrial policy. Finally, there is speculation about the bearing of these issues on Mexican- United States relations.

THE SCOPE OF INDUSTRIAL POLICY

There is no generally accepted definition of industrial policy and we do not need one for this paper. It is enough to note some of the main objectives and methods of industrial policies and to sharpen the description by pointing out some things that are not industrial policy and how they are related to it.

On that note, the first firm line to be drawn is between industrial policy and the macroeconomic policies that have been the main concern of American economists for several decades. These are largely fiscal and monetary policies concerned with such major objectives as growth, stability, the broad allocation of the gross national product, inflation, interest rates, exchange rates, and, often enough, other intermediate targets concerned with the larger functioning of the economy.

Industrial policy is primarily concerned with other matters, so there is no reason to suppose that there is a necessary clash between it and macroeconomic policy. They are certainly not substitutes for one another. A failure in either is likely to cause trouble for the other; success in one can make the problems of the other easier to deal with. It is not impossible that some of the difficulties with American macroeconomic policies in the 1970s stemmed from a failure to deal with structural difficulties in the labor market, concerning energy, or whatever. Great success in macroeconomic policy--as in periods of strong growth, full employment, and price stability--often reduces the pressure for special measures of industrial policy because it opens opportunities and makes adaptation easier. One way of summarizing much of the difference between the two fields is to say that while macroeconomic policy may be concerned with creating full employment, industrial policy is concerned with what kinds of jobs people have and what they do.

No sharp line can be drawn between industrial policy and foreign trade policy. A general policy of trade liberalization and expansion, such as the United States has followed since 1934, can hardly be called an industrial policy. Nevertheless, it has had a great impact on the structure and performance of the American economy. The selective protection that has accompanied liberalization-- whether through not greatly reducing import barriers in certain industries or imposing special restraints (as in textiles since the 1960s and on other products for shorter periods)--has an industrial-policy dimension since it says that some industries should be supported in ways that others are not. To the extent that one can ascribe the protection or lack of it entirely to the political strength or weakness of the interests affected, one might dismiss the relevance of industrial policy. But as soon as a measure is justified by claims concerning the importance or special situation of the industry, area, or people involved, or some general national goal, then there is at least a gesture toward industrial policy thinking. Naked protection is no longer regarded as the natural order of things and a rationale for protective measures has to be given.[2] The focus may be the level of unemployment in a major industry or unfair competition from abroad, but it is often necessary to invoke a broader national interest in the future of the industry in question or the impact of its decline on the rest of the economy. It goes without saying that such claims may be self-serving, hypocritical, or unjustified, but it would be an odd field of public policy that could only be defined objectively and in cerebral terms and was immune to the play of politics.

Another industrial policy aspect of trade policy is the use of adjustment assistance to help the adaptation of the economy to shifts in trade and production and to cushion the impact of the removal of import barriers on the people most affected. When the United States inaugurated such measures in 1962 (not very successfully), they were related to the decision to make across-the-board, though not necessarily universal, tariff reductions instead of refraining from tariff cuts that might "injure" a particular industry, as had been the declared policy before then. There are also political considerations, since the availability of adjustment assistance may make politically and socially acceptable measures of import liberalization that would be rejected if they would otherwise force too much change, too quickly, or hurt some people more than the rest of the society thought decent or politically prudent.

Although industrial policy often involves interference with market forces, it can also take the form of stimulating competition and making markets work better. In many countries, the nurturing of a "national champion" in a certain field is deemed necessary to create an enterprise big enough to compete globally; in the United States, the antitrust laws exemplify an approach which stresses gains in efficiency in the economy through competition, however controversial the choice of criteria may be. If regulation of industry is industrial policy, so must deregulation be.

Although the antitrust laws apply generally (with certain exceptions), they mean different things in different industries. That is equally true of other measures directed at the performance of the economy generally, such as steps to increase productivity, labor market measures, training programs, much of the help for R&D, and, for that matter, many tax policies, especially in the allowances they make for investment (more useful to capital intensive industries than to others; different again if different kinds of investments are given quicker writeoffs, etc.).[3] Still other kinds of measures, such as those concerned with environmental regulations, regional and other locational concerns, the building and maintenance of infrastructure, cannot be thought of as narrow industrial policies, but one also cannot ignore the fact that their impact on the structure and performance of the economy gives them an industrial policy dimension.

As some of these examples suggest, industrial policies can concern the performance of the whole economy and not simply its structure. Nevertheless, much industrial policy is primarily structural in the sense that it is concerned with which kinds of activities are most desired. The criteria may be economic efficiency, employment, international competitiveness, security of supply, national security in the sense of supporting a defense establishment, or simply maintaining a diversity of activities judged healthy for the economy. These structural concerns often entail policies directed toward individual industries and such activity makes up a large part of industrial policy in many countries. The share is increased by the fact that governments are often slow to act until difficulties pile up, which tend to be concentrated (or apparent) in specific industries. Sometimes the focus is on individual enterprises. Some may be chosen instruments to pursue certain national industrial-policy goals. The existence of others may be threatened and their collapse judged unacceptable. In the latter case--bail-outs--there is apt to be a specific concern with the way labor and management in the concern have contributed to the difficulties and how they can be brought to help in removing them. As in a bankruptcy, creditors come into the picture and different types of creditors may be treated differently.[4] Whether policy focuses on an industry or a firm, the predictability of the response to what the government does is crucial but not easily assured (at least in the United States). Government guidance of business plays a large part in the industrial policy of some countries but goes against the mores of others (again the United States). Cooperation, or its lack, between management and labor is a basic fact that has to be taken into account in industrial policy. So do other interactions among groups in the economy and the distribution of power among them. Such facts shape the kinds of industrial policies different countries can effectively pursue; therefore, it can often be said that industrial policy is not simply what the government does but how the whole nation behaves.

Sectoral policies are unlikely to be uniform for all sectors in the same country. Andrew Shonfield has argued that discrimination is the essence of industrial policy. Quite different measures may be taken in different industries and the objectives may diverge as well. One is engaged in industrial policy when trying to keep an industry in being even if it requires permanent protection or subsidy or if one is trying to make an industry efficient or if one is helping with the removal of resources from an industry that is to be abandoned. Sectoral industrial policy measures may be taken to change the national pattern of production by introducing and nurturing new industries or fostering the growth of some that have not expanded as rapidly as is thought desirable.[5] The current concern in so many countries with becoming producers of high-technology products is a familiar example of this. Similarly, one can say that in developing countries a wide range of measures have to be thought of as industrial policies because their purpose is to change the structure of the economy.

Naturally, there are significant differences among the kinds of measures that can be used to pursue these diverse ends and in their costs, tradeoffs, probabilities of success, and consistency with which countries adhere to them. Measures taken in one field may be inconsistent with those in another. The intent of a policy may be different from its result. The policy may be a response to a problem, not the thought-through pursuit of a well-charted path expected to lead to a certain goal. Grover Cleveland spoke for many governments when he said, "we face a condition, not a theory." One of the most trenchant French critics of French industrial policy said, "a collection of interventions by the state does not necessarily constitute an industrial policy."[6] That seems reasonable but more countries have such collections than have comprehensive and consistent sets of policies. The original French Plan for modernization and reconstruction devised by Jean Monnet was an exception and the fading of that ideal was part of what prompted the remark just quoted.

From this rough and abbreviated sketch one can draw several conclusions about the discussion of industrial policy. (1) Rigorous definitions are neither realistic nor useful. (2) Though one may say "policy," one is more often dealing with "policies" or "measures" than with comprehensive and coherent lines of action that are consistently followed over long periods. (3) It is rarely a meaningful statement to say one is "for" or "against" industrial policy. All these conclusions pertain with particular force to the United States.

DE FACTO AMERICAN INDUSTRIAL POLICY

Certainly the United States does not have a full-blown, comprehensive, and thought-through industrial policy, much less a consistent or coherent one aimed at goals on which its people are agreed. There is no doubt, though, that there are any number of American measures that shape the structure and performance of the economy and that would in another country be called "industrial policy." Not all are clearly focused or well calculated to achieve specific results whose purpose is widely recognized and accepted. Not all that have such goals achieve them. Many produce significant side effects. Not infrequently industrial-policy measures have long outlived their original purpose and are sustained by momentum and vested interest.

Although the term "industrial policy" has virtually no place in American history, policies affecting the structure of the American economy have been common. From Alexander Hamilton's Report on Manufactures of 1792, through "internal improvements" stressing roads and canals in the early nineteenth century, and the later railroad policies that opened the West, on to the rather different kinds of measures used to regulate business and establish antitrust principles, Americans have argued about measures that in other countries would be called "industrial policy." Probably the tariff should be included in the list although it was more a reaction to events than the planned protection of infant industries that is sometimes depicted.[7] In this century, some elements of the New Deal and the conscious shaping of the economy for the needs of World War II (and on a smaller scale in the first World War) carry on the process.

In this paper, there is no need to try to draw detailed lessons from these historical matters.[8] One impression may be in order: when problems are big enough and are recognized, and especially when the manner of doing things that has served well in the past no longer seems adequate, Americans seem capable of breaking out of old patterns, experimenting, and departing from attitudes attributed to them by conventional wisdom (such as their supposed aversion to planning). That certainly was part of the explanation of the New Deal when the prosperity of the 1920s collapsed. The 1970s were quite different, but again old ways were challenged. The recovery of 1983-1984 may have taken the edge off such reactions, but the decade is not yet over.

At least one shift has taken place. The acceptance of the idea of a de facto industrial policy is now sufficiently well established to have displaced the conventional wisdom of only a few years ago that said that industrial policy was a completely alien concept in the United States because, with relatively minor exceptions, the country was committed to letting market forces direct the process of change. When the Organization for Economic Cooperation and Development (OECD) set about studying national industrial policies in the late 1960s, the official American view was that there really was no such thing because "the American philosophy of economic progress" had never called for coordinated government intervention.[9] In 1984, the Congressional Budget Office said, "The federal government extends financial aid to business as part of its constitutional duty to promote industry and commerce."[10] Although the report referred to only one aspect of industrial policy, its point of view was widely shared so that there was very nearly a new conventional wisdom.

Although the shift in thinking is marked, it is not easy to describe the de facto industrial policy of the United States. The rough sketch of the first section has already given some idea of what is involved; the United States does not engage in every one of the activities mentioned there, but it does take many such measures. On the following pages we can only deal in a selective fashion with some major elements. They are divided, somewhat arbitrarily, into categories that are not altogether coordinated: sectoral policies (those directed at individual industries); trade-related measures; investment policies; competition; R&D; and, finally, a miscellaneous group of measures concerned with labor markets, education, productivity, and some other elements.

Sectoral Policies

The oldest and best established American sectoral policy concerns agriculture and it is worth noting that its supposed success has been cited by some people as evidence of what a proper industrial policy should be. Another fairly old policy is support for the shipping and shipbuilding industries, largely on the grounds of national security. In other fields of transportation--roads, rail, air travel, and inland waterways--there are fairly clearly defined policies and a good bit of public support of one sort or another, but these are not often thought of as sectors. Fisheries, electric power (especially its introduction into rural areas), lumbering, mining (in general and with special attention to certain minerals), banking, securities and commodity trading, communications, and housing are other activities that benefit from what could be said to be American sectoral policies.

Large defense spending is often cited as an American industrial policy. There is no doubt that some industries have benefited, notably civil aviation and, in early phases, computers and other electronic sectors. But there is strong support for a contrary view that defense spending has diverted talent and other resources to non-competitive activities to a degree that has more than offset the advantages attributable to the spillover of defense spending to the civilian economy. Much the same can be said about the space program and putting a man on the moon. Energy--at least since 1973, but with some earlier history--has been the subject of various sectoral policies and can be said to show how hard it is to arrive at a comprehensive policy on these matters in the United States--and to carry it out.

In manufacturing, three sectors stand out: textiles, steel, and automobiles.[11] In each case the dominant policy has been protection, but the focus has been on the sector as a whole and there have been either some elements of additional sectoral measures or at least possibilities warranting discussion.

When the problems of the cotton textile industry moved the Kennedy administration to seek an international agreement permitting special trade restraints, there were a number of lines of action under consideration that were intended to make the industry more internationally competitive and generally more efficient. These included various forms of government aid, labor-management cooperation, and some possible restructuring. Once the trade controls were in place, little attention was given these matters, although some analysts believe that government-financed technical assistance played a significant part in modernizing a number of small firms. In the early years of this exceptional protection, company officials frequently complained that the antitrust laws were preventing them from forming units large enough to be efficient, but as time has passed, much regrouping has taken place as the result of mergers, expansions, bankruptcies, and withdrawal from the industry. The conventional view nowadays is that much of the textile industry--but not much of the apparel industry--is internationally competitive. That is clearly true of some firms that export; for others import controls seem important. What is not clear is whether this proves that the protective policies combined with internal competition were a success even though they imposed substantial costs on consumers, according to the best estimates. Not much is heard of the logic of concluding that "success" might mean the industry could do without protection.

When the steel industry issue first came up it was through the industry's complaint, in the Kennedy administration and before, that government pressures to keep down prices were hindering the financing of new investment. In the Johnson administration there was restraint on imports in the form of government requests to foreign producers to limit shipments to the United States. These measures were said to be temporary and were subsequently dropped. When the import issue appeared in a more acute form in the Carter administration, the rudiments of a sectoral policy were sketched in the Solomon report[12]: an industry investment program to be helped by tax measures; revision of environmental controls to postpone or reduce their impact on costs of production; labor-management cooperation; a tripartite committee of management, labor, and government to oversee the measures and discuss the problems of the industry; and the trigger-price mechanism (TPM). This last proved to be the most sustained and troublesome measure. An innovation, it established a formula for determining prices for imported products below which a speedy procedure for antidumping or countervailing duty investigations was to be inaugurated. Although steel companies remained free to make antidumping or countervailing complaints, the Treasury said it would not have sufficient staff to pursue these cases while administering the complex TPM.

As time passed, the trigger price was raised but imports increased more than the companies liked and the industry made complaints of dumping and subsidized imports. The government, wishing to abate the strains on American-European relations that the suits were expected to bring, dropped the TPM, and by a process that has to be abridged here arrived at agreements between the United States and the European Community limiting imports of a number of steel products. (The Japanese had held down exports all along.) Then the industry pressed for quotas from smaller suppliers as well. A new dispute with the Community was set off by measures to protect the U.S. market for specialty steels and the industry asked for new legislation limiting imports to 15 percent of domestic supplies.

Behind the protective barriers some new investment began to take place; internal competition sharpened as the market share of small mills grew; some diversification out of steel by major producers took place; and there were some mergers. The tripartite mechanism amounted to little, but labor concessions became an important element in the delayed process of adjustment. Then the International Trade Commission recommended protection for certain products, provided that the resulting financial gains were invested. Spokesmen for the steel industry accepted the idea of linking protection with investment but insisted that they needed quotas covering substantially all products that would limit imports to 15 percent of domestic shipments for at least five years. As the steel industries of all the industrial countries are undergoing difficult adjustments

and as the future expansion is likely to be in developing
countries, new international efforts may be made that would
provide a framework for the shaping of more clear-cut
American measures.

In automobiles the sequence is simple: the Chrysler
bailout; Japanese export restrictions, first as a short-term
measure and then continued; serious cuts in labor costs
through negotiation; investment and some organization of
production by the major firms; some increase in foreign
investment in the United States; and agitation by the union
for domestic-content laws intended to induce more investment
and limit the ability of the domestic firms to import
components. All these steps had elements of industrial
policy going beyond simple protectionism, but lacked either
a reasonably clear-cut strategy or any overt effort by the
government to make the public assistance (persuasion of the
Japanese) conditional on the industry's performance
(investment, prices, etc.), although this had been talked
about.

Even this sketch of the sectoral policies of the United
States shows that the term does not convey very much about
the content of the policies. For the most important
manufacturing industries there is only the shadow of action
beyond protection, but the rationale for the protection
concerns the problems of the sectors even though the modus
operandi and goals are poorly worked out. Up to a point it
can be argued that what has been done is to give the steel
and automobile industries time to make major adjustments
through some mitigation of import competition but without
throttling it altogether. There has been nothing like the
general subsidization common in other countries, but also
little help or pressure to bring about change.

Trade-Related Measures

The industrial-policy dimension of general trade
liberalization coupled with selective protection has already
been laid out. Almost, but not quite symmetrical, is export
promotion, a general policy the United States shares with
most other countries (although the methods differ). Not
usually thought of as industrial policy, the disposition to
favor exports (and measures that effectively pursue the aim)
do have an influence on the structure of an economy; even if
the gamut of exports is large, some sectors benefit more

than others. More important, the need to measure success by achievements in competitive world markets provides a different bias from that of industrial policies based on ideas about what a country should produce at home.

Export promotion tends to lead to competition in the financing of exports and induces practices that look to others like subsidies. DISC (Domestic International Sales Corporation) was meant to be an American response to countries that relied heavily on VAT (value-added tax) which was, under traditional practices and GATT (General Agreement on Tariffs and Trade) rules, adjusted for imports and exports. An unfavorable report by a GATT panel has led to a change in American law. Probably more important in its impact on the shape of the American economy is Export-Import Bank financing. This tends to favor large projects and major capital goods; without it the civil aircraft and power-plant equipment industries would probably ask for other forms of help. It is common for American businessmen to complain that their government gives them less help in selling abroad than their competitors in Japan, Europe, and Canada get. It is, however, a settled part of American trade policy to bargain for the opening of foreign governmental procurement to American firms, both through the GATT code on the subject and bilaterally, as in the negotiations with Japan about the government communications monopoly.

Most trade-related industrial policy measures are concerned with imports. The significance of adjustment assistance has already been mentioned. Although much could be said about what has been done poorly and what could be done better, it is enough at this point to add the activity to the list. The same is true of so special a feature of American policy as the 806/807 provisions about the reimportation of products exported for processing abroad, a matter of special interest to Mexico.

The fair-trade laws are not ordinarily thought of as industrial policy measures, but this is illogical for several reasons. (1) As already explained, acting to influence the way markets and competition work has significant industrial-policy dimensions. If one chooses to let the structure of an economy be shaped by competition, there has to be some concern with being sure competition takes place and is judged to be "fair." (2) If policy stresses the adaptation of the economy to economic change in the world, it is crucial to know to what one is supposed to adapt; the logic of markets and competition is not generally thought to apply to "unfair" competition, but there is no generally agreed definition of what is fair and the American tendency to presume that all government aid is illegitimate is at odds with thinking in most of the rest of the world. (3) Measures to countervail the effects of foreign subsidies are responses to the industrial policies of other governments. One can say the same thing about antidumping duties if one thinks of industrial policy as comprising the strategies of enterprises. (4) Although the laws are applicable to all products, they are in fact only invoked from time to time and since they require findings of "injury," they are selective in their use. Moreover, the definition of an industry is a key element in the application of the laws. No one would suggest that they are used in all possible cases where they are relevant; thus they have the element of selectivity or discrimination that Andrew Shonfield said was a key characteristic of industrial policy. (5) The result of starting fair-trade procedures is often to bring about an agreement with foreign governments or producers that can resemble measures of international industrial policy. To avoid the disturbing and often uncertain effect of the fair trading laws, foreign governments sometimes enter into orderly marketing agreements or other forms of nominally voluntary export restraint, usually for a given period. The United States government may unilaterally use escape clause measures to limit imports, or raise the barriers to them, even if foreign competition is not alleged to be unfair, so long as it "disrupts" the domestic market. To the extent that the time during which protection exists is used to permit the domestic industry to become more competitive, or at least to permit the orderly withdrawal of resources from the industries in difficulty, we are in the realm of industrial policy. In the United States it has been exceptional to have an explicit link between the import restraint and the adaptation process. The case of the shoe industry was one of the few in which it was, although it had previously been considered possible not only that they should be used in combination, but also that adjustment aid might be an alternative to import restraint under the escape clause. If escape-clause protection is limited to a specific period, it is implicit that the protected interests are on notice that afterwards they must fend for themselves. There may also be declining protection during the period (reducing tariff rates or enlarged quotas). This is a formula for adjustment without government intervention, provided the government adheres to the original deadline, but even with the extensions that are common, similar results can be achieved.

Faint as they have been, links between temporary protection and adjustment other than in the form of a time limit have not been totally absent. The original setting of the trigger price mechanism in steel was related to tax measures, investment plans, and environmental regulations. When Japan undertook a temporary reduction of automobile exports to the United States, there was a general assumption that American automakers could be competitive after completion of an investment program (General Motors), or a degree of reorganization (Chrysler), or fuller global integration of production (Ford). It was often said that increased tariffs for five years would give the Harley Davidson motorcycle company a fair chance to meet Japanese competition (or go out of business quietly?).

The list of de facto industrial policy devices should also mention export controls. Applied primarily for national security purposes (except in the case of feared domestic shortages of some foodstuffs), these can have the effect of limiting the ability of certain industries to serve world markets, which may affect their viability. If other countries do not apply comparable limits, these security or political measures can alter the structure of the international economy, as in the distribution of production of nuclear plants, oil field supplies, and various kinds of high-technology equipment. As the export controls apply to technology as well as products (and may be more stringent there), they have a bearing on investment patterns of American industry, at home and abroad, and create chronic international clashes over extraterritoriality which themselves have industrial policy dimensions.

Investment Measures

As the last example suggests, many "trade" measures also encourage or discourage investment, one of the major fields of activity of most countries' industrial policies. Ostensibly, the United States has had no clear-cut policy to guide investment, but in practice many government measures are at play. Some are tax concessions intended to stimulate investment in specific industries. Other more general tax cuts are not uniform in their effects on investment in different industries or types of activity.[13] Still other tax measures and additional kinds of governmental measures, such as loan guarantees, favor certain types of activity, such as small business, rural electrification, and so on. State and local programs to encourage investment by the provision of tax concessions, purchase commitments, the building of infrastructure, the provision of cheap energy, etc., that may also involve the use of federal funds or guarantees, presumably have some influence on the location of investment and perhaps the allocation among activities, though the impact on its level is a matter of controversy.

Foreign investors in the United States also benefit from these arrangements and sometimes from others negotiated with state and local authorities. American law limits or forbids foreign investment in certain fields, but these are fewer than in many countries and there is sound basis for the general statements of officials in recent years that the country welcomes foreign investment. The great accumulation of funds by OPEC countries stimulated concern about the size of some foreign investments and the alienation of control over some activities and enterprises, but this did not result in any clear-cut policies of restraint. A degree of high-level screening might possibly be brought to bear on certain transactions, but there is no overt record of this being done.

"Buy American" practices and other arrangements for preferring domestic sources of supply can be said to stimulate foreign investment in the United States, at least in some fields. This is also true of access to federally financed R&D, at least insofar as a distinction is drawn between American-based firms and others and not between those that are owned by Americans rather than foreigners.

Private American investment abroad was encouraged by national policy in the early postwar period in the belief that it would contribute to overcoming the dollar gap, to the recovery of Europe and Japan, the development of poorer countries, and to the creation of a multilateral world economy. It is questionable how important the various federal programs were compared with the stimuli given by opportunities abroad and foreign barriers to American exports. American policies aimed at keeping open investment opportunities, reducing restriction and the threat of expropriation and, so far as possible, promoting national treatment can all be said to aim at promoting further investment. These policies are structural, not only as between activities in the United States and abroad, but in the sense that some industries are more apt than others to take advantage of possibilities that exist abroad or are burdened by the lack of them.[14] There is also a link with trade policies, that is, whether the investment is intended to produce for foreign markets or shipments back to the United States.

In the 1960s, policies promoting American investment abroad were attacked on the grounds that they reduced the growth of the American economy and exported jobs. The extreme measures advocated for a time by the AFL-CIO have been dropped, but the issue is not entirely dead and surfaces from time to time whenever measures are taken that are meant to stimulate investment inside the United States or put disposable funds in the hands of American firms. It could also be said that the official policy on these matters now purports to be neutral as between domestic and foreign investment.[15] The case is questioned by those who cite tax laws that defer the tax on overseas investment until the profits are repatriated and some other measures, such as insurance for overseas investments. The 806/807 practices can be put in the same category although they do not require the foreign operation to be an American investment. It is widely believed that fear of antitrust prosecution has led a number of major American companies to concentrate on expansion abroad instead of at home. The Reagan administration launched an effort to negotiate bilateral treaties that will improve prospects for American direct investments abroad, but whether this can be said to depart from neutrality is not clear, especially as its results have yet to be seen.

The most important recent development in American policy toward private American investment abroad concerns the treatment of foreign performance requirements. These are measures which have to be thought of as reflecting foreign industrial policies (or sometimes just trade policies) that presumably influence the behavior of American firms and may influence both trade and investment in the American market and perhaps American exports to the countries imposing performance requirements. The so-far successful challenge to some Canadian procurement requirements illustrates what can be done through invocation of existing trade commitments; alternatives that are likely to appear concern counterpressure by the American government against efforts to impose other requirements that are thought to be undesirable and possibly countermeasures (such as denying export licenses for certain technologies if they are essential to the performance of R&D or certain other activities abroad).

Competition Policy

The major points about this range of issues have already been made. There is, however, a specific link with foreign trade and investment that needs to be underlined.

The antitrust laws have historically focused on the American market and measured degrees of concentration in those terms. They reach out to practices abroad that are intended to influence sales to the United States. Increasingly, the question has been raised whether the past emphasis is suitable to a market that is open to import competition and whether the measure of market size should be global lest the ability of American firms to compete be reduced. This last was a consideration in the argument over the case against IBM that was eventually dropped. A recent refusal of the Antitrust Division to sanction a steel merger was based in part on the limitation of imports that made it impossible for foreign producers to increase their competition. The FTC (Federal Trade Commission) approval of the General Motors-Toyota venture in California was permitted in spite of a comparable limitation on imports, although a dissenting view of the FTC staff argued that permission should be given only if the import ban were lifted. (GM had lobbied for an exemption from the Japanese export control for shipments connected with the venture.) Another perspective on that transaction comes from those who ask whether such an agreement between the two biggest national producers should have been allowed and if it is not necessary to think in terms of global as well as domestic concentration and oligopoly.

The situation is uncertain and confused but there is no doubt that the pursuit of policies in these fields impinges on industrial policy considerations. That extends as well to the extraterritorial reach of American policy in various fields, the limited degree of international cooperation in these matters, and the approach of the U.S. government to the efforts of foreign governments to apply antitrust or pro-merger and compulsory cartel laws to American firms (IBM in the European Community; American firms in the uranium cartel).

A variety of measures intended to support and encourage small business has to be taken into account in a list of structural policies. These have so far had little international relevance, but efforts are being made to encourage or help small firms to engage in export business. Export financing through the Export-Import Bank can also have an industrial policy dimension, as was illustrated by the controversy as to whether support should be given to the export of steel-mill equipment to Korea at a time when steel imports from Korea were being restricted and, it was argued, there was global excess capacity in the field. The resulting compromise--a guarantee and not a loan--reflected the fact that what was regarded as burdensome for one American industry was an advantage for others. There was also a relation to earlier practices, under which foreign aid funds were not permitted to be spent for certain activities that would compete with American production, or current efforts to instruct American representatives in multilateral agencies to take such issues into account when credits are proposed.

R&D

An industrial policy par excellence, public support for R&D has been a major source of discussion in the United States. The practice itself is well established and goes far beyond spending for defense or such activities as putting a man on the moon and the space program on which much attention has focused, and which have sometimes been termed by foreign critics the true American industrial policy. Too many issues are involved to be reviewed here: levels; the distribution between basic research, applied research and the development of commercially viable processes and products; the allocation of activities (and funds) among universities, business, and governmental establishments; who pays for what; the pooling of research among business firms; access to publicly financed research; the alleged growing irrelevance of patent laws to fast-changing technological fields; and so on.

Other Policies

Time and space forbid a consideration of many other aspects of the de facto industrial policy of the United States. It should be kept in mind that the criterion is not the conscious use of these measures for industrial policy purposes, their structural effects, or their contribution to improved performance. These policies range from education (basic, specialized, vocational, and continuing); productivity; labor market measures including security, retraining, aid in finding jobs, and job creation; wage setting procedures; measures favoring union organization or resistance to it; to the tax system and its variety of subsidy-like and discriminatory measures. Many of these have already been mentioned. A good survey is the Congressional Budget Office document mentioned above.

PROPOSALS FOR CHANGE

A variety of motives is behind the beliefs of those people who think that the United States should pay more attention to industrial policy issues. Some think the reason the economy does not work as well as it should is that the old categories of policy, mostly macroeconomic measures, are no longer sufficient. Others stress the need for greater consensus on the objectives and priorities of the American economy and more cooperative methods of pursuing these ends. Some call for more government leadership, while others think that much of the trouble with the American economy stems from the fact that the presence of the government has become too weighty and pervasive. People of either view can agree that because foreign governments engage so extensively in industrial policies and related trade measures, the United States is in danger of having its economy shaped by the policies of others if it does not take countermeasures. There is widespread agreement that a dominant aim in the long run must be international competitiveness, but there is much disagreement as to how this is to be achieved and what it means about the future of basic industries that have been in difficulty in recent years. Technological leadership and national security are objectives that guide the thinking of some people. Others believe that industrial policies should aim to make change easier by helping the withdrawal of resources from declining industries and cushioning the impact on workers and communities. Whatever new measures they may advocate, people increasingly recognize that there is a need to examine what is currently being done--the de facto industrial policy--to see if existing measures serve desirable national purposes in an efficient and equitable manner.

These motivations overlap and sometimes contradict one another. In choosing their objectives, and policies to promote them, Americans are not likely in the foreseeable future to adopt a clear and comprehensive set of principles and pursue them consistently. Nevertheless, the weight given to the different motives mentioned will do much to shape the general character of what is done and how it affects the structure and performance of the American economy, whether it is called industrial policy or not. It is, therefore, worth devoting the rest of this section to a brief discussion of some of the kinds of measures that have been proposed.

Omitted from this list are proposals that are primarily procedural and organizational, important as these are to carrying out effective policy. There are, for example, the AFL-CIO's proposals for tripartite government-business-labor bodies to shape national industrial policy generally and to handle the affairs of each major industry; and suggestions for new bodies to deliberate about such matters in which all interest groups would be represented. Some people advocate giving such bodies power and money, others would establish agencies concerned with particular problems or activities. Congressional-executive relations are involved as well as those among the states, cities, and regions. Business-labor cooperation without government interference or direct relations between each of these groups and the government appear in different schemes.

In much the same vein, the list that follows omits measures that are concerned primarily with improved management or labor practices, such as those intended to secure more cooperation, greater flexibility, improved participation in decisions and adjustment, better quality, longer range views, and the like. Measures that depend on some degree of international agreement or that are largely concerned with action taken in common with foreign governments are held over for the following section.

Even apart from these omissions, the list that follows cannot be an exhaustive inventory. On almost every topic there is a variety of proposals that differ in what appear to be significant ways. (Is it God or the Devil who is in the details?) Only rarely are proposals comprehensive, consistent, and so fully thought out that one can be sure how they are intended to apply to all cases. Often the vagueness or ambiguity is intentional and necessary in the search for public support. To provide a thorough taxonomy of the proposals would require much time and space since the variables include objectives, strategy, tactics, methods,

and options. Instead, the list is rough, using approximate
categories and simply suggesting the kinds of action that
have been proposed. In one way or another, most of the
general ideas in circulation have been covered, but readers
should bear in mind that, as the survey of de facto
industrial policy has shown, any number of additional ideas
might be included which are left out to avoid repetition or
because they have so far only been discussed in relatively
specialized circles (for example, the possibility of making
changes in the bankruptcy laws and procedures that would
take account of either industrial policy-objectives or the
condition of particular industries).

1.   Guidance in one form or another characterizes
most proposals.   Nothing as simplistic as "picking the
winners" is necessarily called for, though removing
obstacles (domestic or foreign) that threaten real winners
may be crucial. The emphasis more generally is on knowing
what the country wants its economy to become and supporting
activities that make for this result. The choice need not
be made by the government alone. Reliance on market forces
can be given much weight, either as something to be departed
from only for clear-cut reasons, or as an objective to be
worked for more systematically than is now the case. Almost
no one believes entirely in this as a complete and
unqualified objective. The tendency to equate reliance on
competition with complete laissez faire and "getting the
government out of the economy" is fallacious.   There is a
good case to be made for making much, if not all,
governmental aid conditional. For example, if protection is
provided either by import controls or asking another country
to restrain exports, the protected industry (or firms)
should have undertaken to make certain adjustments or follow
certain policies or achieve certain results. In many cases,
no machinery exists for doing this, or any legal basis
either, but such problems are not taken into account in this
list.

2.   A new RFC. The term is shorthand and a tribute
to the popularization by Felix Rohatyn of the idea that a
government agency with funds can play a key part in
industrial policy and particularly in restructuring the
economy.   The idea has been adopted by the AFL-CIO in its
rather full-blown program for industrial policy and appears
in one form or another in many other proposals, but is
explicitly rejected by some people, including spokesmen for
the Reagan administration. The idea is not as clear-cut as
it sounds, even in Rohatyn's writings where it has been
assigned, at one time or another, a number of different

functions.[16] Some proponents emphasize an alleged shortage of capital for long-term investment; sometimes the government presence as guarantor is a key factor, or the leverage on private capital from either an easing of terms by the government's participation or simply conditioning aid on the contribution of others. A public voice to guide the use of capital, reorganization of management in a firm as part of the arrangement, fitting investments into an agreed pattern of cooperation for dealing with an industry's problems, are all aspects of the RFC idea that have been stressed by one person or another. Sometimes specific needs are alleged in high-technology industries, such as the provision of the large sums needed to bring technological novelties into commercial production before the investment of venture capital that financed their start has been paid off. It is also argued that in almost any kind of targeting strategy, such as to provide support to become competitive against imports, funds are apt to be needed and should not have to be raised by separate legislation for each case. Union pension funds have been suggested in some labor statements as a possible source of contributions, provided their use will expand job opportunity in the industry from which the workers earn their living.[17]

    3.   Protection in various forms is a frequent ingredient of industrial-policy proposals. Measures to make effective use of the time gained by escape clause actions, orderly marketing agreements and the like have been touched on above. They exemplify one version of conditional aid. Instructions to the International Trade Commission to point to vulnerabilities, measures that would reduce injury and increase competitiveness, and so on, when they hear claims for escape-clause action would provide one method of doing this. Arrangements for market sharing between domestic production and imports have played a part in proposals for textiles, shoes, and other industries in the past, not always with the understanding that quotas would be lifted after a period. There is an element of this in the rules governing preferences for some developing country products and it would be one of the ways of meeting claims that industries of a certain size in specific fields are needed for national security or health. The steel industry has proposed that imports be limited to 15 percent of domestic supply "expressly to permit and encourage capital investment in the modernization of the domestic steel industry." If the level of investment was not "at appropriate levels" the Secretary of Commerce could suspend the quotas. Although the initial legislation would be for five years, this is the

sort of arrangement that easily perpetuates itself.[18]

Although some people would object to calling the fair-trade laws protection, there is little doubt they have such effects. A major emphasis of several business and labor groups has become the strengthening of these laws, the speeding up of their use, and the reduction of the discretion left to the executive branch in applying them. Any emphasis on American adjustment by the play of market forces has to make some provision for the fairness of competition; any effort to keep down trade barriers has to reckon with the uncertainty stemming from the use of these measures; any emphasis on adjustment and competitiveness in American industry has to allow for the fact that the use of these laws does nothing to help that process at home unless it is already under way and has no effect on unfair competition in third markets. In many respects the subject merges with the international measures discussed in the next section which can reduce the pressures for using the fair-trade laws in the United States by checking foreign practices that offend them.

4. <u>Subsidy</u> <u>and</u> <u>procurement</u>. Although direct subsidies are used less in the United States than in other countries, the preference economists have usually shown for subsidies over tariffs and the ability to target subsidies and discriminate among their recipients (helping a few weak producers instead of protecting a whole industry) make them natural instruments of industrial policy, and suggestions for their use are likely to increase. A more popular form of subsidy in the American system is tax concessions and these ought to be looked at in the light of industrial policy considerations. In the defense economy there is a variety of forms of government aid to business, including the building and leasing of plants, which have potential applications as subsidy techniques to meet other needs. The defense experience also provides examples and warnings about preferential procurement by government agencies (states and cities as well as the federal government) which are standard in foreign industrial policies and seem likely to be used more widely in the United States with their advantages and disadvantages if the industrial-policy approach catches on.

5. <u>Research</u> <u>and</u> <u>development</u> with public support is so central to almost all industrial-policy thinking that it has to be put on this list even though nothing much can be added to what was said above. Apart from the issues mentioned earlier, a key current one is the extent to which government financing of advanced work in such matters as computers is going to come through the defense budget. Such

expenditures raise the question of who is eligible to
receive the support, the classification of the results, and
the extent to which it is proper and feasible to direct the
spending so that the results are valuable commercially as
well as in security terms.

6.   Domestic-content legislation for automobiles is
being advocated by the United Automobile Workers and has
fairly wide political support. The concept is applicable to
other industries as well.   It is, in many respects, an
application of the concept of performance requirements that
is widely used in other countries and in the automobile
industry (but not by Japan, the principal target of this
legislation).   It also underlines a difference in interest
between the workers and the companies in the automobile
industry which is not found in most cases in which the two
sides combine to ask for protection.   Even if the
legislation is not enacted, which seems likely, the threat
exercises some pressure on foreign companies to invest in
the United States and on American companies to be careful
about the amount of foreign procurement for domestic sales
they undertake.   In other respects as well, this idea
focuses attention on the interrelations of trade and
investment in shaping the structure of economies and
influencing their levels of activity.

7.   Adjustment assistance is being actively
reexamined and new legislation is almost certain to be
proposed during the next few years. Two key issues will be
whether companies as well as workers should be helped and
whether sources of change other than import competition will
be taken into account. In terms of effect, the key issues
are how closely assistance can be linked to the creation of
new jobs, improved concepts of retraining, and whether the
existence of new methods will make change politically more
acceptable.   Closely related are other kinds of measures to
improve labor market mobility, including possible
experiments with wage subsidies geared to the employment of
displaced workers.

8.   Competition policies seem bound to have a larger
place in future discussions of American industrial policy
than in the past. Much of what was said earlier boiled down
to a business view that a relaxation of the antitrust laws
was required to permit American companies to compete in
world markets or to cope with foreign cartels or national
champions at home. The need was challenged by many analysts
and the prevailing view in the Antitrust Division and among
many outside antitrust lawyers was that there was enough
flexibility to permit virtually any activities that truly

increased competition. Clarification of what could be done for the pooling of R&D has opened new possibilities; links between merger activity and trade barriers have been discussed above. The underlying question is whether antitrust decisions--not only whether to prosecute, but what to accept in consent decrees and how to judge cases that are fought to a verdict--can and should be influenced by standards of national industrial policy that go beyond the combination of precedent and lawyers' and judges' opinions about what is competition under century-old laws.

As this and the earlier discussion suggest, the issue is no longer one of how much concentration should be permitted, but rather how competition can be promoted so as to strengthen American firms. An American scholar of business practices concluded after a survey of Japanese policies and business performance that one of the principal lessons the United States and other western countries could learn from Japan concerns the importance of:

> ...competition policy. This would include policy aimed not just at traditional antitrust objectives, but also policies aimed at stimulating the creation and nurturing of maverick entrepreneurial firms like those who have been Japan's competitive flagships. There is need especially for a competition policy that promotes competition among Western firms _before_ when unsuspecting, unaware oligopolistic, "industry colleagues" are hit by Japanese price-cutting and Japanese quality carried to the West by firms bred of sterner stuff in the arch-competitive Japanese domestic market. [19]

That view is not yet conventional wisdom but it is gaining enough ground to show how far-reaching the industrial policy debate is likely to become. It is a reminder, too, of the fact that policy prescriptions based on models of atomistic competition and common economic assumptions about market-clearing mechanisms give poor policy guidance when oligopoly prevails.

9. _State and local activities_ of an industrial-policy character pose a range of problems. How much federal coordination should there or can there be? Is the only test the use of federal funds or guarantees to stimulate investment in one place rather than another? Should distinctions be made between inducing new activities and

supporting existing ones? Among types of industry? Does rivalry among states help or hinder the market process? What difference does it make if the alternative location is in a Canadian province? There are constitutional barriers to practices that interfere with interstate commerce but they do not automatically cover all local or state activities that influence these processes.

There is the related issue of the extent to which the rise and decline in levels of economic activity in different regions should be a matter of public concern and what should be done about these forces of change. Is it more important to leave them free, or to take measures to protect those damaged by the results? Should tax laws be neutral? If they favor innovation, do they necessarily weigh more heavily on old centers than new ones? It is alleged that tax writeoffs now favor new building and thus tend to draw firms away from existing centers. Comparable issues can be found in labor laws to the extent that federal legislation or action establishes nationwide standards or permits local variations that affect labor costs and union activity.

10. Infrastructure throughout the American economy is generally thought to need more attention than it has had in recent years. Meeting the needs presents fiscal problems, but for the purpose of this paper the question is whether an assessment of what is needed should be seriously influenced by industrial-policy considerations. For example, is rebuilding what exists the primary guide, or does there have to be a reassessment of allocation by type of activity (road, rail, airport, pipeline, seaport) or area (inner cities, new sources of water, electric power)? While some infrastructure needs can be derived from an assessment of industrial change, the processes of change and structural shift can also be influenced by what is done about infrastructure. These are not the kinds of questions that normally come up when Congress allocates funds for the repair or maintenance of infrastructure--at least not on a national basis.

11. Environmental tradeoffs have been recognized for some time as crucial to business performance, growth rates, and other crucial matters such as the absorption of investment funds and levels of productivity. They touch industrial-policy concerns in many ways, whether the emphasis is on sectoral considerations (smelting, coal v. oil, etc.) or the problems of regions and localities and the distribution of costs (as in acid rain). The need for clearer methods of calculating costs and benefits, better ways of making decisions stick for a period of time, and

persuasive distributions of power and responsibility among those who are affected in different ways (polluters, pollutees, third parties whose jobs, supplies, markets, and costs are dependent on what is done or not done about economic activities run by others) is great. These issues will be discussed for a long time; just what their link with industrial-policy considerations will be remains to be seen.

12. Energy policy is bound to reappear as a central question for the United States. The issues are too well known to need repetition and their relevance to Mexico is clear. All that needs emphasizing here is that whether one thinks of energy as a sector or not, it affects many sectors and how it is handled is a crucial matter for much of the rest of the economy. A simple example, also relevant to Mexico, concerns costs and prices in energy as they affect the raw material costs of the petrochemical industry which in turn becomes a question of how American practices compare with those of other countries. (Is domestic use subsidized or highly taxed? Is there a difference between the domestic price and the export price, or discrimination as to use?) Although somewhat obscured in current discussion, one of the most basic considerations of energy policy is security of supply.

13. Labor policies have been mentioned from time to time in this paper without being fully explored. In addition to what has already been said about regional differences, labor-market mobility, security, and other matters, it is important to recognize that if an economy is undergoing as substantial structural changes as appears to be the case for the United States, much of the burden will fall on working people. Whether the "security net" is adequate or has to be strengthened for those especially hard hit is a question that points to one series of issues. Another concerns the means by which there can be a change from the exceptionally high wages (and other labor costs) that were built up in such industries as automobiles and steel which are now undergoing some of the greatest changes to viable new levels, and how the wage rates can be kept from creeping back to levels that will cause new problems. This clearly depends on much else in the industries, not just labor costs, but questions are bound to arise about the way wage levels are negotiated, how they are geared to productivity, the flexible use of the labor force, profits, and other factors.

Two further large questions arise. Organized labor now comprises less than 20 percent of the labor force. How is the rest to be represented in processes shaping industrial

policy? What is the validity of the feeling that is strong
in the AFL-CIO that the 1981-82 recession, other national
economic difficulties, and the general political situation
are being used to attack unions and reduce their strength
drastically? What is the remedy? As the largest single
resource of an economy is its people, an industrial-policy
approach that ignores such matters is unlikely to be
satisfactory in the long run.

14. Piecemeal industrial policy, which is far more
likely to appear in the United States (and already exists)
than anything comprehensive and thought-through, presents a
variety of difficulties. Action in one field not matched in
another is the breeding ground of second bests--if one can
reach that high. Inequity is more apparent than any
objective rationale for special treatment. "What you do for
him you have to do for me" can be a disastrous prescription
for public policy, as the history of protectionism shows.
How can the selectivity (or discrimination) inherent in much
industrial policy be successfully carried out in the light
of these facts?

Many other problems arise from an uneven and to some
extent erratic application of industrial-policy approaches.
Is there anything that can be done about this in the
American system?

15. Government failure is as common as market
failure. Any given failure is likely to have very large
consequences, as has been demonstrated by much academic
analysis showing the dangers of a concentration of decisions
in one place rather than having them spread over many
centers. Fiorello LaGuardia summed up the matter when he
said, "If I make a mistake, it's a beaut." George Eads has
provided a balanced argument pointing to the contribution of
past governmental measures to the difficulties that are now
supposed to be dealt with by industrial policy and warning
about the limited capacity of the U.S. government for
dealing with such matters.[20] These are factors that cannot
be left out of account and are bound to have an important
effect not only on how measures of industrial policy are
carried out, but whether they are adopted at all. For many
people, the inability of the U.S. governments (again the
plural is advised) to do the things they undertake to do in
an acceptable manner turns the tables against doing anything
at all; but that does not necessarily produce better results
either.

INTERNATIONAL MEASURES

Not only does part of the stimulus for American thinking about industrial policy come from the activities of foreign governments under this rubric, but many of the measures urged, resisted, or taken in the United States concern foreign economic relations and the whole system of international economic cooperation which has done so much to make this period different from all previous times. The subject is too large to be taken up here, but a few signs must be posted since what the United States does or does not do on a wide range of industrial-policy matters is likely to be shaped, if not determined, by what happens in the rest of the world. The items that follow simply list some key activities or issues; their connection with what has gone before should be reasonably apparent.

1. GATT negotiations of the future will deal with such sectoral matters as agriculture, high technology, and services; adjustment questions such as the use of safeguards; industrial-policy practices insofar as they are covered by codes, notably those on subsidies and government procurement; the special interests of developing countries in access to the markets of older industrial countries.

2. Outside GATT there are discussions about the management of structural change that involve a wide range of issues touched on in this paper and by national industrial policies. The OECD, preparations for the western summits, and quadripartite trade discussions all sometimes touch on these matters; what if anything, is decided may well also involve the future of GATT, but that remains to be seen.[21]

3. Existing sectoral arrangements--notably those in textiles, steel, and automobiles--touch the first two categories, but also provide separate foci which bear directly on what is done in the United States about these industries.

4. High-technology discussions between the United States and Japan have displaced the aborted GATT discussions as the central focus of possible progress in these crucial industries. It is impossible for an outsider to make a firm judgment about the scope and likely outcome of these negotiations, but it seems clear that their potential is great. One possible result is that the two governments, with the assent of the industries, will arrive at understandings about what kinds of practices are acceptable in supporting high-technology industries and which will be unacceptable. For example, it might be agreed that certain

kinds of R&D could quite properly be supported by public funds, whereas others had to be treated as costs of production for private firms. The American concern with Japanese targeting might be alleviated by clarification of practices on both sides. Reasonable arrangements might be made for reciprocal access to R&D, bidding for government contracts, and commercial markets.

Should the two countries reach broad enough agreements on these matters, they might, as the leaders in the field, open their arrangements to other countries and offer them as the bases for multilateral agreements in GATT. (It would be wise of them to make their arrangements potentially compatible with GATT obligations from the outset.) An alternative result might be much more negative. Resistance on either side or demands that go beyond the acceptable might result in barriers on either or both sides, the diversion of Japanese cooperative efforts toward Europe to support the resistance to American firms there, and a general deterioration of the possibilities of reaching new understandings. Either outcome would have significant implications for American industrial policy. Both will be affected by the growing internationalization of the industry, an almost independent process that cannot be pursued here.

5. <u>Relations</u> <u>between</u> <u>the</u> <u>United</u> <u>States</u> <u>and</u> <u>developing</u> <u>countries</u> that concentrate for the moment on debt issues, the American system of preferences, and relations in GATT almost all touch the problems raised in this paper. They affect not only trade barriers, but the kinds of challenge to which American industrial policy has to respond; this raises questions about "fair trade," global "excess capacity," future development financing, structural change in developing and older countries, which are mostly expressions of ideas about industrial development and are often undergoing change.

6. <u>Canada</u> has special relations to American industrial policy for a variety of reasons: the major trading partner; the high level of American investment in Canada that makes much trade intracompany trade; the importance of Canada as a source of raw materials of various sorts; geography that makes some north-south currents stronger than east-west ones within the same country; a substantial removal of trade barriers over the last 35 years; a high degree of Canadian economic dependence on what happens in the American economy; a high degree of Canadian sensitivity to this relation which is reflected in various measures of economic nationalism; and a wider range of

attitudes that create intra-Canadian differences about the proper course of action vis-a-vis the United States.

With regard to issues discussed earlier in this paper, it is important to bear in mind: the defense production-sharing agreement that nominally eliminated preferential procurement in that field; the automotive that creates a kind of free trade modified by performance requirements on the Canadian side; other Canadian controls over investment, some aspects of which have been challenged by the United States in GATT with partial success; important trade union links across the border; the development of provincial industrial policies that are sometimes more highly developed and cogent than those of the federal government and that affect foreign trade and investment in ways that can escape federal control; Canadian regional policies and other measures which, while initially focused on internal matters, can substantially affect relations with the United States; numerous close energy links between the two countries involving a substantial number of unresolved problems.

Of particular relevance to the issues raised in this paper are the negotiations between Ottawa and Washington about the possibility of overall free trade between the two countries. Even if general free trade does not result, more limited agreements may be reached. There has, for example, already been an understanding about consultation and prior notification before the invocation of safeguard action by either country. Canadian concern about how American steel quotas might be administered (and allocated) provide another indication of what might be done.

7.   A summary of these lightly sketched international dimensions can be reduced to saying that what the United States in the end does or does not do about the wide variety of industrial-policy approaches mentioned in this paper will be heavily influenced by what the rest of the world does, whether that comes in the form of foreign measures that have an impact on the United States, the response of other countries to what, if anything, the United States proposes, and the impact of national industrial policies on the international economic cooperation.[22]

IMPLICATIONS FOR MEXICO-UNITED STATES RELATIONS

If only because so many factors are involved, there can be no safe predictions about the course the United States will follow in industrial policy. Nevertheless, one can say with assurance that whatever the United States does or does not do about industrial policy will affect Mexico-United States relations.

If the United States were to embark on anything approaching a comprehensive industrial policy, it would be of concern to Mexico whether the primary objectives were to help the American economy adapt to change by reducing the size of old industries or to support such industries even if they were not fully competitive on world markets. A policy of fostering the growth of new industries and services would have still other effects. The situation would not be very different if, instead of a general industrial policy, the United States simply dealt more systematically than in the past with certain industries. Measures that focused on high technology might not only expand production of such products, but lead to new processes in old industries that would overcome some of the disadvantages of high labor costs. And, if the United States did nothing except the sort of thing it has done for years without calling it industrial policy, there would still be problems for Mexico-United States relations connected with existing or new trade barriers, claims of unfair import competition, concern about the markets for the products of new investments, prices and supplies of energy, and many other factors.

Mexican measures concerned with development, investment, and trade will also affect the bilateral relation. This will be true even if new approaches are adopted that emphasize greater selectivity in protection and the choice of activities to be supported. Depending on the selection, issues may be exacerbated. Any constraints on imports resulting from balance-of-payments pressures and the burden of debt will add to the number of problems. Perhaps, though, cooperation on the debt issue and its connections with trade and investment will open new opportunities of adjusting policies in both countries in ways that are mutually helpful both in their economic consequences and in reducing friction.

Much depends on how long the balance-of-payments constraints on Mexico persist and what the future flow of financial resources looks like. The exchange-rate issue is another factor affecting what both governments are willing and able to do in relating with one another and the rest of the world. With these problems in mind it may be useful to list some of the issues that people concerned with Mexico-United States relations will have to worry about in the years to come. Although they are familiar as questions of trade policy or in other fields, they belong in the present context since they have implications for the structures of both economies.

1. Subsidies (and related practices, some connected with exchange rates) that are seen in the United States as distorting competition. These are not about to disappear in Mexico. They often trigger the use of fair-trade rules in the United States, a field that may well become more troublesome in the future. Does it make sense to think of an agreement indicating what practices might avoid the use of countervailing duties? Would an intergovernmental agreement beyond what now exists on subsidies and countervailing duties suffice to block private resort to the remedies provided in American law?

2. Performance requirements have been a tool of some importance for promoting Mexican industrialization. Many American companies have conformed without too much difficulty but the U.S. government is now challenging some such practices in other countries, notably Canada. There is a growing concern with the matter in the American labor movement, in Congress, and perhaps in the business community as well. Is there a possibility of Mexican-United States agreement on these matters or does it have to be part of a broader multilateral understanding?

3. American investment. In an article which seems to lay out some of the major themes of American trade policy for a second Reagan administration, former U.S. Trade Representative William E. Brock put particular emphasis on the need "to improve the environment and to increase the prospects for meaningful flows of private direct investment to developing countries over the longer term...."[23] This is an old theme in Mexican-American relations but seems to be getting a new emphasis. Although Brock speaks of "low-key bilateral consultations" with Mexico instead of an effort to negotiate the kinds of treaties being sought with other countries, one should wonder how this issue might evolve, especially since it is so intimately linked to the structure of the two economies and the pattern of trade between them.

4. Technology transfer is closely related to direct investment and sometimes to trade barriers; it is easily made the target of performance requirements. Two tendencies in the United States ought to be borne in mind as possible

sources of future trouble. One is concern in some parts of
the business community that exports have been lost through
too-hasty transfer of some technologies to foreign
competitors. The other is the move--mostly resisted by the
business community--to impose more restrictions than in the
past on the export of technology in all forms even to
friendly countries. The products of publicly financed R&D
are particularly vulnerable to the latter pressure.

    5. <u>International negotiations</u> of a variety of sorts,
bilateral and multilateral, are under way. How are these to
be taken into account in the handling of Mexico-United
States relations?

    6. <u>Complementarity</u> is a theme running through a
number of the papers for this conference. One can see that
it would make sense in a number of fields to provide both
Mexican and American producers the advantages of access to a
large market by a sensible division of labor emphasizing the
respective advantages of the two countries in resources,
labor costs, location, and technology. This kind of
intra-industry specialization has certainly contributed to
development in many parts of the world, but what does one do
to promote it? The processes of working out such a division
of labor are complex; they involve judgments that often go
wrong. Americans tend to say the risks should be left to
private entrepreneurs in a free market, but do not always
live up to that formula when jobs or other matters are at
stake. It is even harder to square such an approach with a
Mexican development strategy and efforts to make the best
use of scarce resources. This would be something like a
joint industrial policy. Does it offer real possibilities?

    This list could be made longer. Perhaps enough has
been said to show how an initial concern with American
industrial policy, insofar as it exists, can lead back to
some familiar territory which has to be traversed in new
circumstances. None of the problems looks very easy. There
is, however, a good case for believing that Mexicans and
Americans can both gain from some intelligent innovation and
will certainly lose if they do the wrong things. In his new
book, Sidney Weintraub has argued persuasively that it is
reasonable to begin talking and thinking about free trade
between the two countries because it is clear that there are
Mexican industries that could benefit, which might not have
been true once upon a time.[24] There is a comparable argument
that applies to some measures of industrial policy in both
countries so far as the material gains go--and at least as
much of a need to start thinking.

NOTES

[1]See the comments on this point in William Diebold, "Adapting Economies to Structural Change: The International Aspect", International Affairs (London) October 1978; and Diebold, Industrial Policy as an International Issue (New York: McGraw Hill for the Council on Foreign Relations, 1980), pp. 6, 7, 289.

[2]This change probably took place in the '50s or early '60s according to Raymond A. Bauer, Ithiel de Sola Pool, and Lewis Anthony Dexter, American Business and Public Policy (New York: Atherton Press, 1965), p. 147.

[3]There is a good example of the overlaps of industrial and macroeconomic policies in the approach to investment. The balance of investment and consumption in the economy is a macroeconomic question; the adequacy of investment for the productivity or competitiveness of a given industry is a matter of industrial policy.

[4]The bailing out of banks raises still other questions and shows the overlap of industrial policy with monetary and financial policies.

[5]The differences among adaptive, defensive, and innovative industrial policies are more fully discussed in Industrial Policy as an International Issue (cited in footnote 1), pp. 5-8; and John Ponder, Takashi Hosomi, and William Diebold, Industrial Policy and the International Economy: The Triangle Papers 10 (The Trilateral Commission, 1979), pp. 42-48.

[6]Lionel Stoleru, L'Imperatif Industriel (Paris, Editions de Seuil, 1969), p. 157.

[7]At least this seems to me to be what Frank W. Taussig was saying in his standard work, The Tariff History of the United States (New York: Putnam, 8th ed., 1931).

[8]I have tried to examine this experience in a bit more detail in the chapter on "Past and Future Industrial Policy in the United States" in John Pinder, ed., National Industrial Strategies and the World Economy, An Atlantic Institute for International Affairs Research Volume (Totowa, N.J./London: Allanheld, Osmun/Croom Helm, 1982), pp. 206-35.

[9]"A presentation made by the United States Delegation

to the OECD, United States Industrial Policies (Paris: 1970) p. 35.

[10]Congress of the United States. Congressional Budget Office, Federal Support of U.S. Business (Washington: GPO, 1984), p. ix.

[11]One could add shoes, which was subject to a program of adjustment assistance, and other industries that have benefited from special measures, such as higher than average protection or special tax treatment, but they are passed over here.

[12]"A Comprehensive Program for the Steel Industry," Report to the President, Task Force, Anthony M. Solomon, Chairman, December 1977, 35 pp. (mimeographed).

[13]An explanation of the difficulties of being precise in these matters, along with many useful figures that cannot be considered in detail here, is to be found in the report of the Congressional Budget Office cited in note 10. There is an excellent discussion of these and related matters in Barry P. Bosworth, "Capital Formation, Technology, and Economic Policy," and the comments by Edwin Mansfield in Industrial Change and Public Policy, Symposium sponsored by the Federal Reserve Bank of Kansas City, Jackson Hole, Wyoming, August 1983, pp. 231-265.

[14]Of course, this could also be said about policies affecting the exchange rate of the dollar, wage levels, etc.

[15]Arguments bearing on this and related matters are well surveyed in C. Fred Bergsten, Thomas Horst, and Theodore Moran, American Multinationals and American Interests (Washington, D.C.: The Brookings Institution, 1978).

[16]A number of the papers have been collected in Felix G. Rohatyn, The Twenty-Year Century (N.Y.: Random House, 1983). Those interested in all the variations, however, may have to track down the earlier versions and uncollected pieces.

[17]Thus the question of who controls the pension funds becomes yet another industrial-policy issue since trustees or managers may not share the views of union leaders in this matter, as is suggested by the dispute as to whether British coal miners' pension funds should be invested in the United States.

[18]American Iron and Steel Institute, Steel Comments, February 10, 1984, p. 4; italics in original.

[19]Lawrence G. Franko, The Threat of Japanese Multinationals--How Can the West Respond? (New York: Wiley, 1983), p. 140. Italics in original.

[20]George C. Eads, "The Political Experience in

Allocating Investment: Lessons from the United States and Elsewhere," in Michael L. Wachter and Susan M. Wachter, eds., Toward a New U.S. Industrial Policy? (Philadelphia: University of Pennsylvania Press, 1981), pp. 453-82.

[21]These large issues are laid out in Miriam Camps and William Diebold, The New Multilateralism--Can the World Trading System Be Saved? (New York: Council on Foreign Relations, 1983).

[22]The main contention of Industrial Policy as an International Issue cited in note 1 was that unless better means were found of dealing with the clashes of national industrial policies, they would probably destroy the system of cooperation in international trade. Nothing that has happened since the book was published gives me any reason to change that judgment.

[23]William E. Brock, "Trade and Debt: The Vital Linkage," Foreign Affairs, Summer 1984, pp. 1037-57.

[24]Sidney Weintraub, Free Trade Between Mexico and the United States? (Washington: Brookings Institution, 1984).

3

The New Industrialization Strategy in Mexico for the Eighties

René Villarreal Arrambide

INTRODUCTION

This chapter deals with Mexico's new industrialization strategy and foreign trade policy. The presentation begins with a review of the industrial policy the country followed until the 1982 crisis. Then follows an overall description of the objectives and strategies adopted after December 1982 for reordering the economy in order to avoid deterioration in productivity and employment. The presentation concludes with a detailed examination of the objectives and the strategy of structural change in industry and foreign commerce, and its application in protective, development, and regulation policies.

EVOLUTION OF INDUSTRIAL DEVELOPMENT UNTIL THE 1982 CRISIS

World War II provided a favorable opportunity for Mexico to initiate its industrialization process based on import substitution. This initial impulse was later strengthened by deliberate promotion by the government, whose principal functions during the 1950s were to protect and finance industrial development in general and to participate directly in the production of oil and derivates, iron and steel, fertilizers, and paper.

During the 1950s, national production grew at an average annual rate of 5.8 percent and manufacturing at 6.3 percent. Industry became the driving force of expansion,

47

substituting with domestic production for the majority of imports of consumption goods,thereby transforming the agro-mining-export character of the economy. Imports of consumer goods were reduced from 25 percent total imports in 1939, to less than 10 percent in 1960. However, the substitution of intermediate and capital goods was not achieved. Imports of these goods increased considerably during that period; intermediate goods increased from 25 to 32 percent of total imports and capital goods from 50 to 58 percent.

In the 1960s, the government continued its policy of import-substituting industrialization, which by then was showing internal disjointedness. An anti-export bias was generating external and internal imbalances and was being increasingly financed with foreign capital. The government continued to support industrialization by the creation of an infrastructure. It also provided costly strategic items, such as oil and electricity, at subsidized prices, which aggravated the public sector deficit. External debt played an increasingly greater role in the financing of the public sector.

During that decade, production of manufactures increased at an annual average rate of 8.3 percent. Progress was made primarily in substituting for imports of durable consumer goods and to some extent for intermediate and capital goods. The proportion of imports in the total offer of intermediate goods diminished from 42 to 22 per cent and of capital goods from 74 to 50 percent. One unfavorable aspect during that decade was that industrial production for export grew only by 3.2 to 3.4 percent, a rate insufficient to finance the sector's imports. In 1970, the trade deficit was $1.039 billion and the deficit for the manufacturing sector was $1.355 billion. The latter was a reflection of imports by the most dynamic industrial branches such as nonelectrical machinery, automotive, electrical appliances, and chemicals. These sectors were not integrated, and required increased direct and indirect imports. Dynamism decreased in the traditional industrial sectors.

In the period 1970-1982, Mexico created a diversified industrial structure. Manufacturing production grew at an average annual rate of 6.8 percent. By 1982, Mexico was second in Latin America in gross national product per capita and in the aggregate value of manufacturing production,, and first in the value of merchandise exports, including oil.

However, starting in the early 1960s, the Mexican economy has shown the negative effects of structural imbalances in industry. The adverse international situation added complications. The 1976 and 1982 Mexican crises were manifestations of the imbalances created by the industrial strategy adopted after 1940. Because of their importance, it is necessary to mention those factors which explain the Mexican crisis.

Above all, Mexico experienced a macroeconomic imbalance. From 1977 to 1981, annual aggregate demand increased by more than 10 percent, while internal production increased by 8 percent; this led to growing import pressure. In addition, inflationary pressures became acute. As a result of the decision to fix the Mexican peso's exchange rate in order to contain inflation, the currency suffered from overvaluation. In December 1981, this over-evaluation was the equivalent of a 32 percent tax on exports and subsidy to imports. This aggravated the damage of the import-substitution process. It also encouraged the tendency toward the single product exportation of hydrocarbons. In addition, the flight of capital caused by economic and noneconomic factors stimulated the resort to more foreign loans. This reinforced expectations of a maxidevaluation and accelerated the flight of capital even more.

The combination of high investment and capital flight left national savings insufficient to cover the demand for credit. From 1978 to 1982, gross fixed capital investment increased further, leading to more foreign loans.

Factors of foreign origin were added, such as the general recession in international trade which affected Mexican exports, the increase in interest rates internationally, beginning in 1980, which meant a greater expenditure in servicing foreign debts, and the drop in prices and the demand for oil in the international market during the second half of 1981, which significantly altered expectation of foreign currency income.

In addition to the macroeconomic problems leading to the 1982 crisis, we should cite those of a structural character which industrialization had been generating. These included imbalances between the industrial and the foreign sectors; the low level of industrial integration, which led to gaps in the production chains of basic and strategic goods; the disjunction of industry from the rest of the economy; the geographic concentration of industry; the use of noncompetitive technology and plants of a technically inefficient size; and the lack of interaction between enterprises of different sizes.

These factors led to an industrial production highly dependent on imports, of low competitiveness, and unable to generate enough productive jobs to respond to national needs. The 1982 crisis demonstrated that national industry, despite its spectacular growth, did not adequately meet the basic demands of the population. Furthermore, the basic imbalances of the industrialization process, accentuated by the macroeconomic and sectoral policies, led to stop-and-go policies which manifested themselves acutely in 1982, when gross domestic product decreased by 0.2 percent and inflation reached 98 percent. The crisis had repercussions which affected the productive units since they faced a reduction in internal demand, increased indebtedness in national and foreign currencies, and unprecedentedly high costs for supplies and imported goods necessary for production. The situation threatened to unleash a generalized failure of the productive plant and an unprecedented increase in open unemployment.

PROGRAM FOR THE DEFENSE OF EMPLOYMENT AND THE PRODUCTIVE PLANT

Facing this pessimistic panorama, the 1982 crisis made clear the need to assure the survival of the productive plant in the short term and then to revitalize it by 1984. The December 1982 "immediate economic rearrangement program" (Programa Inmediato de Reordenación Económica - PIRE), had a set of guidelines to deal with inflation, the unstable exchange rate and the shortage of foreign exchange, the protection of employment and the productive plant, and restoring the bases for sustained growth. As part of PIRE, the "program for the defense of the productive plant and employment" (Programa para la Defensa de la Planta Productiva y el Empleo) was established in February 1983.

The strategy of this program was to orient demand toward domestic production, utilizing the public sector's purchases to promote an efficient substitution of imports. Production was also promoted in the northern border area. Imports of goods that could be produced locally were strictly controlled.

Because of foreign debt problems, the program supported business enterprises in their dealings with foreign creditors through the establishment of the "commission for the protection of exchange risks" (Fideicomiso para la Cobertura de Riesgos Cambiarios, or FICORCA), which took over the obligation to pay the foreign-exchange debts of national enterprises.

The foreign currency shortage forced strict rationing to meet debt-service commitments and the need to import vital supplies to keep productive plants going. A program to encourage nonpetroleum exports was developed.

Special funds were created or expanded to support business enterprises with cash-flow problems and to help them obtain priority items needed for the production of basic goods, goods for export, and to assist cooperatives and small and medium-sized industries.

An evaluation of the program made in 1983 concluded that a generalized bankruptcy of enterprises and an increase in the rate of open unemployment had been prevented. However, all the problems affecting production were not resolved. The strategy in 1984 aimed at the gradual and selective expansion of demand and supply, especially by greater utilization of existing productive capacity. Public and private investment projects of high priority were continued and new national private investment was supported, as was foreign investment on a selective basis.

INDUSTRY AND FOREIGN TRADE: STRUCTURAL CHANGE STRATEGY

Dealing with the problems of the Mexican economy requires more than emergency programs. It was necessary to transcend the emergency with an integrated strategy to radically change the organization, and hence performance, of industry in order to avoid repetition of the vicious cycle of growth-recession.

The strategy of the De la Madrid administration is designed to achieve a new industrialization pattern and specialization in foreign commerce. It is designed to achieve balance relationship between industrial growth and foreign trade, greater industrial integration and intersectoral articulation, and greater international competitiveness.

The strategy seeks to offer answers to questions faced by all societies: what and how much to produce?; how to produce, taking into account two dimensions, technical-productive and political-economic?; where to produce?; with whom to produce?; and for whom to produce?

It is necessary to stress several specific issues in the Mexican case.

First: We must decide which industrial branches

should have production priority.

    <u>Second</u>: Which technologies will allow us to move during the current transition into a new technological pattern?

    <u>Third</u>: Which technical relations are the proper ones to achieve an efficient production that responds to the country's productive resources and which allows for the industrial plant's competitive operation in seeking optimum output levels?

    <u>Fourth</u>: We must define the strategic criteria for industry's geographic location, taking into account the sectoral order and the demands placed by regional development.

    <u>Fifth</u>: What must be the specific participation of each productive element within the context of our mixed economy under governmental direction and democratic planning?

    <u>Sixth</u>: Who will be the principal beneficiaries of the structural change?

    These questions will be faced from six interrelated orientations of structural change:

    1.   The industrialization strategy and the specialization pattern in foreign commerce.

    2.   The new industrial technological pattern.

    3.   The rationale for the industrial organization.

    4.   The industrial location strategy.

    5.   The participation of the industrial sectors in production and foreign trade.

    6.   The social dimensions of the strategy.

1. The <u>Industrialization</u> <u>Strategy</u> <u>and</u> <u>the</u> <u>Specialization</u> <u>Pattern</u> <u>in</u> <u>Foreign</u> <u>Commerce</u>

    The Mexican pattern of industrialization is designed to integrate three groups of activities by differentiating by (1) the destination of products, (2) their dynamism, and (3) their effect on other economic activities.

    Those activities which are least vulnerable to external factors are those branches of industry which have the greatest degree of integration with the rest of the economy and which have had consistent dynamic growth. These are designated as the Endogenous Industrial Sector (Sector Industrial Edógeno - SIE). This sector relies largely on national resources and does not depend on substantial importation of raw materials for its operation; as a result, its foreign exchange requirements are minimal. Its coefficient of primary raw materials in relation to the total material required is 35 percent, and only 32 percent of this is imported. In quantitative terms the SIE generates 75 percent of total manufacturing output and 72 percent of the jobs. From 1972 to 1981, the average annual growth of its production was 6.3 percent.

The second group, called the Export Industrial Sector (Sector Industrial Exportador - SIEX) is made up of those branches of the endogenous sector that have an exporting tradition and successfully trade in the international market and have an exporting tradition. The principal characteristic of these branches is that they offer cost advantages and generate a positive balance of foreign exchange. Producing competitively to international standards, the sector contributes 40 per cent of the total manufactured exports.

The third group, called Import Substitution Industrial Sector (Sector Industrial Sustitutivo de Importaciones - SISI), has contributed little to productive integration within the economy. This last sector has made a minimal contribution to industrial integration and intersectoral articulation. The raw materials it requires for production represent 20 percent of all national imports and its coefficient of imports to value added is 30 percent.

The structural-change strategy considers the SIE to be the development lever. It will enjoy selective import protection and be linked to the total productive sector of the country. Because of its importance in total manufacturing production and employment, as SIE production and productivity levels rise, so also will the welfare of the population. This will also lead to selective improvement in export potential and intersectoral articulation because the input demand by this sector is representative of industrial output generally.

Because of the great vulnerability of the Mexican economy to developments in other countries, strengthening the exporting industrial sector is essential. Increasing exports has first priority, especially of those branches that contribute most to generating net favorable foreign-exchange balances. The short-term goal of consolidating this sector was pursued through the devalued exchange rate. The medium term objective is to regain markets for those goods which have cost advantages but lost export dynamism. The long-run objective is to modify the pattern of specialization in foreign trade so that capital goods and intermediate materials can be obtained domestically by means of import substitution into activities with export potential.

The import-substitution sector has been the most problematic throughout the industrialization process. Its future treatment will be markedly selective, based on two fundamental considerations. First, indiscriminate substitution of imports will be eliminated. In the past, indiscriminate import substitution has not resulted in an efficient industrial structure with widespread domestic linkages. Second, optimal integration of industry does not mean that all goods required for investment or national consumption must be produced internally. Over the medium term, many products are not desirable for substitution purposes because of their high cost. The objective is to promote the selective substitution of those strategic materials which are readily available and of capital goods that foster priority linkages with the endogenous and exporting sectors.

2. Industrial Integration and Intersectoral Linkages

Another aspect of the strategy is intersectoral linkage. Not only does the strategy seek to integrate productive chains of priority manufacturing branches, but also to promote effective linkage between manufacturing and other economic sectors. The objective is to achieve more efficient performance of the total national production system.

This means that industrial integration should strengthen those industries that generate materials and capital goods used in the primary, construction, energy, communications, transportation, commercial, and service sectors so that these, in turn, may efficiently supply those materials required of them by industry. The main effect of the linkages across sectors is to increase job opportunities and national income.

3. The New Industrial Technological Pattern

The new industrialization plan must develop a

technological base consistent with present and future needs
of the country. This technological pattern must foster
industrial integration and intersectoral linkages and foster
better and more rational utilization of the country's
resources. The road to this new technological pattern is
based on three strategies: a) defensive, in the case of
mature and conventional technologies; b) assimilative, for
new technologies; and c) taking the offensive, in the case
of leading technologies. These strategies will be applied
to the productive branches according to their present
technological state and the expected economic and social
consequences.

Conventional technologies will be promoted in those
activities important for the production of basic goods. New
technologies will be applicable to those industries likely
to increase the competitiveness of Mexican products abroad.
Leading technologies will be studied meticulously before
use.

Finally, technological innovation will take place
within productive plants of proper scale and with the
support of research and development centers linked to the
industry. To the extent that these linkages take place, we
can speak about Mexico going into an effective transition
toward a new technological pattern.

4. Rationale for the Industrial Organization

One of the problems noted above is the lack of cohesion
between productive units of different sizes. The strategy
for the parastatal (state-owned enterprise) industrial
sector gives priority to those enterprises that subcontract
a significant portion of their production. To achieve
flexible and efficient subcontracting, we will look
especially to the consolidation of medium-size enterprises
capable of subcontracting in order to reinforce this
relatively weak link in the structure of enterprise sizes.
The linkages among enterprises of different size will not
only increase the efficiency of national industry by
reducing production costs, but will also contribute to the
generation of productive employment since small units, which
will be consolidated and joined to subcontracting chains,
are capable of generating employment with a modest amount of
capital.

Another fundamental aspect of the strategy refers to

the promotion of plant sizes consistent with the market structure of the country. That means discouraging the proliferation of enterprises in activities in which demand is saturated and to search for new industrial projects in plant sizes that can effectively develop economies of scale made possible by the market.

5. Industrial Location Strategy

The current geographic distribution of the industry is the result of industrial policies followed during more than four decades. There has been a tendency to concentrate production in consumption centers, there generating attraction poles for the industry in two or three large-sized marketplaces. The objectives of the industrial location strategy are: to apply policies of decentralization more effectively to prevent new disfunctions in the territorial structure of the industrial plant; and to take advantage of the natural and human resources the country has in its various regions.

This strategic orientation will differentiate among branches and regions and push for the consolidation of medium-sized cities as centers for new industrial development. The new strategy will be implemented mainly by means of investment programming on national, regional and local levels, complemented, in the case of private investment, by more selective financial management, fiscal incentives, and the purchasing power of the public sector.

6. Mixed Economy Under Governmental Leadership

The structural change strategy is taking place within a mixed-economy system under the government's leadership. The strategy seeks to take maximum advantage of the potential and experience of each economic agent so as to foster collaboration among them. Since the mixed economy is part of a market system, industrial and commercial policies will not displace the market, but rather reorient it selectively and regulate it based on national development objectives.

7. Social Dimension of the Structural Change

This strategy is designed to achieve continuous generation of better-paid jobs, a more egalitarian distribution of income, and the satisfaction of the population's basic needs. These three achievements are to come about from self-sustaining, permanent, and cohesive development, which will increase national income and incorporate a greater part of the labor force into modern productive activity.

POLICIES FOR THE PROTECTION AND DEVELOPMENT OF FOREIGN TRADE

The policies for rationalization of protection and foreign-exchange budgeting have a short-term goal of avoiding decay of the foreign sector and of maintaining the productive plant in operation, including its level of employment. The medium-term goal is to contribute to the consolidation of an efficient, internationally competitive production system in terms of prices and quality, reducing inter- and intrasectoral distortions, and protecting the capital-goods industry.

Regarding export development policy, we will modify the pattern of specialization of foreign commerce, offering both overall and selective support to the branches defined as being part of the exporting sector. The exchange rate will be realistic, thereby rationalizing the use of foreign currency, and directed by a flexible policy that will contribute to the prevention of speculation and sudden movements of capital. The policy for border areas and duty-free zones will promote exports and expand financial backing to the twin-plant industry in order to stimulate employment in those areas. Policy for international business negotiations will seek to avoid indiscriminate use of foreign exchange by promoting unconventional means of trade, such as barter and bilateral agreements.

INDUSTRIAL DEVELOPMENT POLICIES

These policies have been designed with selective criteria. Financing policy seeks to guarantee the availability of financial resources for priority branches and achieve an optimum relationship between internal and external resources. The policy for the parastatal industrial sector is designed to make its investments consistent with the overall strategy, reorient its purchasing toward the domestic market, and repair its financial structure. Technological development policy will seek to develop a national, self-determined technical foundation, increase the efficiency of national industry and its competitiveness abroad, and raise productivity in those activities that form part of integrated productive chains of basic and general consumption goods. The industrial-structure policy will be founded on technical and economic criteria to promote higher levels of competitiveness based on optimum plant sizes, and degree of concentration in terms of the magnitude of the national market, capturing export potential, and using appropriate technology.

The policy for investment programming will give priority to public and private projects of greatest financial and strategic relevance for structural change by identifying those that form part of the productive chains. The strategy is to increase the availability of basic goods for popular consumption, substitute for imports where this is called for, and promote exports. The policy for fiscal incentives will support viable regional development and reduce indiscriminate support to large industries. The system will concentrate in the medium term on priority activities that contribute to the substitution of imports and industrial subcontracting. The policy for integral support to small- and medium-sized industries will be to consolidate this sector, which contains the majority of national enterprises, so that, through subcontracting, it becomes vigorously involved in industrial production.

REGULATION POLICIES

As a complement to the policies discussed above, regulation will reinforce market mechanisms in areas of particular importance for the protection of basic consumption and guarantees national leadership of industrial development. Price policy will be integral in the sense that there will be congruence between price controls, guaranteed prices, public sector prices, tariffs, subsidies, and transfer prices. With respect to subsidies, we shall seek transparency and selectivity. The public sector's prices and tariffs will be adjusted as needed, based on financial restructuring. Price control and registry will take place within a reduced universe of products whose impact is fundamental to the popular economy or to the production costs of priority activities.

Finally, policy for direct foreign investment will selectively promote the inflow of foreign capital, with the goal of helping national productive activity, the real transfer of technology, and the modernization of the industrial plant. Direct foreign investment regulation will be designed to assure its complementarity with national investments and avoid foreign domination of priority industrial branches.

Taken together, this is the new industrialization strategy of Mexico for the 1980s. Bilateral relations between Mexico and the United States must take place within this strategy and within a framework of reciprocal collaboration and mutual interest.

4

Industrial Strategy in the United States and the Impact on Mexico

Sidney Weintraub

INTRODUCTION

Countries have national development styles. These are not immutable but rather change with the country's stage of development. Discussions on major changes in trade and industrial policy are going on right now in both Mexico and the United States. Underdeveloped, primary commodity exporters have little need for protection, but tariffs and other indirect taxes are common to raise revenue. As a country embarks on an industrialization program, the typical pattern is to add tariffs or nontariff measures to protect infant industries. The protective pattern is rarely uniform; domestic production is shielded against competitive imports more than are imports of goods not produced at home. Once this differentiation is introduced into the import-protection pattern, levels of effective protection for various activities become jumbled. Capital-goods production, which does not exist at the infant stage, is frequently admitted free of duty. Intermediate goods, on the other hand, are rarely afforded duty-free entry and this complicates the cost structures of national producers who must pay higher prices than competitors for the same intermediate products. This competitive disability leads to elaborate schemes of drawbacks or export subsidies.

The free traders of the world for industrial products are almost invariably highly developed (highly industrialized) countries. Even in these countries, free trade in industrial goods is an ideal, a limit to be approached, but the approach has been consistent and accelerated since the end of World War II, except for the current flirtation with protectionism.

61

Complex theoretical constructs have been developed to justify these behavioral patterns of perceived national self-interest. It is hardly an accident that Adam Smith and David Ricardo did their thinking in the then leading industrial nation of the world or that a Latin American institution, the Economic Commission for Latin America, was the first to elaborate a coherent, modern-day theory justifying import-substituting industrialization (ISI). It took brilliance in each of these cases to theorize in a way that galvanized official policy, but the basis for the theorizing and the galvanization grew out of particular national experiences and situations.

The history of U.S. trade and industrial policy reflects this stages approach, not perfectly but reasonably precisely. The United States became gradually less protective as its industrial structure became more competitive internationally. There were lapses in this progression, such as the highly protective Smoot-Hawley tariff, but these are explainable (even if not justifiable) in their historical context. What was referred to earlier as the current "flirtation" with protectionism has erupted most vociferously in those U.S. industries which have lost international competitiveness, particularly automobiles, steel, and machine tools. There would be no General Agreement on Tariffs and Trade (GATT) as we know it, and there would have been no successive negotiating rounds of tariff and trade liberalization under the GATT without U.S. leadership. It is not surprising that developing countries complain after each round of these negotiations that they are not satisfied with the outcome. These GATT negotiations sought to approach the limit of free trade in industrial goods and developing countries do not yet see this as their limit.

Mexican industrialization policy similarly reflects this progression of philosophy from ultra-protection to gradual liberalization. Mexico has not yet completed its extreme ISI stage, but there have been intermittent efforts during the past fifteen years to write a partial finis to this chapter of Mexican industrial development. Because of the state of its industrialization, one can expect Mexico to abandon its extreme protectionist stage as it emerges from its present economic crisis. Leading Mexican trade and development theorists are rarely thoroughgoing ISI advocates today, but rather proponents of gradual import liberalization. One battle between the protectionists (mostly the small industrialists) and advocates of greater import openness (in the name of improving industrial

competitiveness) was fought out in 1979 when Mexico declined
to join the GATT. The protectionists won that skirmish but
the issue of extreme protection versus gradual import
liberalization has since returned.

The purpose of this essay is to examine U.S. trade and
industrial policy at this moment of U.S. economic history.
The analysis will cover the philosophic antecedents to the
current policy debate, the nature of the debate itself, and
the probable consequences for Mexico of potential outcomes.

CHANGING U.S. TRADE PRINCIPLES

Foreign officials who must deal with the United States
on trade matters know from bitter experience that the U.S.
constitution gives the Congress the power "to regulate
commerce with foreign nations...."[1] In discussing this issue
in The Federalist Papers, Madison had in mind the experience
under the Articles of Confederation and his primary concern
was to prevent "unceasing animosities" by "the relief of the
States which import and export through other States from the
improper contributions levied on them by the latter."
Hamilton devoted his discussion of this issue to the need
for "unrestrained intercourse between the States" to bring
out the "unequalled spirit of enterprise" which would make
the new country "the admiration and envy of the world."[2] The
conflict between the executive and legislative branches with
respect to this provision was not at the center of the
constitutional debate. The wisdom of the founding fathers
in establishing what today is called a common market or
customs union is not questioned,[3] but foreign nations might
wish that they had also centralized the power to regulate
commerce in the hands of the President rather than spread it
among what is today 535 individuals, each with his or her
own local or state agenda. Many U.S. trade policy conflicts
with foreign nations derive from the constitutional decision
on the branch in which to lodge this authority.

U.S. history is replete with tariff conflicts. There
undoubtedly would have been conflict no matter where primary
responsibility for trade policy was placed, but it is
undeniable that the U.S. constitutional provision on trade
regulation is tailor-made for engendering strife between the
branches. The Congress has recognized this and has followed
the practice of simultaneously delegating authority for
trade policy to the executive branch for specific purposes

for limited periods while retaining the prerogative to impose contrary policies. The Congress finds no inconsistency in railing against export subsidy practices of others while legislating U.S. subsidies, such as those inherent in the legislation on U.S. Domestic International Sales Corporations (DISCs); nor is it unusual for the same individual to advocate the freest possible trade in, say, agricultural products while seeking to protect industry within his state or district through domestic-content legislation for automobiles. One should not make too much of these inconsistencies; they are not unique to U.S. trade practice. What does stand out in the U.S. system is the need for the Congress to periodically sacrifice its primacy in the regulation of international commerce so that the U.S. government can conduct trade negotiations with other nations.

These limited renunciations of dominance were used in the 1930s under the reciprocal trade agreements program. They were used more extensively after the GATT came into existence and precise delegations were granted to the executive branch to reduce tariffs, and in due course to deal with nontariff measures, in successive rounds of multilateral trade negotiations. The bicycle metaphor became an article of faith among U.S. trade policy officials; some delegation of tariff-reduction authority was necessary, no matter how limited, in order to prevent the Congress from imposing protective measures. The contradictory authorities--constitutional favoring the Congress, and limited legislative authorities to the executive--could function efficiently only when both existed at the same time. The system could not stand still without rekindling protectionism. These successive delegations of authority set the pattern for the worldwide trade liberalization that has taken place since World War II.

The tension between the two branches is never absent. When the executive branch traded away the American-selling-price (ASP) method for calculating U.S. tariffs for various products, particularly some benzenoid chemicals, in the Kennedy round, the Congress refused to ratify the action on the grounds that the executive branch had exceeded the authority granted to it.[4] In order to deal with the many complex nontariff measures negotiated in the Tokyo round (the multilateral trade negotiations, or MTN), a deal was struck under which the Congress not only delegated some authority but also participated actively in the negotiations themselves in return for what became known as a "fast-track" process of approval of the results.[5] The constitutional-legislative authorities for trade negotiations have thus become extremely complex, involving congressional primacy, limited delegations to the executive, maintenance of congressional authority despite these delegations, and actual congressional participation in what are essentially executive activities in the conduct of foreign policy. The system works, but so do Rube Goldberg contraptions.

The point that must be made is that foreigners have come to understand intellectually, even though they often bridle viscerally, that they must conduct two trade negotiations with the United States, one each with the executive and legislative branches, and that they may get whipsawed in the process.[6] Neither of the two branches is reluctant to threaten foreigners with congressional restriction if they fail to reach agreement in some negotiation with the executive branch.

Despite this organizational complexity, the basic aspects of U.S. trade policy have been reasonably consistent since the 1930s, and particularly in the period since World War II and the formation of the GATT.[7] There have been lapses from this consistency, but they were seen as exceptions. Looking ahead, it is no longer clear whether the lapses or the basic principles will dominate.

Among the constant principles which have dominated U.S. trade policy until recently have been adherence to the unconditional most-favored-nation (MFN) clause, the doctrine of reciprocity, the striving for steady reduction in protection (at least among industrial nations), and the settlement of disputes through negotiation, conciliation, or arbitration.

The MFN clause has been breached repeatedly since the formation of the GATT, in the establishment of customs unions and free-trade areas, the institution of tariff preferences by industrial countries in favor of developing countries, and in one-way free-trade mechanisms, such as those under the Lomé agreements between the European Community (EC) and developing countries in Africa, the Caribbean, and the Pacific, and most recently by the United States in favor of countries in the Caribbean Basin. The United States has concluded a two-way free trade agreement with Israel and is negotiating one with Canada.

The MFN principle in its unconditional form was discarded at U.S. and European initiative in the negotiation of some key nontariff codes in the MTN. In these codes, those on subsidies and countervailing measures and government procurement, like treatment was not extended to all GATT contracting parties but only to those nations which subscribed to the codes. This conditional form of MFN is a reversion to a practice abandoned by the United States in the 1920s.

One can argue with much logic that each of these derogations from the unconditional MFN principle was justified in light of the existing circumstances, but the totality of the exceptions and the accumulation of new departures means that the MFN clause (in Article I of the GATT) is now embedded in U.S. trade practice only when it is convenient. The European Community reached this situation much earlier. MFN is no longer a principle but a tactic. The implications of this reality are far from clear regarding either future U.S. trade policy or international trade practice.

Reciprocity in U.S. trade practice meant from the 1930s forward that tariffs and other trade barriers would be reduced only as part of a negotiation in which there was a quid pro quo. It was a trade-liberalizing concept. There was a derogation from the principle in part IV of the GATT in favor of developing countries, but this was more a codification of reality than a substantive departure from actual practice. One can argue whether it was wise to codify the reality and thus forsake the principle, particularly since this was done primarily to dull the attraction of the then-forming United Nations Conference on Trade and Development (the effort failed), but the action was not protectionist on the part of the industrial countries. (It may have fortified the developing countries in their protectionism, however. This was an example of countries taking protective positions commensurate with their stage of development.) More recent U.S. reciprocity proposals have been protectionist rather than liberalizing. They would close access to the United States for particular products, or even across the board, unless a trading partner was seen to give the United States comparable entry into its market for a given product or for U.S. products generally. One analyst has referred to this as "aggressive" as compared with the "passive" reciprocity that existed earlier.[9]

This aggressive reciprocity has not been put into practice. What has happened so far is that the United States has threatened retaliation in the name of reciprocity in the hope that the threat need not be carried out. The idea for the threat arose in the Congress and is an example of the importance of congressional primacy in the regulation of U.S. trade.

In past U.S. trade negotiating rounds under the GATT, the U.S. tactic was to put on the table for negotiation all,

or practically all, that the executive branch had to offer
as the result of specific congressional authorizations. If
comparable concessions were not offered by others, proposed
tariff reductions were withdrawn to achieve what was deemed
to be reciprocity. The new tactic is different. It would
put maximum retaliatory threats on the table and seek
concessions from others as a price for withdrawing the
threats. The difference between the two tactics is
profound.[10] Like the progressive abandonment of the MFN
principle, the long-term implications of this new tactic are
unclear but troublesome for the expansion of world trade.

The U.S. trade-liberalizing bicycle is not now moving
forward and, as experts predicted would be the case,
protectionism is increasing. Early in the Reagan
administration, the U.S. Trade Representative made what he
called a "statement on U.S. trade policy" on behalf of the
administration.[11] It called for the "maintenance of open
markets at home and abroad," adherence to the "principle of
reciprocity," the need for adjustment of an industry or
shifting to other activities when "other nations have a
natural competitive advantage," the avoidance of "trade-
distorting bilateral deals," and stating as an overall goal
the achievement of "free trade, based on mutually acceptable
trading relations." Some three years later, one commentator
referred to the executive branch, along with the Congress,
as the free-trade "villain."[12] The commentary cited
administration rhetoric which encourages industry filings of
"unfair" trade-practice complaints (i.e., countervailing and
anti-dumping duty petitions), the forcing of export
restraints on trading partners, granting import relief to
the specialty steel industry, the prolongation of restraints
on Japanese auto sales, and the tightening of the already
stringent system of textile and apparel quotas.

It is not fair to say that the Reagan administration is
protectionist, or even more protectionist than its recent
predecessors. It is true, however, that it has catered to
protectionist interests in particular cases even as it
advocated free trade as a longer-term objective. This,
however, is in the mainstream of U.S. practice for more than
forty years. The key difficulty that this administration
had to contend with was that the economic times conspired to
heighten protectionist sentiment in the country, or at least
in the Congress, because of a severe economic recession,
high unemployment, a series of record-high U.S. trade
deficits, and the decline of many basic U.S. industries at a
time that new competitors were coming on the scene to join
the traditional competitors. The administration can be

faulted for not trying to counteract these protectionist
pressures by seeking new trade-liberalizing legislation--the
most common protectionist neutralizer of the past. It has
instead pandered to protectionism by adopting the
restrictive definitions of reciprocity and fair trade.

The objective of free trade stated by the U.S. trade
representative early in this administration was also in the
mainstream of executive-branch positions of the past two or
three decades. One is nonetheless impressed by the felt
need in recent academic writing to make the case once again
for free trade--a case which a few years ago one would have
thought was accepted wisdom for the United States.[13] The
arguments for free trade are familiar: efficiency; widening
of choice; achievement of economies of scale; advancement of
technology through the spur of competition. The arguments
against free trade are similarly familiar: the need to
develop infant industries (the stages approach to trade and
industrial policy discussed at the outset of this essay);
national security (this case is being made in the United
States as this is written for the machine-tool industry);
and most important, that markets are not competitive. That
the free-trade arguments must again be rehearsed in the
academic literature in the United States is a sign of the
protectionist times. It may also be a symptom of the
changing industrial position of the United States. This
will be taken up in the next section since this is at the
heart of the debate now taking place in the United States
regarding trade-industrial-regulatory policy.

Raymond Vernon has made the point that even though
basic trade policy principles may be in eclipse--in the
United States and industrial countries generally--it is
important to keep the GATT alive to perform its dispute-
settlement function and to serve as a launching pad for
future trade initiatives.[14] The GATT, in fact, is being
increasingly bypassed in national trade actions. There is
support for a new safeguard clause for imposing import
restrictions precisely to arrest the erosion in the use of
GATT's escape clause prescribed in Article XIX.[15] Recent
U.S. protective actions, such as voluntary export restraints
(VERs) limiting Japanese auto sales and earlier VERs
affecting other exporters and other products, and U.S.
protection against steel imports, have taken place outside
the GATT framework. U.S. behavior in connection with
complaints by other nations about the consistency of the
U.S. DISC legislation with the articles of the GATT gave the
clear impression that the United States did not welcome the
use of the GATT dispute-settlement procedure in this case.[16]

This same Canadian trade expert has characterized recent U.S. safeguard behavior as a contingency system of protection, that is, the use of anti-dumping and countervailing duty procedures, rather than of GATT Article XIX. The latter requires compensation when duties are raised on a commodity which is "bound" in the GATT (that is, when a concession has been "paid for" by another country under the old passive system of reciprocity). This contingency protection also involves negotiations outside the GATT for VERs and orderly marketing agreements. This new system, he argues, has led to "power-oriented rules."[17] Another writer has made the same point, that the new protectionism has shifted from firm rules to administrative discretion and, concurrent with this, to a lack of openness in the determination of protective steps.[18]

Taken together, these departures from GATT principles, and even from the GATT itself, could lead to far-reaching changes in the rules under which international trade is conducted, coupled with the absence of a central institution to provide decisions that would be heeded on what the rules are. The United States is not the only culprit in the deterioration of previously accepted rules and principles. Developing countries, including those that are relatively advanced economically, opted out of key rules from the outset. The West Europeans have established a preferential system encompassing not only themselves but countries on their periphery and former colonies. The great danger is precisely what Grey has noted, that in a system without rules, or with rules that can be bent with impunity, trade relations are transformed into an exercise in comparative power. It is not clear that there can be many winners under such a system, but the most probable losers will be the weaker countries, the developing countries.

Mexico has already been affected by this change in the form of protectionism. Mexico was not a signatory to the code on subsidies and countervailing measures and therefore did not receive comparable treatment under the code from the United States to that given to signatories. In practice, this meant that subsidies granted by Mexico were countervailable when the goods entered into the United States even if there was no injury or threat of injury to a competing U.S. producer. A bilateral agreement has since corrected this. Mexico never joined the GATT and was thus a free rider in the system of rules and principles established in that institution. Mexico benefited from the MFN principle; and it received the fruits of duty reductions negotiated by others under the practice of passive reciprocity. Mexico hoped during the heyday of the dominance of world oil suppliers that it could practice bilateralism to its advantage by trading access to its oil for other benefits.[19] This strategy is less viable when there is an oil glut and most of the leverage is on the side of the oil importer. A coherent and transparent system of rules for the conduct of international trade can only be of benefit to Mexico, especially now as it seeks to expand markets and diversify the product content of its exports. Its absence from the GATT has made Mexico a bystander in the international debate taking place regarding trade policy, but it is an interested party and its renewed application to enter GATT is a reflection of this reality.

ELEMENTS OF CURRENT U.S. DEBATE

A series of issues has come to a head simultaneously in the United States. These are: declining growth in productivity after 1973, and into the 1980s; a large merchandise trade deficit, close to $150 billion in 1985; the decline of some basic U.S. industries, particularly automobiles and steel; the breakdown of the GATT, at least its central tenets; the emergence as major trade competitors of newly industrializing countries (NICs), many of which wish to be treated differently (preferentially) even as they compete vigorously; the international financial (debt) crisis; and the deregulation of large elements of the U.S. economy. Suggested remedies for dealing with these issues are still inexact. They run the gamut from scapegoating others (hence the use of the phrase "fair trade" and the introduction of aggressive reciprocity); changing the mix of U.S. fiscal and monetary policy (which, it is argued, will lead to lower interest rates and the depreciation of the overvalued dollar); or adopting vigorous new programs to stimulate "sunrise" industries (high tech) and restructure (increase productivity) or shift out of "sunset" industries (such as autos and steel).

Most of these issues are not new; what is new is the intensity of their simultaneous eruption in the United States. The pervasiveness of the debate reflects the accumulated seriousness of the issues. Dealing with the problems these issues pose involves policy inconsistencies. Protectionism is the offspring of economic recession and unemployment, but the recent vigorous upswing of the U.S.

economy has led to the growth of the merchandise deficit. The fair-trade offensive is directed primarily at NICs, such as Brazil and Mexico, even though it is recognized that resolution of the international debt crisis requires sustained export increases by these countries. The stimulation of sunrise industries may require subsidies even as the United States criticizes the subsidies of others. Restructuring basic industries has involved import protection even as the United States cites free trade as its objective.

Other papers prepared for this conference discuss what is meant by "industrial policy" by different advocates.[20] In many of its manifestations, industrial policy is trade policy under a different label. The need to adjust to changing competitive positions, avoid overvaluation of the exchange rate, provide adjustment for workers damaged by imports, and respond in some manner to subsidization by others that damages domestic industry, have long been elements of trade policy. The intention of those advocating a U.S. industrial policy must be to go beyond trade policy, or put differently, to change the objective from free trade to that trade which emerges from the specific stimulation of certain favored activities, or the protection of particular industries. Different advocates have focused on various kinds of industries: "high value-added emerging industries"[21]; "key linkage" industries such as autos and steel[22]; and machine tools.[23] Others have focused on techniques: tax incentives, loan guarantees, and other types of subsidies[24]; labor-management-government cooperation[25]; a subsidized lending institution similar to the Reconstruction Finance Corporation[26]; and import protection, sometimes conditional on action by the industry and sometimes not.[27] Except possibly for the idea of labor-management-government cooperation, each of these suggestions is explicitly selective; a specific industry is chosen, by some technique, and it is targeted for assistance.

Targeting has, in fact, become the word of art to describe the working of industrial policy. Japan is criticized for targeting the auto industry for penetration of the U.S. market. Brazil is chastized for targeting the steel industry and then using subsidies for penetration of the U.S. market. Industrial policy advocates want to target U.S. industries for development and as a means to restore what is believed to be the declining competitiveness of U.S. industry. Critics of this suggestion obviously are concerned about who does the targeting.

The purpose of this essay is not to enter into the virtues and defects of industrial policy (because of the many varieties which exist, it would take a volume to do this), but rather to analyze implications for U.S. international trade policy and for Mexico. Practically all of the techniques suggested for targeting--subsidies in one form or another and protection, conditional or otherwise-- would involve a further departure of the United States from its free-trade goal. One rationale for this departure is that others follow this practice and if they will not desist, the United States must join them. This is similar to the argument in favor of discrimination and for bilateralism. The road to free trade, using this justification, must first pass through obstacles previously condemned--discrimination, bilateralism, and now subsidization and protectionism.

It may be that there are forms of industrial policy, such as greater labor-management-government cooperation, that will not require greater subsidization and protection. However, industrial policy as practiced in those sectors in which we have known it--agriculture and defense industries in the United States and elsewhere, the regulation of trade in textiles and clothing, the rationalization of the steel and auto industries--has involved a mixture of subsidy and protection. Indeed, when there is a significant subsidy granted by the government, the logical consequence is to protect the government's investment by limiting imports. This is the history of agriculture in international trade. There may be exceptions to this combination of heavy subsidy and protection against imports, but this author is unable to cite any.

The goal of industrial policy is to encourage the growth and development of emerging industries or to ease the transition to a new competitive situation of existing but no longer competitive industries, or both. The techniques for accomplishing either or both of these objectives involve promotion (tax concessions, subsidized loans, financing of research, subsidized export credits, and other comparable measures that imply a a fiscal burden) and/or protection (import restrictions, generally nontariff in nature). As the title of this essay indicates, the methods for encouraging new industries or easing the adjustment or structural burden for old industries can also encompass regulatory change.

There have been proposals to alter U.S. antitrust laws to permit horizontal mergers (between companies in the same industry) and vertical mergers (a corporation taking control

of a supplier or a company to which it sells goods and
services) in the name of efficiency. "Bigness in some kinds
of business activity may have to be encouraged rather than
discouraged. So too might certain kinds of collaboration
and information-sharing within strictly enforced limits."[28]
The two authors from which this citation was taken make the
point that, as in tax policy, the United States should
practice targeting in regulatory policy.

Antitrust rules have been eased to provide limited
immunity for joint export efforts. Many persons advocate
doing something similar for joint research.[29] A senior
official in the Carter administration proposed a procedure
for official certification of an industry as distressed
(using such criteria as the proportion of idle installed
capacity, change in profits, change in employment, and
percent of the domestic market supplied by imports) after
which mergers would be permitted.[30] Under most of these
suggestions, conditions would be imposed on the industry
(such as making new investment), and on labor (limiting wage
benefits or actually reducing wages), as a price for
antitrust immunity. The point is usually skirted, but the
antitrust immunity may in these cases be coupled with
temporary and declining import restrictions to ease the
adjustment of the industry.

The conceptual backdrop to the various proposals for an
industrial policy is the conviction that the United States
is deindustrializing, that it is losing out in the
competitive struggle with other nations which use all the
promotion, protective, and regulatory techniques of
industrial policy. The very titles of the leading works in
this field make clear the sentiment behind the proposals:
The Deindustrialization of America (which deals primarily
with sunset industries); The Next American Frontier (which
stresses emerging industries); and "Reconstructing America"
(which focuses on the promotion instruments of industrial
policy). The opponents of industrial policy challenge both
the diagnosis and the prescription.

Robert Lawrence has stated bluntly: "Most of the
stylized characterizations about U.S. manufacturing
performance are inaccurate."[31] His evidence includes the
following: Compared with other industrial countries, U.S.
manufacturing industries did not fail to invest in physical
capital or in research and development between 1973 and
1980. After 1973, the United States was the only major
industrial country with positive growth in labor inputs into
manufacturing. Of the 52 sectors making up manufacturing,
only 11 had declines in employment due to trade between 1970

and 1983. "Without the jobs created by manufacture trade
between 1973 and 1980, U.S. industrial employment would have
declined."[32] Manufacturing employment did decline by 1.5
million between 1980 and 1982, and Lawrence states that
one-third of this was due to trade. He argues, based on
econometric analysis, that the erosion in U.S. trade
performance was due to the global recession and the
appreciation of the dollar. His prescription, therefore, is
to get U.S. macroeconomic policy correct rather than to turn
to selective policies of protection and promotion.

Lawrence is not alone in this view. Charles Schultze,
his colleague at the Brookings Institution, has expressed
doubt about the targeting aspects of industrial policy.[33]
Philip Trezise has commented that "...the impressive
economic growth and social stability of postwar Japan are
not owing in any decisive degree to the microeconomic
decision making that is often held up as a source of
Japanese accomplishments...."[34]

The debate in the United States on the nature and
direction of its industrial structure and the role of trade
in shaping this deals with substantial issues. The
opponents of industrial policy make their case in two
essential ways: The U.S. industrial sector will perform well
if the macroeconomic policy context permits this to take
place. (This context refers primarily to lower U.S.
interest rates and a more depreciated dollar.) Targeting at
the specific industry level is almost certain to be fraught
with political intrigue, as past U.S. experience has
demonstrated.[35] The opponents of industrial policy generally
share the objective of free trade among industrial
countries.

Those who favor some form of industrial policy make a
series of counterarguments. The question is not really
targeting, or selective policies, since that is implicit in
every tariff, nontariff measure, and tax, export credit, and
subsidy decision, but whether the targeting is coherent and
consistent. The United States has an industrial policy,
they argue. Why not have an efficient one? These persons
are not necessarily opposed to the free-trade objective, but
they tend to consider it irrelevant because of what other
countries are alleged to be doing and the deterioration in
any event of the basic tenets of the GATT system.

IMPLICATIONS FOR MEXICO

Many aspects of U.S. trade and industrial policy already are affecting Mexico. They could hardly do otherwise in light of the importance to Mexico of the U.S. market for manufactured goods.[36]

In the trade-policy field, many of the petitions for what in the United States is called "fair-trade" relief (requests for countervailing and anti-dumping duties) have been directed against Mexican industries. There is no reason to believe that the practice of making fair-trade petitions will diminish. The extent to which they will affect Mexican products depends on the need of Mexican exporters for subsidies, and this depends largely on the export incentive provided by the peso-dollar parity.

Mexico already faces some discrimination in the U.S. market. Mexico is not a beneficiary country under the Caribbean Basin Initiative. The degree of discrimination this will involve depends on the amount of investment attracted to beneficiary Caribbean and Central American countries and the degree to which these export platforms produce goods competitive with goods produced in Mexico. The most likely competition will be with maquiladora, or assembly, industries in Mexico. When goods from these industries are exported to the United States, the U.S. duty is imposed on the value added in Mexico; for most comparable products produced in the Caribbean Basin, there will be no U.S. import duty.

The issue of reciprocity as practiced in the United States can affect Mexico in several ways. The most visible relates to "graduation" from developing country status, particularly for preferential entry into the United States for designated Mexican products. The graduation issue is part and parcel of the reciprocity issue in U.S. trade thinking. The pattern of decision-making is that countries as advanced as Mexico, and other NICs, are less entitled to nonreciprocal treatment than less advanced countries and, therefore, the NICs should "pay" for the trade concessions they receive. The issue has not been a major one thus far; Mexico has been graduated from preferential treatment for only a few products. The issue may become more pressing if the U.S. trade deficit grows further.

The most serious aspect of recent international trade-policy developments, however, probably relates to the abandonment of principles and diminution of devotion to rules. Such abandonment could not but affect Mexico whether or not it enters GATT.

The promotion aspect of industrial policy involves a variety of subsidies for the selected industries. Mexico has practiced such selective promotion and this has led to disputes with the United States. If selective subsidization or promotion becomes the practice in the United States, this almost certainly will lead to disputes with Mexico. The protection aspects of industrial policy must lead to comparable disputes, as they already have when practiced by one or the other country.

However, U.S. promotion of emerging industries--what is loosely labeled high tech--need not adversely affect Mexico. The stage of Mexican development does not yet permit direct competition with the United States in most of these industries. To the extent that the United States focuses on these industries, and not on its less-competitive basic industries, this may leave scope for a beneficial division of labor between the two countries.

The industries most pregnant for conflict are those in which U.S. competitiveness is declining and Mexican competitiveness is increasing. This may be true for steel. It may be the case for cement. It may be true in the future for automobiles. The extent of the conflict will depend on the success of the structural adjustment in the United States and the rapidity with which Mexico builds its competitiveness.

There are other industries--and these may be the majority--in which the two countries can become complementary. This is possible for two of the industries cited above, autos and steel, and many others, such as petrochemicals and electronics. Complementarity involves specialization of each country in different aspects of production within these industries. This already exists to some extent, e.g., the production of small engines in Mexico for automobile assembly in the United States, the use of Mexican maquiladora in the electronics industry, and a greater concentration in the United States on higher derivative petrochemicals rather than the basic products in which Mexico may have a comparative advantage.

The United States is in the midst of a significant debate on its trade and industrial policy. The debate concerns basic trade principles and even the predictability of future trade practices. The debate deals also with the techniques that will be employed for adjusting the U.S. economy to its changed position in the world. There may be clear decisions from this discussion, but the more likely outcome is a continuation of the debate for an extended period even as discrete decisions are made on trade policy and industrial adjustment.

The decisions made will affect Mexico and will influence the outcomes of comparable debates taking place there. The two countries can only profit from regular consultation on these issues since what each does will condition what the other is able to do.

NOTES

[1]Article I, section 8 of the U.S. constitution.

[2]The relevant papers are numbers 42, 45, and 56 by James Madison and number 11 by Alexander Hamilton. The citations are from The Federalist Papers (New York: Mentor Book, 1961 edition with an introduction and commentary by Clinton Rossiter).

[3]The common market that is the United States is not questioned, but individual states sometimes take actions that contradict the acceptance of this common market. These take the form of "buy state" provisions for state government procurement. Recently the governor of New York proposed allowing grocery stores in that state to sell wines, but only New York State wines. The proposal was overturned in the courts.

[4]The ASP negotiation is discussed in John W. Evans, The Kennedy Round in American Trade Policy: The Twilight of the GATT (Cambridge, Mass.: Harvard University Press, 1971); and Ernest H. Preeg, Traders and Diplomats: An Analysis of the Kennedy Round of Negotiations under the General Agreement on Tariffs and Trade (Washington, D.C.: Brookings Institution, 1970).

[5]Twenty-third Annual Report of the President of the United States on the Trade Agreements Program - 1978 (Washington, D.C.: U.S. Government Printing Office, 1979).

[6]One senior Mexican official has referred to the Congress as the biggest U.S. nontariff barrier.

[7]Raymond Vernon, "International Trade Policy in the 1980s: Prospects and Problems." International Studies Quarterly, 26:4 (December 1982), pp. 483-510.

[8]The free-trade agreement with Israel was the first for the United States under the GATT.

[9]William R. Cline, "'Reciprocity': A New Approach to

World Trade Policy?" In William R. Cline, ed., Trade Policy in the 1980s (Washington D.C.: Institute for International Economics, 1983), pp. 121-158.

[10]The new technique resembles disarmament negotiations in the sense that the threat becomes a bargaining chip.

[11]William E. Brock, "Statement on U.S. Trade Policy." Before the Joint Oversight Hearings of the Senate Committee on Finance and Senate Committee on Banking, Housing, and Urban Affairs, July 8, 1981.

[12]I. M. Destler, "Why Reagan is a Free-Trade Villain." Column in The New York Times, March 18, 1984.

[13]Some examples are C. Fred Bergsten and William R. Cline, "Trade Policy in the 1980s: An Overview." In Cline, ed., Trade Policy in the 1980s, pp. 6-66; and Alan V. Deardorff and Robert M. Stern, "Current Issues in Trade Policy: An Overview." Department of Economics and Institute of Public Policy Studies, University of Michigan, April 15, 1983 (mimeo).

[14]Vernon, "International Trade Policy in the 1980s...."

[15]Alan Wm. Wolff, "Need for New GATT Rules to Govern Safeguard Actions." In Cline, ed., Trade Policy in the 1980s, pp. 363-391.

[16]Rodney de C. Grey, "A Note on U.S. Trade Practices." In Cline, ed., Trade Policy in the 1980s, pp. 243-257. See also John H. Jackson, "The Jurisprudence of International Trade: The DISC Case in GATT," The American Journal of International Law, 72:4 (October 1978), pp. 747-781.

[17]Ibid., p. 250.

[18]Max W. Corden, The Revival of Protectionism (New York: Group of Thirty, 1984).

[19]The administration of José Lopez Portillo signed various bilateral agreements, with Japan and Sweden to name just two, explicitly designed to trade oil availability from Mexico to nonoil concessions from the other country.

[20]See particularly the paper by William Diebold, Jr., "Industrial Policy in the United States."

[21]Robert B. Reich, "Beyond Free Trade," Foreign Affairs, 61:4 (Spring 1983), pp. 773-804.

[22]Ira C. Magaziner and Robert B. Reich, Minding America's Business: The Decline and Rise of the American Economy (New York: Vintage Books, 1983).

[23]Gary Hart, in his campaign for the Democratic nomination for the presidency.

[24]Reich, "Beyond Free Trade."

[25]Stan N. Lundine, "Now is the Time for a National Industrial Strategy." Challenge, 26:3 (July/August 1983), pp. 16-21.

[26]Felix Rohatyn, "Reconstructing America." New York Review of Books, March 5, 1981.

[27]Harald B. Malmgren, "Notes for a U.S. Industrial Policy." Challenge, 23:6 (January/February 1981), pp 19-23.

[28]Ronald E. Muller and David H. Moore, "America's Blind Spot: Industrial Policy." Challenge, 24:6 (January/February 1982), p. 10.

[29]Microelectronics and Computer Technology Corporation, of Austin, Texas, is an example of joint research for the next generation of computer technology.

[30]Stuart E. Eizenstat, "A New Antitrust Law." New York Times, op-ed column, April 22, 1984.

[31]Robert Z. Lawrence, "The Questionable Case for Selective Industrial Policies." Brookings Discussion Papers in International Economics No. 10, December 1983, p. 6.

[32]Ibid., p. 12.

[33]Charles L. Schultze, "Industrial Policy: A Dissent." The Brookings Review, 2:1 (Fall 1983), pp. 3-13.

[34]Philip H. Trezise, "Industrial Policy Is Not the Major Reason for Japan's Success." The Brookings Review, 1:3 (Spring 1983), p. 13.

[35]Murray L. Weidenbaum, "Industrial Policy Is Not the Answer." Challenge, 26:3 (July/August 1983), pp. 22-25.

[36]Gerardo M. Bueno, "U.S. Influence on Mexico's Economy." The Mexican Forum, 4:1 (January 1984), pp. 13-16.

PART TWO

Industry Studies

5

The Petrochemical Industry in Mexico

Francisco Barnés de Castro
and Lars Christianson

INTRODUCTION

The world is going through a transitional period of great importance for the life of nations. Just as societies evolved from agricultural to industrial, so now the most developed countries are experiencing a change from an industrial society to one essentially oriented toward information and service activities: that is to say, a society in which an increasingly important segment of its population is dedicated to create, process, and disseminate information and to provide specialized services, rather than to manufacture goods. Simultaneously, these countries are reorienting their research and development activities toward generating technologies which are more and more complex and sophisticated, allowing their business enterprises to maintain a competitive position in relation to the emerging industries that are now starting to proliferate in developing countries.

A cause of this change has been the accelerated development of international trade, which has brought increasing interaction of nations. The world has become so interdependent that it is no longer possible to think and act in an isolated manner, on the basis of autarchic national economies; instead it has become necessary for all of us to recognize that each country forms part of a global system which transcends frontiers, ideological divisions, and geographic barriers.

Commercial relations between countries which are traditionally producers of raw materials and those with high industrialization levels, producers of capital goods and manufactured products, are also in an evolutionary period.

83

Their interchange has altered as the countries on the road to development integrate themselves gradually into the international manufacturing trade, augmenting their production and export of goods of increasingly greater aggregate value, which replace or complement their traditional exports of raw materials. As a consequence, the industrialized countries tend to orient themselves toward the export of products of greater aggregate value with higher technological content.

The chemical and petrochemical industries do not escape these changes. The production of petrochemicals for general use (petrochemical commodities) is tending to move to countries rich in hydrocarbons. The industries in the most developed countries are being oriented instead toward technology-intensive products (TIPs), as their budgets for research and development demonstrate.

Some countries have recognized the need for change and are limiting the growth of their petrochemical industries with the expectation that those petrochemical raw materials which they once processed will now originate, under more favorable commercial conditions, in those regions having it as a natural resource; Japan is such a case. On the other hand, the petroleum-producing countries, in different ways, wish to initiate or expand the production of petrochemical products with increasingly higher percentages of integration. Some are doing this independently and in association with the principal multinational enterprises. It is within this context that one must place the development prospects of the petrochemical industry in Mexico.

BACKGROUND

Legal Framework

The legal framework for the petrochemical industry is based on the 1917 constitution of the United Mexican States, which states in Article 27, among other considerations, that direct control over oil and all solid, liquid, or gaseous hydrocarbons belongs to the nation and that this is an inalienable and imprescriptible domain. It also states that the exploitation, use, and development of these resources by private individuals or corporations duly formed under the laws of Mexico may not take place except by means of concessions granted by the federal executive power, under rules and conditions stipulated by law.

In order to establish the basic rules of the petrochemical industry's development under Article 27, the regulation-law for the oil industry was passed in November 1958, and is now in effect. Its fundamental concepts were more specifically defined through the rules and regulations for petrochemical matters, which went into effect on February 9, 1971. The following points should be highlighted regarding the regulations:

1. The petrochemical industry is based on the use of chemical and physical processes to create compounds derived totally or partially from the transformation of oil, gas, and their derivatives.

2. The petrochemical field is clearly delineated between that which is reserved to the nation and a second area in which private Mexican nationals or private corporations with a minimum of 60 per cent Mexican capital may participate. Private initiative participates in a determining way in this second area.

3. Provision is made for the legal formation of the Mexican Petrochemical Commission, whose objective is to promote the harmonious development of the national petrochemical industry, oversee its compliance with the relevant rules defined by legislation, and provide it with guidelines as set out in government plans and programs. The Commission also acts as an auxiliary organ for technical consulting in petrochemical matters for the Department of Energy, Mines and State-Owned Enterprises.

The Commission consists of a president and officers, who are, respectively: the Secretary of Energy, Mines, and State-Owned Enterprises (SEMIP); the Secretary of Commerce and Industrial Development (SECOFI); and the Director of Petróleos Mexicanos (PEMEX). The Commission includes a technical secretariat under the General Directorate of the Parastatal Chemical and Secondary Petrochemical Industry of SEMIP.

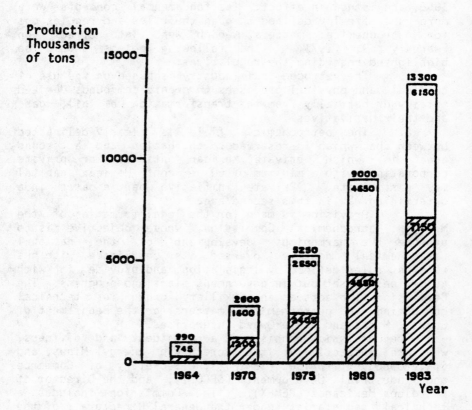

Production
Thousands
of tons

FIGURE 5.1
Evolution of the Petrochemical Industry in Mexico

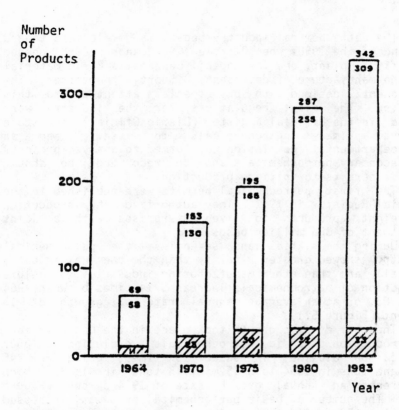

FIGURE 5.1 cont.

Historical Development of the Mexican Petrochemical Industry

The petrochemical industry began its development toward the end of the 1950s when Petróleos Mexicanos (PEMEX) opened its first plant, one for dodecil-benzene, a basic material for the manufacture of detergents. Shortly thereafter, the government decided to pay special attention to this industry. The first regulations for the industry were issued in the Official Register (Diario Oficial); the state reserved primary petrochemicals to itself, and an interdepartmental commission was formed to analyze projects for secondary petrochemicals and to recommend who should receive permits to initiate production.

The first petrochemical permits were published in the Official Register in 1961. They authorized the production of eight products to five enterprises with a joint investment of 300 million pesos.

During the sixties and seventies, the petrochemical industry showed greater vitality than the chemical industry generally and than other manufacturing industries. Volume production of petrochemicals increased 14 times between 1964 and 1983, or at an average annual rate of growth of 15 percent (Figure 5.1).

The most dynamic growth took place in the basic sector. The production of basic petrochemicals, excluding sulphur and carbon dioxide, increased 29 times, going from 245 thousand tons in 1964 to 5.15 million tons in 1983, which represents an annual growth rate of 19.4 percent (Figure 5.2). The number of basic petrochemical products increased from 11 to 33 during that period.

The production of petrochemicals in the secondary sector increased 8.3 times during the 1964-1983 period, at an average annual growth rate of 11.8 percent; the increase was from 745 thousand tons in 1964 to 6.15 million tons in 1983 (Figures 5.3-5.9). Of the secondary sector industries, chemical fibers, synthetic resins, and intermediate products stand out, showing growth greater than 13 percent annually in the last few years. The number of secondary products increased from 58 to 309 in the period mentioned.

Between 1961 and 1983, 359 petrochemical permits were issued to 163 enterprises for the installation of plants with a joint capacity of 10.456 million tons (Figure 5.10).

Foreign investment in the secondary petrochemical industry represents 26.3 percent of the total private investment permits authorized in the sector; of these, 64

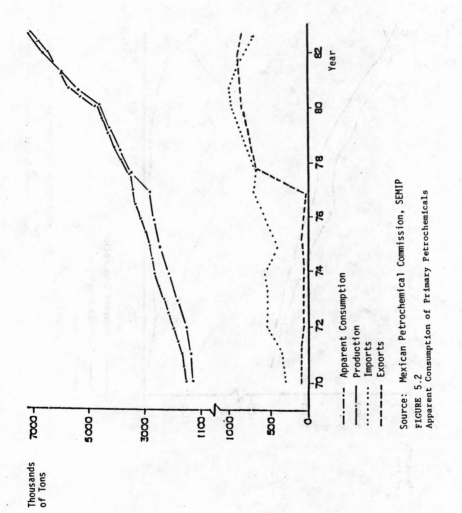

Thousands
of Tons

Year

Apparent Consumption
Production
Imports
Exports

Source: Mexican Petrochemical Commission, SEMIP

FIGURE 5.2
Apparent Consumption of Primary Petrochemicals

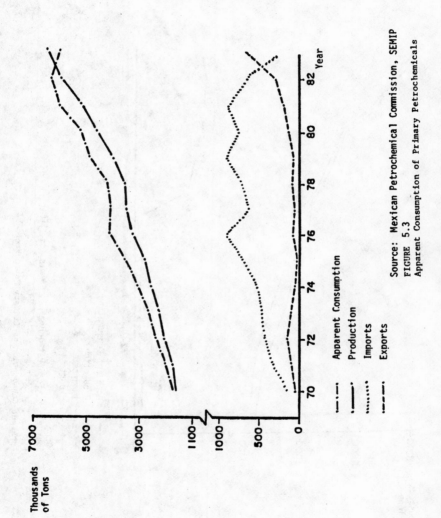

Thousands
of Tons

Apparent Consumption
Production
Imports
Exports

Source: Mexican Petrochemical Commission, SEMIP
FIGURE 5.3
Apparent Consumption of Primary Petrochemicals

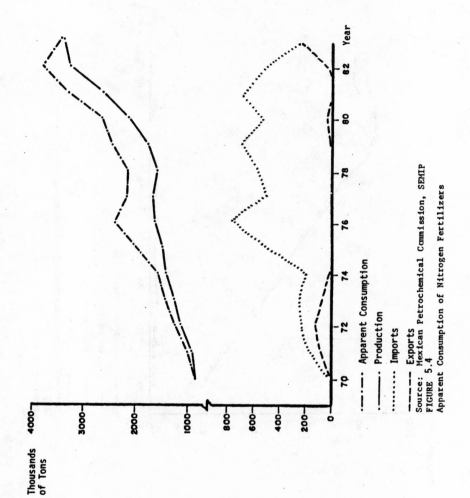

Thousands
of Tons

·—·—· Apparent Consumption
········· Production
·········· Imports
——— Exports
Source: Mexican Petrochemical Commission, SEMIP
FIGURE 5.4
Apparent Consumption of Nitrogen Fertilizers

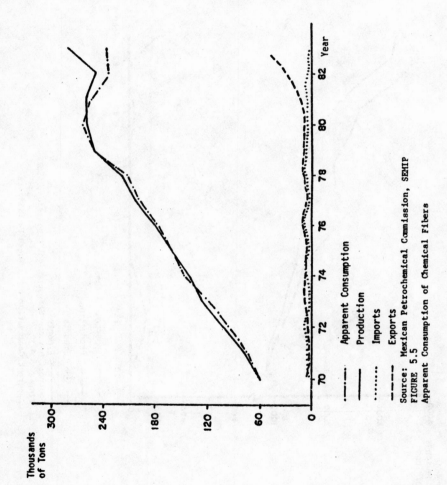

Thousands
of Tons

Apparent Consumption

Production

Imports

Exports

Source: Mexican Petrochemical Commission, SEMIP

FIGURE 5.5

Apparent Consumption of Chemical Fibers

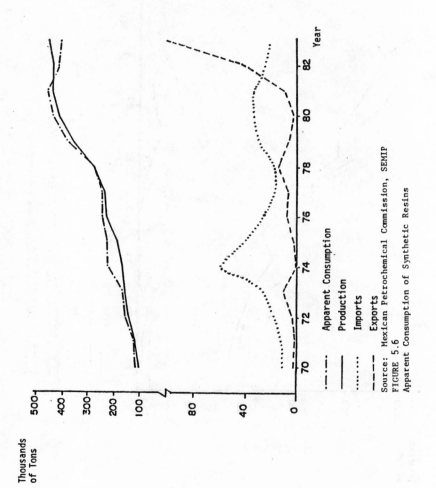

Thousands
of Tons

Year

Apparent Consumption
Production
Imports
Exports

Source: Mexican Petrochemical Commission, SEMIP
FIGURE 5.6
Apparent Consumption of Synthetic Resins

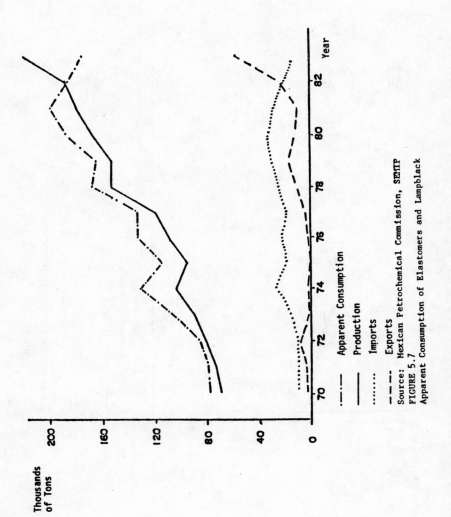

Thousands
of Tons

Apparent Consumption

Production

Imports

Exports

Source: Mexican Petrochemical Commission, SEMIP

FIGURE 5.7

Apparent Consumption of Elastomers and Lampblack

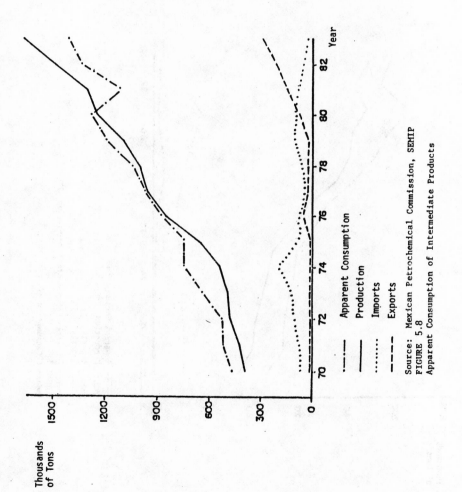

Thousands
of Tons

Source: Mexican Petrochemical Commission, SEMIP
FIGURE 5.8
Apparent Consumption of Intermediate Products

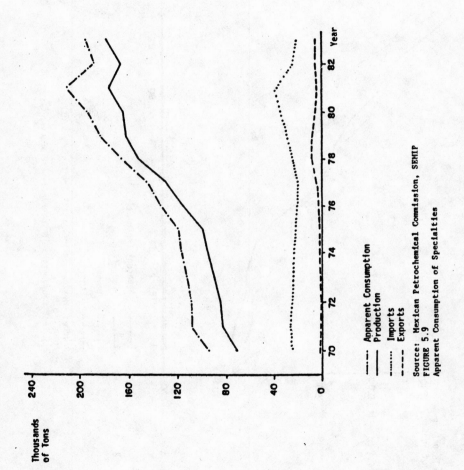

Thousands
of Tons

Apparent Consumption
Production
Imports
Exports

Source: Mexican Petrochemical Commission, SEMIP
FIGURE 5.9
Apparent Consumption of Specialties

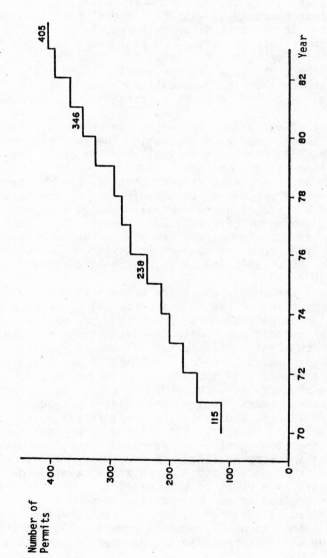

Source: Mexican Petrochemical Commission, SEMIP
FIGURE 5.10
Petrochemical Permits Granted

percent were for U.S. investment.

Supply has lagged behind demand in basic as well as secondary petrochemicals, with the exception of 1983, when the large fall in national demand allowed the channeling of more production for exports. With respect to production value, the level of self-sufficiency has not surpassed 85 percent during the last twenty years (Figure 5.11). Not even under the extraordinary conditions prevailing in 1983 was it possible to have a positive balance in petrochemical trade.

In spite of sustained increases in exports, imports have grown faster, gradually increasing the sector's deficit to a maximum of $876 million in 1981; the deficit declined to $158 million in 1983 (Figure 5.12).

It is worth noting that petrochemical product imports have averaged 6.7 percent of all imports during the last 15 years, while exports of petrochemical products were only 1.7 percent of all exports (Figure 5.13). During the last 15 years, the industry's deficit represented an average of 18 percent of the total trade deficit (there were trade surpluses in 1983, 1984, and 1985), reaching a maximum of 39 percent in 1977.

Analyzing separately the trade balance for each major commodity, using the Petrochemical Commission's classification of petrochemical products[1], one observes that all have been deficit prone with the exception of chemical fibers, which have fluctuated around a position of equilibrium (Figures 5.14-5.20). Chemical fibers, synthetic resins, elastomers (lampblack and chemorubbers), and intermediate products have succeeded in achieving a surplus only in recent years, while the primary petrochemicals, nitrogen fertilizers, and specialty areas remain in deficit.

It is unlikely that this situation will be drastically altered during the next few years. Thus, the primary petrochemical industry is likely to remain in deficit until the end of the decade and have an annual average deficit during the next five years of $200 million. On the other hand, it is logical to expect that the surplus in the trade balance attained in 1983 for secondary petrochemicals will decrease as the country recovers economically and that a trade surplus will not reappear in prosperous times until

---

[1]In this classification, ammonia, polyethylene, and polypropylene are considered primary petrochemicals.

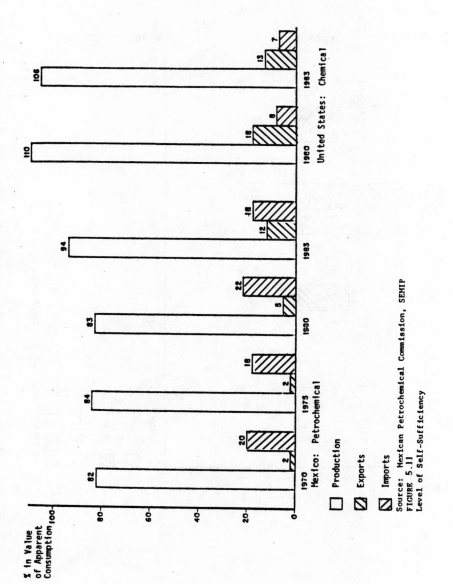

% In Value
of Apparent
Consumption

Mexico: Petrochemical

United States: Chemical

Production

Exports

Imports

Source: Mexican Petrochemical Commission, SEMIP

FIGURE 5.11

Level of Self-Sufficiency

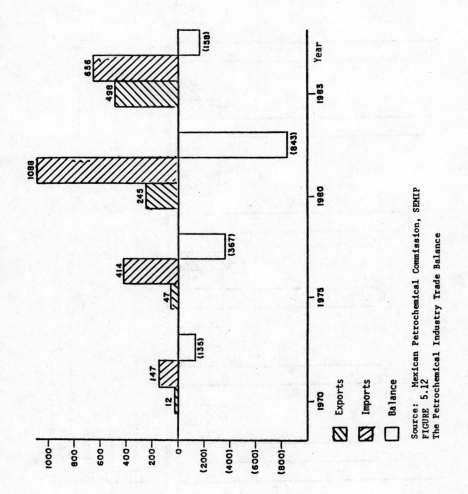

Source: Mexican Petrochemical Commission, SEMIP
FIGURE 5.12
The Petrochemical Industry Trade Balance

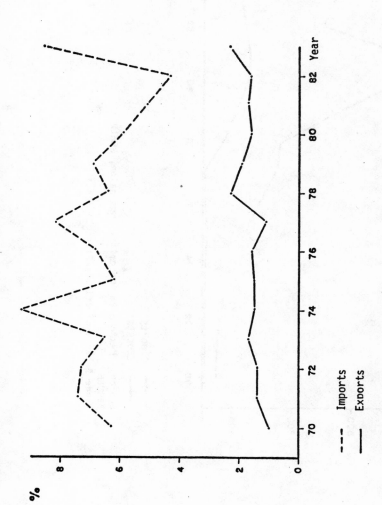

Imports ----

Exports ——

Sources: Mexican Institute of Foreign Trade, and the Mexican Petrochemical
Commission, SEMIP.

FIGURE 5.13
Relative Importance of the Petrochemical Industry in the Trade Balance

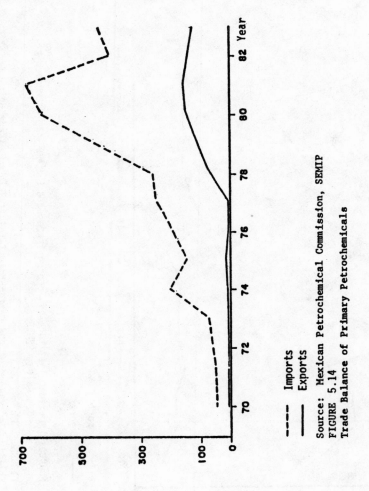

Millions
of U.S.
Dollars

- - - - Imports
———— Exports

Source: Mexican Petrochemical Commission, SEMIP
FIGURE 5.14
Trade Balance of Primary Petrochemicals

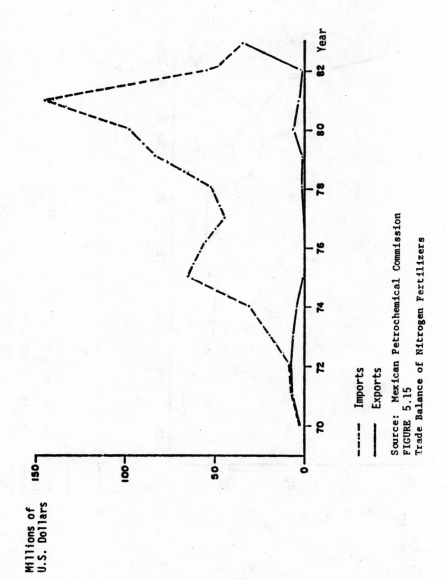

Millions of
U.S. Dollars

Imports

Exports

Source: Mexican Petrochemical Commission
FIGURE 5.15
Trade Balance of Nitrogen Fertilizers

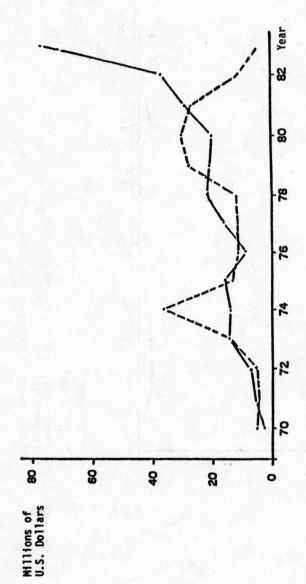

Millions of
U.S. Dollars

----- Imports

——— Exports

Source: Mexican Petrochemical Commission, SEMIP
FIGURE 5.16
Trade Balance of Chemical Fibers

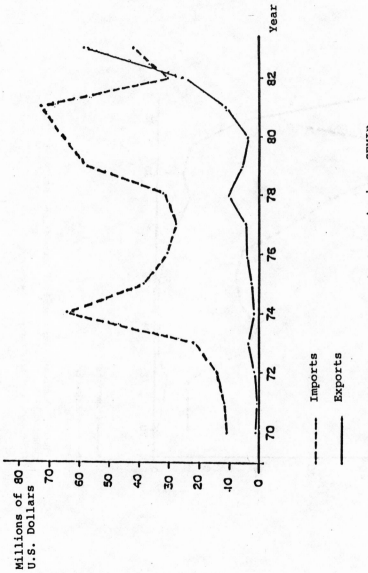

Source: Mexican Petrochemical Commission, SEMIP
FIGURE 5.17
Trade Balance of Synthetic Resins

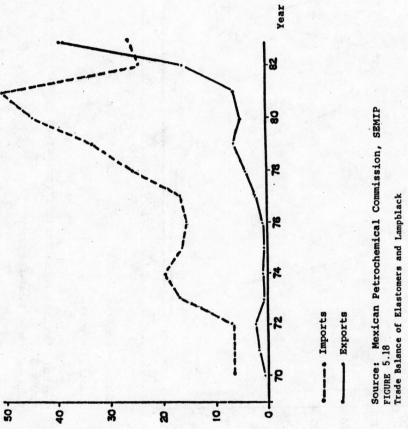

Millions of
U.S. Dollars

Year

●———● Imports

———— Exports

Source: Mexican Petrochemical Commission, SEMIP
FIGURE 5.18
Trade Balance of Elastomers and Lampblack

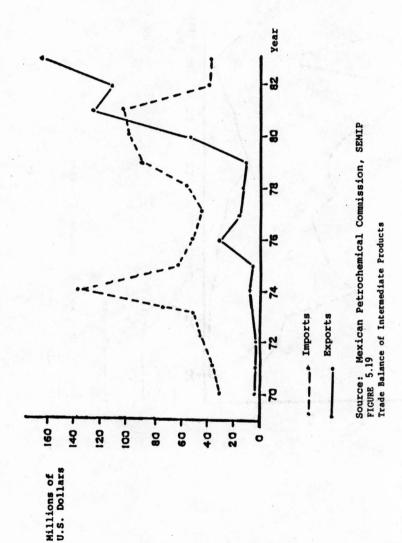

Millions of
U.S. Dollars

Year

- - - ▸ Imports

•——— Exports

Source: Mexican Petrochemical Commission, SEMIP
FIGURE 5.19
Trade Balance of Intermediate Products

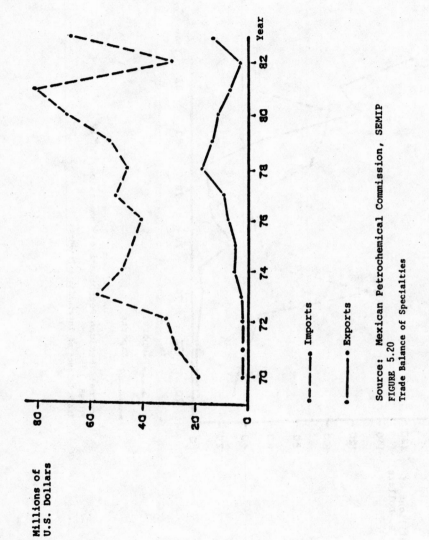

Millions of
U.S. Dollars

●—— ● Imports

●——● Exports

Source: Mexican Petrochemical Commission, SEMIP
FIGURE 5.20
Trade Balance of Specialties

production is expanded in national plants.

It is interesting to note the modest importance of petrochemical product trade between Mexico and the United States. In 1983, total Mexican exports of petrochemical products were equal to only 6.9 percent of U.S. petrochemical imports, and such imports by Mexico equaled only 5.4 percent of U.S. petrochemical exports (Figure 5.21). The trade balance for products other than oil has been historically unfavorable for Mexico (Figure 5.22), particularly for chemical and petrochemical products.

DEVELOPMENT STRATEGY

Mexico's industrialization has been characterized by a higher rate of growth in manufacturing than in the rest of the economy; however, even this growth has been limited by structural deficiencies. Notwithstanding these deficiencies, Mexico has a diverse infrastructure and industrial base, a solid national entrepreneurial capacity, and projects in progress to permit sustained development of the industrial plant.

The industrial development of Mexico has been stimulated over the years not only by microeconomic policies but also macroeconomic measures to stimulate the economy. However, imbalances were generated in the balance of payments and the domestic financing capacity and inflationary forces were set in motion which finally forced an economic slowdown which halted industrial growth in 1983. The national petrochemical industry did not escape these developments.

The National Development Plan 1983-1988 (NDP), published in 1983, gave priority to the petrochemical industry in order to meet the growing domestic demand and generate cash and savings in foreign currency by shifting from imports to exports. The petrochemical industry is also important to support the development of a national capital-goods industry and for its direct and indirect ability to create jobs.

Among the guidelines established by the NDP in the petrochemical field, the following stand out:

1. To secure an ample, assured, and diversified supply of primary petrochemicals for the production of basic goods. In order to accomplish this, the traditional shortage of supply in relation to demand must be overcome.

110

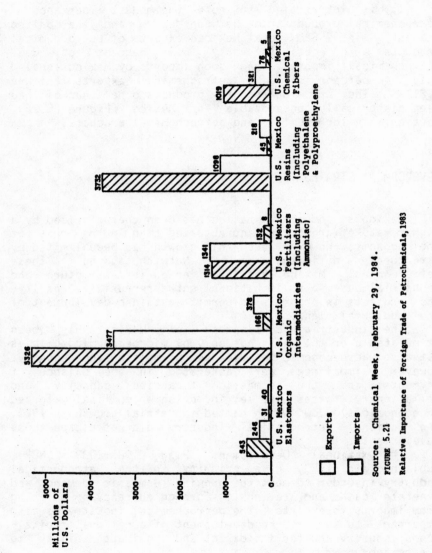

Millions of
U.S. Dollars

5000
4000
3000
2000
1000
0

U.S. Mexico
Elastomers

543 246 31 40

U.S. Mexico
Organic
Intermediaries

5326 3477 166 378

U.S. Mexico
Fertilizers
(Including
Ammoniac)

1314 1341 132 8

U.S. Mexico
Resins
(Including
Polyethalene
& Polyproethylene

3732 1098 45 218

U.S. Mexico
Chemical
Fibers

1019 321 76 5

□ Exports

□ Imports

Source: Chemical Week, February 29, 1984.

FIGURE 5.21

Relative Importance of Foreign Trade of Petrochemicals, 1983

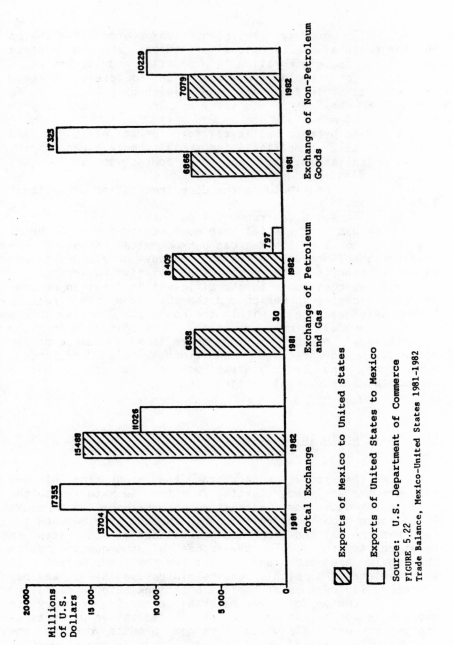

Millions
of U.S.
Dollars

20000-
15 000-
10 000-
5 000-
0

17353
15704
11026
15488
1981
1982
Total Exchange

6838
30
8409
797
1981
1982
Exchange of Petroleum
and Gas

17325
6866
10229
7079
1981
1982
Exchange of Non-Petroleum
Goods

Exports of Mexico to United States

Exports of United States to Mexico

Source: U.S. Department of Commerce
FIGURE 5.22
Trade Balance, Mexico-United States 1981-1982

2. To promote the integration of production chains for the rational use of natural resources and to promote greater national integration in production and facilities.

3. To promote the generation of foreign exchange from exports of intermediate and finished products. To accomplish this, it is necessary to participate actively in international markets.

4. To promote the installation of an efficient and internationally competitive industrial complex, encouraging technological assimilation and development activities and improving plant productivity.

5. To contribute to the decentralization of national life.

6. To avoid environmental pollution.

Three basic strategies have been delineated to guide the development of the Mexican petrochemical industry: the integration of production chains; regional development; and selective exports on the basis of comparative advantage.

Oil may contribute to the efficient integration of some production chains in Mexico and thereby favor the creation of new develoment poles within the country. Oil also offers great potential for successful competition in the international market. Since there is an abundance of raw materials, advantageous conditions, human resources, experience, and basic infrastructure, it is possible to achieve much industrial integration.

Productive Chain Integration Strategy

When the steps necessary for the production of any product are analyzed, starting from the raw material to the finished product, some interesting observations can be made. These concern both the relationship in each step between the required capital and labor and the balance of each step in relation to others. The development of subsequent steps in the chain are occasionally limited by the lack of intermediate and highly capital-intensive steps and may therefore lag because of these limitations (Figure 5.23).

It is common for a raw material exporting country to eventually become an importer of the derivative products of its own raw materials which it cannot produce due to the intensity of capital required. A balance in the production chain is thereby lost and this introduces an imbalance in foreign trade.

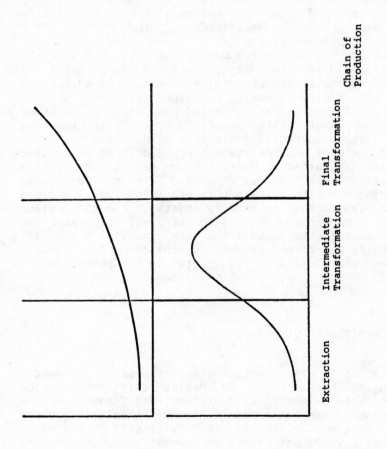

FIGURE 5.23
Value Added, Relation of Capital to Labor

Mexico has few choices for rational and optimal integration of production chains; the petrochemical industry stands out sharply among these. A large portion of the production of this industry goes to other industries; many of the latter are labor intensive, such as the textile industry, home appliance manufacturing, and plastics for industrial and automotive use.

Production chains require much equipment, much of which can be fabricated locally. It is therefore fundamental to devote attention to the production of the required capital goods, giving special emphasis to high-investment phases, since the benefit of higher value added by labor is obtained by the production of capital goods, in contrast to the low labor utilization in capital-intensive production.

In a world of advanced technology and large production scales, the integration of capital goods may be of little benefit, since the volumes involved are small and local manufacturing tends to utilize obsolete technologies because it is unable to keep constantly updated. For this reason there are not many opportunities to carry out integrated and sustained activity to justify the development of a capital-goods industry based on production chains of consumable goods; the opportunities are greater in the petrochemical industry.

Regional Development Strategy

Population is often concentrated in large urban centers in developing countries. In Mexico this concentration exists mainly in Mexico City, Monterrey, and Guadalajara.

This phenomenon is in fact a vicious circle; industry generally develops close to the markets it is trying to supply; that development offers employment opportunities and stimulates migration to the industrial development centers; this increases the market, generating more industry, demanding more employment, and so forth.

It is imperative that we reverse these trends by creating new development centers in Mexico. The petrochemical industry can contribute to decentralization by attracting manufacturing industries and petrochemical suppliers to new development centers. The petrochemical industry can attract capital goods industries.

Selective Export Strategy on the Basis of Comparative Advantage

Since commercial and financial exchange with other countries is a necessity for Mexico, especially now in view of the country's foreign debt and foreign currency shortage, it is evident that exports must be further developed. Export activities must be selected to provide the advantages the country seeks and at the same time offer attractive and competitive products to the world. The petrochemical industry offers much potential in this context because of the local availability of raw material, the possibility of achieving the integration of production chains using a high percentage of locally-produced capital goods, and the availability of human resources and basic infrastructure.

DEVELOPMENT PERSPECTIVES

This section will establish the desirable development scenario for the national petrochemical industry and analyze the effort required to achieve the specified goals.

Growth expectations for domestic demand in the industry depend on the recovery of the national economy. In addition, the petrochemical industry faces mature markets, and penetration of a product will be slower than in the past. The growth of apparent consumption foreseen for the next few years (Table 5.1) is therefore inferior to that of the past.

It is possible to improve and consolidate Mexico's export position by taking advantage of the experience gained in the early 1980s, when important efforts were made to compete in the export market. It is therefore possible to reduce Mexico's dependency on imports through selective substitution oriented toward the integration of productive chains. It is possible to have a more solid position by the end of this decade than that of the preceding decade.

The goals for each of the petrochemical industry's sub-categories are shown in Table 5.2 and in Figures 5.24 and 5.25. If the foreign trade goals are achieved, and keeping in mind the expected growth of domestic demand, the scenario for 1990 would be that presented in Table 5.3. According to this scenario, the level of self-sufficiency attained by national production, in relation to apparent

TABLE 5.1
Expected Increase in Apparent Consumption of Petrochemical Products
(thousands of tons)

	Apparent Consumption (1983)	Apparent Consumption (1990)	TMCA (1983-1990) (%)	Percent Increase (1983-1990)
Basic Petrochemicals	7,044	12,500	8.5	78
Nitrogen Fertilizers	3,478	6,400	9.0	84
Chemical Fibers	241	400	8.0	66
Synthetic Resins	384	660	8.0	72
Elastomers and Lampblack	177	270	6.2	53
Intermediate Products	1,350	2,170	7.0	61
Specialties	195	300	6.2	54
TOTAL	12,869	22,700	8.5	76

TABLE 5.2
Projected Scenario for the Petrochemical Industry Trade Balance
(percent of apparent consumption by volume)

	1980-1983 Period		1990 Objective	
	Exports	Imports	Exports	Imports
Basic Petrochemicals	14.4	15.3	8	3
Nitrogen Fertilizers	1.9	15.7	10	2
Chemical Fibers	9.1	2.3	20	2
Synthetic Fibers	9.1	6.5	20	5
Elastomers and Lampblack	14.7	13.6	30	10
Intermediate Products	14.5	6.3	20	3
Specialties	2.5	15.3	5	15

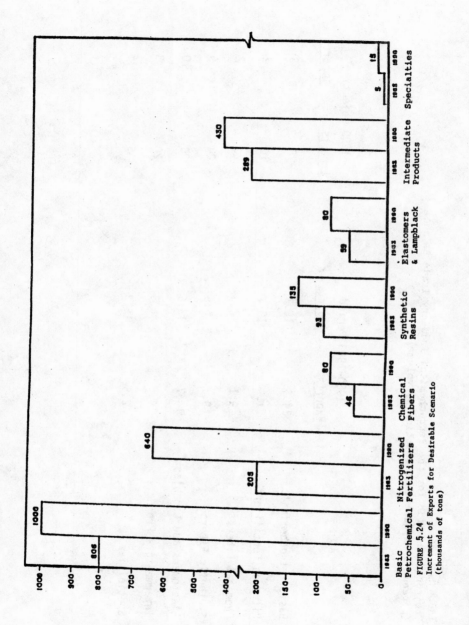

FIGURE 5.24
Increment of Exports for Desirable Scenario
(thousands of tons)

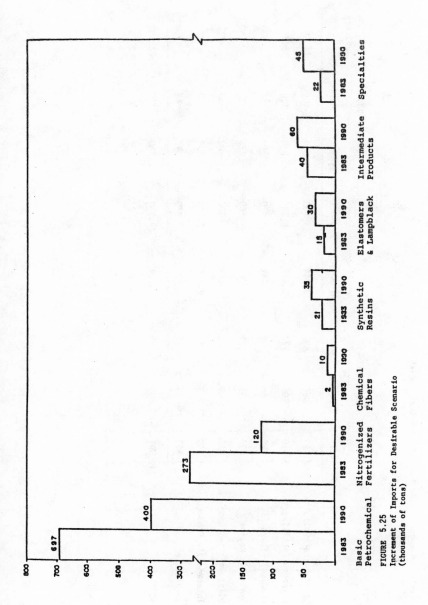

FIGURE 5.25
Increment of Imports for Desirable Scenario
(thousands of tons)

TABLE 5.3
Projected Scenario for the Petrochemical Industry
(thousands of tons)

	1983				1990			
	Production	Exports	Imports	Apparent Consumption	Production	Exports	Imports	Apparent Consumption
Basic Petrochemicals	7,153	806	697	7,044	13,100	1,000	400	12,500
Nitrogen Fertilizers	3,410	205	273	3,478	6,920	640	120	6,400
Chemical Fibers	285	46	2	241	470	80	10	400
Synthetic Resins	456	93	21	384	760	135	35	660
Elastomers and Lampblack	221	59	15	177	320	80	30	270
Intermediate Products	1,599	289	40	1,350	2,540	430	60	2,170
Specialties	178	5	22	195	270	15	45	300
TOTAL	13,302	1,503	1,070	12,869	24,380	2,380	700	22,700

consumption, would surpass the 103.4 percent achieved in 1983 and reach 107.4 percent in 1990. The level of exports would be reduced from 11.6 to 10.5 percent of domestic consumption, although exports would be composed of products with greater aggregate value; imports would be reduced from 8.3 to 3.1 percent of apparent consumption.

The balance of trade in the industry could go from a deficit of $158 million in 1983, to a surplus of around $300 million for 1990 (Table 5.4).

The magnitude of the effort necessary to achieve this outcome is as follows (Table 5.5): it is necessary to increase production by 11.1 million tons, or 83 percent above the level of production reached in 1983, or an average annual growth rate of 9 percent.

To achieve this production, it will be necessary to increase installed capacity by a little more than 15 million tons, which would imply a total investment of $8.2 billion during the period until 1990, or an investment in the order of $1.2 billion annually. Approximately 25 percent of this investment will be used for the acquisition of technology and to import equipment not made in the country, and the remaining 75 percent will be invested in goods and services of national origin.

The principal products projected for export by the end of the decade are some primary petrochemicals, nitrogen fertilizers, intermediate products, synthetic fibers, large volume resins, synthetic rubber, and lampblack; imports will consist mainly of primary petrochemical products and specialized products of all types.

COMPLEMENTARITY AND CONFLICT

The need for balanced development to maintain socio-political stability must be placed within an international context in which countries will seek to optimize their commercial exchange based on the principles of comparative advantage and selective specialization. Neighboring countries like Mexico and the United States should base the development of national industries on complementarity with each other, within a competitive framework of commercial exchange. This is the analytic framework in which the possibilities of complementarity and conflict between Mexico and the U.S. in the chemical and petrochemical industry are discussed in what follows.

TABLE 5.4
Trade Balance for the Projected Scenario
(billions of dollars)

	1983			1990		
	Exports	Imports	Balance	Exports	Imports	Balance
Basic Petrochemicals	124	442	(318)	250	280	(30)
Nitrogen Fertilizers	20	36	(16)	75	15	60
Chemical Fibers	76	5	71	135	20	115
Synthetic Resins	58	43	15	90	70	20
Elastomers and Lampblack	39	26	13	55	50	5
Intermediate Products	167	37	130	290	60	230
Specialties	14	67	(53)	40	140	(100)
TOTAL	498	656	(158)	935	635	300

TABLE 5.5
Increases Required During 1984-1990 Period to Reach Projections

	Increase in Production (Thousand Tons/Year)	Increase in Installed Capacity (Thousand Tons/Year)	Required Investment Billions USD
Basic Petrochemicals	5,950	8,500	4,300
Nitrogen Fertilizers	3,510	4,400	700
Chemical Fibers	185	265	800
Synthetic Resins	305	435	350
Elastomers and Lampblack	100	140	210
Intermediate Products	940	1,300	1,600
Specialties	90	160	240
TOTAL	11,080	15,200	8,200

The accelerated development of international markets, the rapid dissemination of technology, and the high degree of competition at an international level have brought a reduction in profit margins of products for general use (commodities). It is therefore rational to install new industrial plants only in those countries which, like Mexico, have clear comparative advantages. These advantages may result from the availability of relatively inexpensive raw materials or a sufficiently developed and protected domestic market. Without these advantages, it is impossible to justify the necessary investments.

The recent global recession reinforced this situation. New investment projects have been concentrated almost exclusively in developing countries like Mexico, which have ample raw materials and other advantages to enable them to compete in the international market, even in a period such as the present, when there is a clear installed overcapacity in industrialized countries.

As a logical response to this situation, large chemical firms of industrialized countries have modified their development strategies by orienting themselves toward technology-intensive products (TIPs) in which prospects exist for large profit margins based on proven research and development capacity, and taking advantage of their strategic position to offer specialized technical services to their clients. The large forms thereby preserve a position of comparative advantage with respect to the infant industries of the developing countries. This is the behavior of a majority of U.S. chemical enterprises.

Mexico, like other developing countries, follows certain methods to encourage the decentralization of development and promote the development of priority industrial activities. To achieve this, the country must provide incentives and apply specific promotion measures, such as fiscal stimuli, preferential credit, accelerated depreciation of investment, and tariff barriers.

The promotional and protectionist measures must be understood within the context of international readjustment and not as subsidies for inefficiency. If this is not understood, or if the developed countries employ protectionist and/or discriminatory measures, the result would be a paralysis of trade. Then, not being able to generate export capacity, the less-developed countries would have less import capacity. In this event, both the industrialized and the developing countries would be injured and tensions between them aggravated.

Traditional enterprises in industrialized countries may

serve mainly local markets, lack a solid structure of research and development, and have a limited response capacity to competition. They see their position as being threatened and have resorted increasingly to requests for protection. Some recent examples of this are for ammonia and lampblack.

There is also the threat that the U.S. Congress could approve restrictive laws to block the import of Mexican petrochemical products. A bill sponsored by Congressman Sam Gibbons, approved earlier by the House Committee on Ways and Means, is of this nature despite the fact that Mexican exports of petrochemical products represent less than 1 percent of the U.S. market.

When complementarity is sought by means of comparative advantage, short-term difficulties generally arise. The country that cedes to another the production of a commodity which the former could produce is, apparently, sacrificing possibilities for employment and economic development; but it also is creating possibilities for production and export of products for which it is better suited.

Difficulties are sharpened when trade is sought between nations unequal in their development. The world is now suffering from a crisis whose origin is, precisely, in the inequality which exists among countries.

The imbalances are not easy to redress, since the causes are profound and complex; they relate to trade relations and internal phenomena. Adjustments in these relations will take time. They will require a determined will to overcome the inertia facing change, and each side must be convinced of the need to reduce tensions caused by inequality. It is important to recognize that there cannot be immediate equality in commercial exchange between the two sides, since the aim is precisely to reduce differences.

The only possibility for the establishment of a sane basis for the harmonious develoment of international commerce and social equilibrium in third-world nations is the gradual reduction of the inequalities produced by unbalanced development and improving the conditions of trade between highly developed and less-developed countries. This should take place in the context of better prices for the raw materials traditionally produced by developing countries and by creating a favorable environment for industrialization and commercialization of manufacturing of higher value added in developing countries.

Total autonomy of production is not feasible today even for the most developed countries. This search for autarchy leads to the limitation of economic, social, cultural, and

political development potential. It is no longer possible
to think in terms of self-sufficient national economies.
The world is an interdependent system. It is important that
we think in global terms and recognize ourselves as part of
a global economy.

6

The Mexican Iron and Steel Industry

Gerardo M. Bueno,
Gustavo S. Cortés,
and Rafael R. Rubio

HISTORICAL EVOLUTION AND PRESENT SITUATION

The Mexican iron and steel industry got its start at the end of the last and the beginning of the present century from the market created by the improvement and expansion of the railroad system. The expansion also stimulated production and commerce generally.

The historical development of the iron and steel industry can be divided into three stages: the first began in 1900 and lasted until 1940; the second started during the Second World War and lasted until 1970; and the last one began in 1970.

The First Stage: 1900-1940

During the first years, iron and steel production was characteristically carried out in small-scale plants which lacked facilities and equipment to transform steel ingots into relatively elaborate finished products. Consequently, during most of this epoch the production shortage was satisfied through imports.[1]

This beginning merits emphasis because it shows that even before the country had begun a formal process of industrialization, the infrastructural basis for the industrialization process was being established. This was the pattern for iron and steel development by the majority of countries in that era. Steel production in Mexico was later conceived as an indispensable input for advancing to higher stages of economic development.

The 1940-1970 Period

The second stage was one in which the industry was consolidated into a relatively important manufacturing activity. This was propelled by supply shortages during the Second World War on one hand and the state's own policy of industrial development on the other. Interruptions in the flow of international commerce created the conditions necessary for the government to foster the country's industrialization possibilities generally. A policy of import substitution was encouraged, and this continued after the Second World War, although for different reasons and with different characteristics.

Three new iron and steel enterprises were created during the second stage, which are now the integrated productive nucleus of the industry. These were: Altos Hornos de México, S.A., which was established in 1931; Hojalata y Lámina, S.A., was created only two years later; and Tubos de Acero de México, S.A., created in 1954. A large number of smaller, semi-integrated and relaminating plants were established.

The state began its participation in the industry by becoming the major shareholder of the Altos Hornos de Mexico, S.A. enterprise, based on debt capitalization by the Nacional Financiera. This participation reinforced the view over time that steel was a strategic or basic input for industrialization. This conceptualization had the additional result that steel products were included in the system of price controls in 1951, based on the government's desire to assure an adequate supply of steel for infant Mexican industries. The number of products subject to price control was still relatively small at that time.

Production growth during this second stage was substantial. Production went from 150 thousand tons of ingots in 1940, to more than one million tons of steel in 1957, and close to four million tons in 1970. The average annual rate of growth of production was 11.4 percent, a figure that greatly surpassed the average rate of growth of manufacturing (7.3 percent annually). The production supported a relatively intense process of import substitution. During the decade of the 1940s, the average annual proportion of apparent national consumption satisfied through purchases abroad was 53 percent; in the following decade, the percentage was reduced to 38 percent; and during the 1960s continued to decline until it reached 7 percent in 1970.

Exports were recorded after 1960, some to the south of the United States and the rest, the majority, to various Latin American countries. However, the total exported was modest and was fundamentally due to the surplus capacity in iron and steel production which resulted from plant expansions adjustment periods in the economy. The balance of iron and steel trade between the United States and Mexico was favorable to the United States during those years.

The iron and steel the industry then and since has maintained the practice of growing in line with the growth of national demand. This strategy is reasonable when internal demand grows at a relatively stable rate, as was the case during most of the period of consolidation. However, the situation changed when there was short-term acceleration in industrial demand. The years of the economic "boom" at the end of the decade of the 1970s show the delicate supply-demand balance in this type of development.

Iron and steel entrepreneurs sought greater productive integration, both backward and forward, during this second stage. Prospecting, exploration, and beneficiation of raw material were significantly increased. One accomplishment was the technological advance in iron mineral reduction known as the direct-reduction process. In 1957, the first soft iron productive plant was established and this placed the Mexican iron and steel industry in the vanguard of this technology.

With respect to forward integration, the enterprises began to produce almost the whole range of iron and steel products from ordinary steel to certain derivative output, such as wire and galvanized products. However, there were (and still are) relatively important gaps, such as sheet iron, tinplate and certain types of specialized steels.[2]

The "inward" orientation of industry based on import substitution reflected the desire of the government and enterprises to avoid problems of turning to international markets, but was also the result of official economic policies to intensify the process of industrialization.

The Third Stage and the Present Situation: 1970 Onward

The third stage can be differentiated from the previous stages in several respects. Production and demand have been out of phase since 1977 and this led to growing imports of iron and steel products, mainly from the United States. Imports satisfied only 10.6 percent of demand in 1976; in 1978, Imports were 22 percent of apparent national consumption; and in 1981, this ratio reached its maximum point of 40 percent.

Most Mexican iron and steel production took place in plants of internationally competitive scale and technologies, but there were further important changes. In 1971, Hojalata y Lámina, in its installations in Puebla, started the first integrated production of non-flats, introducing the use of continuous casting to Mexico. In the following years, especially after 1972, there was a relatively rapid process of substitution under which several integrated enterprises using open-hearth furnaces were reconverted to oxygen converters. In 1976, operations began in the newest integrated plant in Mexico (SICARTSA).

However, there were delays in adopting new technologies in Mexico. For example, Japan introduced the advanced oxygen converting furnace process in 1956, and continuous casting in 1961, while Mexican utilization was delayed by 10 to 16 years respectively.

The principal features of the industry are the following:

a. a public sector, responsible for 56 percent of total vertically integrated steel production using the advanced oxygen converting furnace;

b. two vertically integrated private enterprises, responsible for 28 percent of production using direct electrical reduction furnaces; and

c. a nucleus of semi-integrated enterprises that rely on electric furnaces for production of the remaining 16 percent of steel.

The public enterprises concentrate on the production of flat products (70 percent of the total), and private firms (integrated and semi-integrated) produce the remaining flats and 100 percent of the seamless pipes.

The steel industry has been growing in importance in the national productive structure. Its contribution increased from 1.07 percent of gross industrial product in 1970, to 1.21 percent in 1980. Its share of manufacturing was 4.51 percent in 1970, and 4.92 percent in 1979.

In 1979, about 77,000 persons worked in the steel industry, which represented 3.4 percent of total employment in manufacturing. Annual growth of employment in the iron and steel industry in the 1970s was 4.8 percent; this was more than the 3 percent employment growth in manufacturing generally. The Mexican iron and steel worker still does not reach the level of productivity of the worker in the industries in more efficient countries. Figures for production per employed person in 1982 indicate that Mexico compares favorably with Brazil but not with Japan (108, 105, and 207 tons per employed worker respectively). The industry probably now confronts its most critical situation of recent years. Its problems are both cyclical and structural. The short-term problems are the result of the recession of the Mexican economy. The most important of these problems are the following:

a. Economic and exchange-rate problems caused a reduction in demand of 31 percent in 1982 and 26 percent in 1983; in other words, demand in 1983 was 50 percent less than that of 1981. Production declined by 8 percent in 1982 and 1.5 percent in 1983.

b. There was low utilization of installed capacity: utilization was 74 percent for the industry as a whole in 1983, and 70 percent for integrated enterprises.

c. The industry had problems in meeting payment commitments, especially abroad. The debt of the iron and steel industry in 1983 was about $3.5 billion, of which 60 percent was contracted by private and the rest by public enterprises. As of mid-1983, 63 percent of this debt had a short-term amortization due date and, of the remainder, 3 percent was long-term;

d. The difficult international situation impedes exports. Petitions to the U.S. Department of Commerce seeking increased duties on iron and steel products imported from Mexico are palpable proof of these difficulties.

The main structural problems of the iron and steel industry are the following:

a. There is inadequate integration of the industry with national productive networks. Those problems concern the supply of raw materials and the lack of coordination with steel-consuming industries.

b. Modernization of the productive plant has lagged.

c. The industry has low productivity stemming from labor problems and a lack of incentives for introducing technological innovations.

ROLE OF THE IRON AND STEEL INDUSTRY IN THE INDUSTRIAL
STRATEGY OF MEXICO

As discussed above, the development of the iron and
steel industry during the last forty years is intimately
linked with Mexico's industrialization policy. This is
typical of other countries as well. The reasons why the
iron and steel industry, in Mexico as elsewhere, have been
considered as basic are fundamentally three:[3]
1. the extensive use of steel as a raw material for
other manufacturing branches and the construction industry;
2. the high capital intensity that characterizes
most iron and steel production processes; and
3. the importance of iron and steel imports directly
and in capital and consumer durable goods in the balance of
payments.
There are three connections between the public sector
and the iron and steel industry. These are: (1) the use of
economic policy instruments and the formulation of
development programs specifically designed to encourage the
iron and steel industry; (2) the direct participation of the
state in national iron and steel production; and (3) the
adoption of a series of concrete measures supporting
development of the iron and steel industry.
As to the first of these, planning for the iron and
steel industry has been carried out in Mexico since the
beginning of the 1960s. A plan for the development of the
common laminated steel industry was prepared at that time
and this contributed to the decision that later led to the
construction of the iron and steel plant in Las Truchas. It
was subsequently decided that the iron and steel industry
merited permanent attention, and this led to the
establishment of a committee for the programming of the
steel industry in the Secretariat of National Patrimony,
with participation by the public sector and the steel
enterprises; the committee still functions within the
Secretariat of Energy, Mines and Parastatal Industry.
The Secretariat of Commerce and Industrial Promotion,
within its industrial planning function, coordinated the
compilation of an integral program for the development of
the steel industry, to which the National Chamber of Iron
and Steel, other public entities, and the iron and steel
enterprises contributed. This program is part of the
national program of industrial development and foreign
trade. The objectives of the integral steel program are to
improve efficiency in the industry and assure that there is

productive capacity available to satisfy both internal and external demand.

Iron and steel are classified under category one since 1978, which means that it is a a producer of strategic inputs for the industrial sector. Based on that classification, the state granted fiscal incentives for: new investment or expansion of installed capacity (for some 20 percent of the value of investment); the generation of new jobs in all parts of the national territory (for another 20 percent); and the acquisition of new machinery and equipment for national production (for 5 percent of the value of the acquired goods). Concessional prices were granted for energy consumption.

However, steel industry incentives were put in the context of other incentives, e.g., for steel consuming industries. The total result was a mixture of incentives and punishments. The incentives included fiscal credits, other facilities for financing, and protection against imports. Among the disincentives are the control of prices of iron and steel products, the obligation of the industry to buy relatively expensive inputs coming from other domestic industries, sudden and drastic changes in the level of protection and, at times, labor policy. The result is that although iron and steel is a "priority" industry, it is not an industry "preferred" by investors.

The second form of state action is direct participation in the production of iron and steel goods. State participation in iron and steel was not initially the result of a deliberate decision by the government. It came about when Nacional Financiera became the majority shareholder of Altos Hornos de México by capitalizing liabilities of the firm. Something similar occurred in 1971 and 1972 with Fundidora Monterrey. Siderúrgica Lázaro Cárdenas-Las Truchas (SICARTSA) was a big project supported from the outset by the state; the intent was for the state to be a minority shareholder, but this was changed when it became clear that private sources would not contribute sufficient capital. In 1978, the role of the public sector as majority partner in the industry led to the creation of Siderúrgica Mexicana (SIDERMEX) in order to coordinate the activities of this government-owned industry.

Other forms of state participation in the iron and steel industry occur in an indirect manner. The public sector is an important consumer of iron and steel products through activities in the petroleum sector, construction, and the production of capital goods. The public sector is also a producer of raw materials, such as coal and iron ore, and it is a shareholder in other enterprises that provide important inputs to the steel industry, such as refractory materials and ferro-alloys.

The relatively large participation of the state in iron and steel activities is not very different from what occurs in other developing countries and even in certain developed countries. The iron and steel industry, with notable exceptions, has become one activity in which state participation is practically inevitable. This is true of England and Italy among developed countries and India among less developed.

The state has also taken other concrete measures to foster iron and steel development, such as the creation of the Mexican Institute for Steel Research, which is dedicated to applied investigation. The Council for Mineral Resources carries out exploration activities that are useful to the iron and steel industry. One other example is the construction of infrastructure of ports and roads for Las Truchas.

PERSPECTIVES, OBJECTIVES AND DEVELOPMENT STRATEGIES

The market for the iron and steel industry will be determined by the success of the economic stabilization program and the mid- and long-term structural change of the economy. Estimates for the mid- and long-term demand for iron and steel products were made under two economic scenarios. Under the first scenario, the stabilization program would meet with reasonable success by the end of 1984, and growth of the economy would be in accord with the rates foreseen in the National Development Plan. This scenario held for but a single year. Under the second scenario, the economic adjustment period would be extended by one more year and later economic growth rates would then be as projected in the Plan. This, too, was optimistic.

Under scenario one, the demand for iron and steel products would have increased at an average annual rate of 9.3 percent between 1984 and 1994, rising from 5.6 million tons of finished products in 1984, to 13.7 in 1994. This growth rate is similar to those of the 1960s and 1970s (9.2 and 10.5 percent respectively, annually). However, the level of consumption in 1981 was 9.4 million tons of finished iron and steel products; if 1981 is used as the base year, the average annual rate of growth for the period

1981-1994 would be only 2.9 percent (Table 6.1).

Under scenario two, the growth rate of product demand would be at 9.1 percent annual average.

The methodology used in the demand projections was based on regression equations for the main iron and steel products, using the economic behavior of the principal consumer sectors as independent variables.

The demand estimates were not analyzed solely from a quantitative point of view; qualitative aspects based on the specialization in certain types of steel and/or the substitution of others were also used.

In both projections, flat steel products show more dynamic growth than non-flats and seamless tube steel. The explanation for this is that those sectors with the greatest demand, such as capital goods, petroleum, petrochemicals, and domestic electric appliances, are to be favored in the federal government's industrial strategy.

With respect to national supply, based on existing capacity and projects for capacity expansion, it is anticipated that the national production of iron and steel products could grow from the 6.2 million tons in 1984 to 10.1 million in 1994; this would be an average annual growth rate of 4.9 percent. This rate would not only be much lower than that of consumption rate (9.2 - 9.4 percent annually), but it would also be significantly lower than past growth.

The resulting supply/demand balance is that in the intermediate term (1985-1988), the steel market will show a deficit, even after including the completion of current projects. The steel shortage may exceed one million tons in 1988. In the long run (by 1994), the deficit could be on the order of 4 to 5.6 million tons (Tables 6.2 and 6.3 and Graphs 6.1, 6.2, 6.3, 6.4, and 6.5).

These estimates of supply and demand imply that the iron and steel market will maintain relative equilibrium until the latter 1980s, but will deteriorate rapidly during the early years of the next decade. This will be true for most products, although the shortage will probably begin with and grow for non-flats.

This analysis suggests that despite the current pessimism about economic conditions the country faces, it is urgent to plan now for new additions to the productive capacity of the iron and steel industry in order to guarantee a sufficient level of capacity in future years.

Similarly, steps must be taken to assure provision of raw materials, especially iron and coal, for years to come. Failure to establish this congruence would cause production bottlenecks and have repercussions on major sectors of the

TABLE 6.1
Mexico: Apparent National Consumption
(thousands of tons)

	84	85	86	87	88	89	90	91	92	93	94
STEEL											
SCENARIO I	7435	8879	10051	11270	12100	12891	13734	14632	15588	16835	18013
SCENARIO II	6969	8641	9210	9791	10609	11418	12458	13500	14629	15579	16436
TOTAL PRODUCTS											
SCENARIO I	5590	6676	7557	8474	9098	9661	10299	10986	11720	12737	13743
SCENARIO II	5240	6497	6925	7362	7977	8585	9367	10150	10999	11801	12560
FLAT											
SCENARIO I	2625	3256	3777	4213	4517	4806	5113	5439	5787	6279	6775
SCENARIO II	2503	3296	3564	3740	4049	4360	4760	5161	5596	6026	6442
NON-FLAT											
SCENARIO I	2648	3075	3407	3864	4130	4409	4707	5025	5365	5848	6315
SCENARIO II	2403	2860	3007	3253	3545	3824	4186	4549	4943	5389	5606
SEAMLESS PIPES											
SCENARIO I	317	345	373	397	421	446	479	522	568	610	653
SCENARIO II	334	341	354	369	383	401	421	441	463	486	512

TABLE 6.2
Mexico: National Production of Steel and Steel Products
(thousands of tons)

	84	85	86	87	88	89	90	91	92	93	94
STEEL	7725	7968	9088	10079	10894	11350	12083	12252	12282	12395	12411
TOTAL PRODUCTS	6291	6539	7378	8210	8873	9413	9918	10072	10123	10160	10173
FLAT	2782	2977	3419	4052	4529	4964	5381	5489	5500	5510	5515
NON-FLAT	3201	3197	3566	3741	3903	3983	4038	4083	4123	4150	4158
SEAMLESS PIPES	308	365	393	417	441	466	499	500	500	500	500

TABLE 6.3
Mexico: Supply-Demand Balance, Using Scenario I
(thousands of tons)

	1984	1985	1988	1992	1994
STEEL	290	(911)	(1206)	(3306)	(5602)

*using Scenario I

( ) = deficit

GRAPH 6.1
Mexico: Supply-Demand Balance: Steel
(millions of tons)

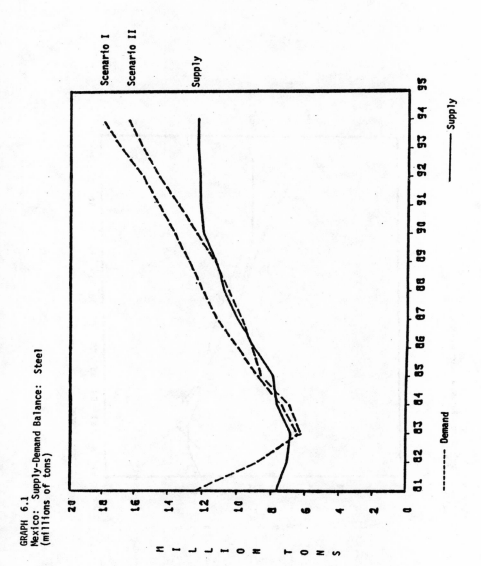

140

GRAPH 6.2
Mexico: Supply-Demand Balance: Steel Products
(millions of tons)

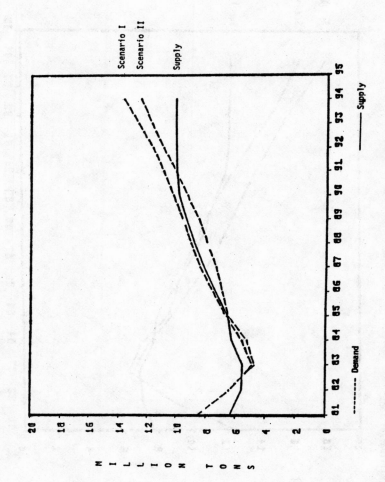

GRAPH 6.3
Mexico: Supply-Demand Balance: Flat Products
(millions of tons)

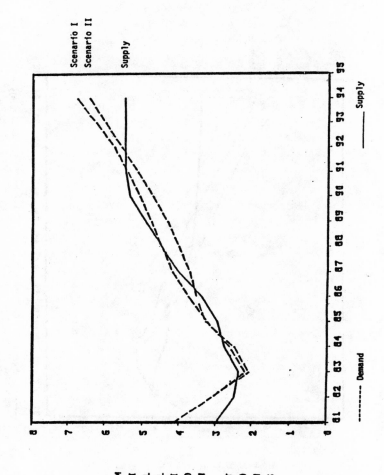

GRAPH 6.4
Mexico: Supply-Demand Balance: Non-Flat Products
(millions of tons)

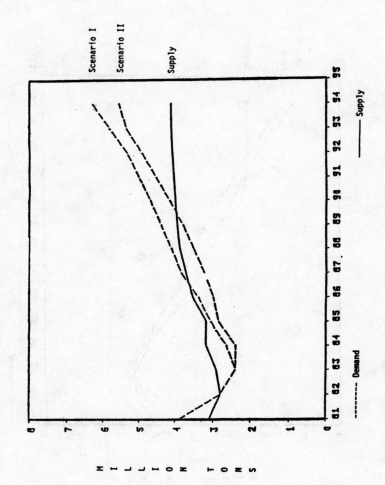

GRAPH 6.5
Mexico: Supply-Demand Balance: Seamless Pipes
(millions of tons)

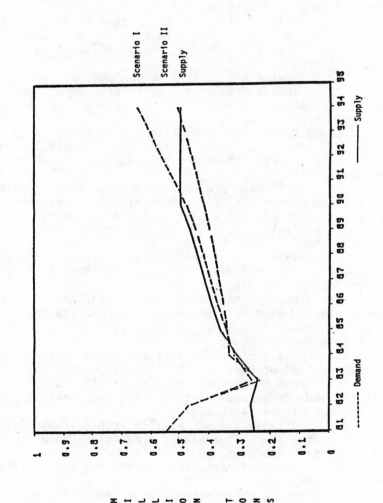

economy.

The quantitative analysis highlights the need to make important changes in the industry to insure achievement of development objectives. If needed current and structural changes are not planned and carried out, the Mexican steel industry will continue to fall behind and lack competitiveness. The iron and steel industry is a force behind other economic activities because it provides basic inputs and, in turn, obtains goods and services from other national sectors.

The following are the principal objectives proposed under the integrated development program of the iron and steel industry. The objectives are classified as general and specific.

The most important general objectives are:

1. Achieve the most efficient articulation possible for inputs and with the principal of steel-consuming sectors in the country;

2. Formulate programs that will permit optimum use of available iron and coal mineral resources and assure future supply of iron and mineral coal by imports, relating these to the extent possible to exports of iron and steel products;

3. Raise the technological level of the iron and steel industry, including the capacity for self-generated technological advance; and

4. Promote the most rapid completion of projects under way and plan for meeting future capacity needs.

With respect to specific objectives, the most important that have been proposed are:

1. Obtain more effective systems of distribution for iron and steel products in the internal market;

2. Promote the use and dissemination of the results of applied research, particularly that related to the technology of specialty steels;

3. Optimize use of installed capacity by eliminating bottlenecks and improving preventive and corrective maintenance procedures; and

4. Improve international marketing systems for iron and steel products.

The iron and steel sector faces one of the most serious financial challenges of its history, since it will need to find resources to finance its growth and to meet the accumulated debt of the past. These needs include the external resources to finance imports of machinery and equipment for the expansion of capacity.

In order to obtain necessary financing, the companies

must achieve profit levels which will enable them to generate internal resources. This implies other related developments, such as the modification of existing relations between the banks and the industry to permit the latter's long-term expansion. Cost and price policies must be compatible with financial goals and permit the necessary cash flow to guarantee the completion of existing investment. While it is foreseeable that the federal executive will control iron and steel prices as part of its official price controls, it is important to find formulas that are reasonably automatic or will allow frequent revision of iron and steel product prices so as not to worsen the financial situation of the companies.

It seems certain that import permits will have to continue for short-term protection for the industry. However, in the medium and long term, this situation should change. Official prices, and particularly the need for import permits, should gradually disappear. The state of the international market for iron and steel must be taken into account in setting tariff levels in order to avoid senseless practices. In order to reduce production in the industry, import protection for raw materials should, in most cases, be close to zero. There is no logic in demanding that an industry be competitive on a world scale and burdening it with the need to buy components from highly protected industries. The efficiency of the iron and steel industry repercussions on investment in other industries, such as durable consumer goods.

Decisions regarding technological techniques under expansion programs will depend on the scale of the projects and on the conditions established for providing raw materials and energy. The technical selection process chosen must also be based on the internal technological objectives of the industry. An effort must be made for a congruence between the technological capacity reached in the country and technological development and application in national projects.

Finally, the state should continue to issue tax rebate certificates to promote exports of iron and steel products, since this is common practice in all exporting countries, but should avoid granting of direct export subsidies.

COMPLEMENTARITY AND CONFLICT IN MEXICO-UNITED STATES
STEEL RELATIONSHIP

The experience between Mexico and the United States in
matters dealing with steel has taken many forms:
1.   The mining company, Minas de Fierro del Pacífico,
was established in Mexico in 1905 as a subsidiary of
Bethlehem Steel Corporation. It obtained a concession on
iron deposits in the zone of Las Truchas, Michoacán, but
this was later revoked due to lack of exploitation.
2.   The American Rolling Mills Company (ARMCO)
participated in 1941 in the formation of Altos Hornos de
México (AHMSA). The investment by the American company was
12 percent of the social capital of AHMSA. The startup
operation of AHMSA was supported by a loan from the
Export-Import Bank of the United States, which was tied to
the purchase of U.S. machinery and equipment. Procurement
of U.S. equipment was repeated with the establishment of
the principal Mexican steel companies.
3.   At the end of World War II, the U.S. steel
industry found itself with excess capacity and a contraction
of demand that forced it to export certain products (black
laminates and galvanized and other plates) into Mexico at a
price lower than the domestic U.S. price. Faced with this
situation, a coalition of Mexican managers and industrial
chambers requested the government to impose import controls,
since the resurgent Mexican iron and steel industry might
not otherwise have survived. The Ministers of Finance and
Economics supported this protection to permit the steel
industry to develop.
4.   Mexico generally has had a deficit in its steel
trade with the United States, particularly in finished steel
and scrap. The only items in which the trade balance
favored Mexico were primary products and ferro-alloys
(Tables 6.4, 6.5, 6.6, and 6.7). Complete information for
1978-1979 is not available for coal and coke trade, but the
evidence is that Mexico purchased most of its imports from
the United States. The proportion of imports from the
United States was between 60 and 70 percent for coal and
more than 90 percent for coke. Mexican exports of these
products is practically nil.
The United States supplies a significant share of
Mexican imports, while Mexican sales are a marginal fraction
of U.S. imports. During 1979-1982, the U.S. share of
Mexico's total apparent consumption was 30 percent. In the
other direction, Mexican exports of steel have not

TABLE 6.4
Mexico-United States Trade Balance[1]
(thousands of tons)

	Mexican Exports to the U.S.	Mexican Imports to the U.S.	Trade Balance[2]
1970	196.8	1029.0	(832.2)
1971	371.1	676.6	(305.5)
1972	399.8	791.9	(392.1)
1973	139.9	304.7	(164.8)
1974	138.3	1489.3	(1351.0)
1975	63.9	1726.0	(1662.1)
1976	158.3	937.3	(779.0)
1977	303.9	546.1	(242.2)
1978	287.5	839.4	(551.9)
1979	232.0	1453.9	(1221.9)
1980	138.1	2599.4	(2461.3)
1981	122.1	1919.7	(1797.6)
1982	220.9	773.3	(552.4)
1983	726.0	578.9	147.1

[1]Includes steel products, primary products, ferroalloys and scrap metal.

[2]( ) = deficit

TABLE 6.5
Mexico-United States Trade Balance: Primary Products and Ferroalloys[1]
(thousands of tons)

	Mexican Exports to the U.S.	Mexican Imports from the U.S.	Trade Balance[2]
1970	1.1	8.7	(7.6)
1971	3.1	9.5	(6.4)
1972	4.8	10.3	(5.5)
1973	6.5	8.2	(1.7)
1974	4.9	75.6	(70.7)
1975	5.0	44.2	(39.2)
1976	2.5	28.7	(26.2)
1977	28.6	19.3	9.3
1978	40.7	16.3	24.4
1979	38.8	17.3	21.5
1980	38.0	39.6	(1.6)
1981	43.2	20.3	22.9
1982	33.8	10.0	23.8
1983	42.4	4.7	37.7

[1]Includes cast iron, soft iron, ferromanganese, ferrosilicon, ferrochrome, and other ferroalloys.

[2]( ) = deficit

SOURCE: Annual Statistical Report, A.I.S.I., several numbers.

TABLE 6.6
Mexico-United States Trade Balance: Scrap Metal[1]
(thousands of tons

	Mexican Exports to the U.S.	Mexican Imports from the U.S.	Trade Balance[2]
1970	4.3	854.9	(850.6)
1971	16.7	583.3	(566.6)
1972	14.0	621.3	(607.3)
1973	6.6	51.4	(44.8)
1974	.9	936.9	(936.0)
1975	.9	1308.9	(1308.0)
1976	6.9	595.4	(588.5)
1977	31.3	324.5	(293.2)
1978	17.8	450.3	(432.5)
1979	20.3	814.2	(793.9)
1980	25.8	1133.6	(1107.8)
1981	33.6	896.4	(862.8)
1982	65.8	379.5	(313.7)
1983	32.6	418.9	(386.3)

[1]( ) = deficit

SOURCE: Annual Statistical Report, A.I.S.I., several numbers.

TABLE 6.7
Mexico-United States Trade Balance: Steel Products[1]
(thousands of tons)

	Mexican Exports to the U.S.	Mexican Imports from the U.S.	Trade Balance[1]
1970	191.4	165.4	26
1971	351.3	83.8	267.5
1972	381.0	160.3	220.7
1973	126.8	245.1	(118.3)
1974	132.5	476.8	(344.3)
1975	58.0	372.9	(314.9)
1976	148.9	313.2	(164.3)
1977	244.0	202.3	41.7
1978	229.0	372.8	(143.3)
1979	172.9	622.4	(449.5)
1980	74.3	1426.2	(1351.9)
1981	45.3	1003.0	(957.7)
1982	121.3	383.8	(262.5)
1983	651.0	155.3	495.7

[1]Includes products from basic steel, and products from steel with a higher degree of transformation.

[2]( ) = deficit

SOURCE: Annual Statistical Report, A.I.S.I., several numbers.

represented more than 1 percent of apparent U.S. consumption, even in 1983, the year of the highest Mexican exports.

The Mexico-United States iron and steel relationship also extends to technological exchange, machinery and equipment purchases, and financing. Mexican companies have shown a high degree of dependency on U.S. sources in this wider context.

5.   Since 1983, the Mexico-United States iron and steel commercial relationship has been affected by accusations that Mexican exports contravene U.S. fair-trade laws dealing with subsidies and dumping. This process was initiated by U.S. Steel in November 1983, when it requested compensatory U.S. import taxes on flats and tube steel products. Subsequently, other charges were made regarding wire and rod products. These charges rarely come to a final determination because the parties involved come to a voluntary agreement involving export quotas for the U.S. market. These charges are part of a tactic that U.S. companies have used since 1982 to restrict iron and steel imports which they believe are being subsidized or sold below their domestic prices. This practice began with the principal steel-producing countries, and now encompasses the steel industries of developing countries. In addition to fair-trade charges, U.S. companies have supported legislation to limit steel-product imports to 15 percent of apparent national consumption.

In response to a preliminary decision which called for countervailing duties of 4.98 percent (the request of the U.S. steel companies was for 35 percent), the Mexican government announced on April 11, 1984, that it would limit sales of flat steel and tube steel products to the U.S. market to 395,000 tons over the following three years. Subsequently, on April 18, 1984, U.S. Steel announced that it was dropping its charges against Mexican exports. It is anticipated that most other cases will follow a similar evolution.

6.   The prospects are that, in one way or another, the flow of iron and steel products to the United States will be regulated. It is unclear whether protection will be applied against specific products, or take the form of a general limitation (say 15 percent of apparent consumption) of steel imports. If the general scheme of protection is applied, this will certainly be accompanied by prorating of total imports among steel-exporting countries. The legislative initiative proposed the following distribution of the 15 percent ceiling: 6 percent for the European

Economic Community; 6 percent for Japan; and the remaining 3 percent for the other countries.

Such a cartel would particularly affect those grouped in the "other countries." In 1983, these countries contributed 9 percent of total U.S. imports and it is expected that they will continue to be a dynamic group among exporting countries. Some of those countries must obtain foreign exchange to deal with the financial problems (Brazil and Mexico, for example), and others inevitably seek an outlet for a growing steel industry (such as South Korea and Taiwan).

As can be seen, the Mexico-U.S. iron and steel relationship has involved both cooperation and conflict. Each industry has, at different times, been protectionist. For Mexico, protectionism represented a way for an orderly transition from an infant industry to one that is completely consolidated. On the other hand, protectionism in the United States is conceived not as a transition toward a mature industry, but rather to support the permanency of a mature industry. Variants of these protective policies are used by most countries with steel industries.

There are three principal factors that will determine the context of complementarity and conflict in the iron and steel industry between Mexico and the United States: (1) the recovery of the demand for steel; (2) the production adjustments in the steel plants of developed and developing countries; and (3) the forms of protectionism used in the steel trade.

If the economic recovery in the principal industrial countries which began in 1983-1984 is maintained for the rest of the decade, it is reasonable to project a steel deficit in 1990; conditions of excess demand may emerge in certain products starting in 1986-1987.

With respect to production adjustments in the international iron and steel sector, it is anticipated that current patterns will continue, but at different rhythms. The closing of old and non-competitive plants will take place more slowly in Europe than in the United States. Japan, for its part, will surely make changes consistent with the development of the international situation. With regard to the iron and steel plant of developing countries, it is probable that their installed capacity will continue to grow at a parri passu with internal needs, even though some countries have already developed excess capacities for export markets (such as South Korea and Taiwan).

With respect to protectionism, the effort by U.S. companies to safeguard their market may lead to segmentation in the principal markets (United States, Europe and Japan) and to to closed competition in remaining markets in which developing countries will be at a disadvantage because of their brief exporting experience, smaller variety of products, and quality considerations.

Within this frame of reference, the following are options for complementarity between the Mexican iron and steel industry and that of the United States:

--Supplying pre-reduced iron mineral. If there is continued expansion of the mini-steel mill concept in the United States, this will demand that pre-reduced iron mineral be substituted for scrap iron (particularly for the types of products these enterprises will produce in the future). Mexico has an installed capacity of 2.1 million tons of sponge iron pellets. In addition, there is the upcoming expansion of the industry, namely, by SICARTSA, with an additional 2 million tons. At one time, a group of semi-integrated companies were considering the installation of a one million-ton plant in the port of Altamira. This decision must take into account the availability of qualified labor, national and international experience, and installed capacity. Of the feasible installed capacity (4.1 million tons), 62 percent is close to port installations of great depth, which would allow handling of transportation at a competitive price. In addition, the Mexican iron and steel industry is in the vanguard of this type of technological process.[4]

--One of the main cost components of American integrated enterprises is for labor. This has particular relevance in the lamination stage, which is labor intensive. If, for reasons of cost, the lamination section does not maintain its capacity utilization in proportion with that of steel, sub-optimum utilization of capacity could develop in the production of steel ingots. One advantage of developing countries, such as Mexico, is lower labor costs than in the United States. In addition, Mexico has experience in the lamination of iron and steel products (particularly traditional carbon steels). These factors--potential idle capacity in ingot steel production in U.S. plants and cheaper labor plus lamination experience in Mexico--could be joined in a scenario in which U.S. ingot steel is sent to Mexican plants to be laminated and re-exported back to the United States. One possibility that could develop under such a scheme is for the Mexican plant to send the ingot steel to its American counterpart for subsequent transformation. This would be similar to the scheme U.S. Steel sought to implement with England.

--Another way in which Mexico could complement the U.S. steel industry is by insuring a supply of ferro-alloys, a raw material for the steel industry in which Mexico has a favorable trade balance with the United States.

Possible features of complementarity of the United States toward the Mexican steel industry include the following:

--Supply of raw materials, such as coal, coke, and scrap. Because of natural limitations, Mexico depends on foreign countries, especially the United States, and the relationship could be stabilized by long-term agreements.

--Finance for the establishment of operations or installations that will yield profit for both industries. This could include financing for expansion of Mexican capacity for iron mineral reduction and lamination of steel products.

--Production of specialty steels. Future Mexican industrial diversification efforts, particularly for capital goods, will require specialty steels which are not completely produced in Mexico and which could be supplied by the United States.

--Production and supply of steel products requiring scale economies. The steel industry in developed countries undoubtedly has the ability to produce some products in non-integrated plants which require highly specialized technology and which would be difficult to produce in smaller markets such as Mexico.

NOTES

[1]Fundidora de Fierro y Acero de Monterrey was established in 1900. Its initial capacity was 90,000 tons of crude steel a year, in integrated form, based on an investment of 10 million pesos.

[2]In 1983, 40 percent of the world production of pre-reduced iron was based on the Mexican patent.

[3]One can even argue that in some developed countries the steel industry takes on magical attributes that exclude it from any process of industrial adjustment. This emphasis is most prevalent in the European Economic Community and the United States, where the technology has been most laggard and protectionist attitudes against imports from developing

countries have been most pronounced.

"As was indicated in earlier sections, 40 percent of the worldwide production of pre-reduced steel during 1983 used Mexican technology.

7

Steel in Transition: Prospects for the U.S. and Mexican Industries

Robert Crandall

MEXICO-U.S. STEEL POLICY: SUMMARY AND POLICY OPTIONS

Mexico enjoys many of the advantages of a large developing country in producing steel. Relatively low wage rates, a large industrial work force, growing internal demand for steel (until the recent crisis), and easy access to raw materials and competitive technology make it an excellent location for steel production. Unfortunately, in the current environment, world steel demand is extremely depressed. Western world steel consumption was fully 25 percent below its 1974 peak in 1983. This weak world market has combined with the difficult external financial situation in many Latin American countries to create major crises in the steel industries in these countries.

Mexico has sought to offset the sharp decline in its internal demand for steel by increasing its exports to the United States, but U.S. producers have successfully repulsed the Mexican exporters with trade suits that argue that subsidized Mexican firms are unfairly injuring U.S. companies. The result has been that Mexico has been forced to accept export restraints, sharply reducing its exports to the U.S. from 600,000 tons of steel in 1983 to less than

The author is a Senior Fellow at the Brookings Institution. The views set forth here are solely those of the author and do not necessarily represent the opinions of the trustees, officers or other staff members of the Brookings Institution.

200,000 tons within three years.

There is little that the Mexican industry can do to solve its steel trade problems with the U.S. as long as the world market remains depressed. It cannot sell steel at higher prices than those obtained in the world market, yet these prices are likely to be below the full cost of Mexican production. As a result, it risks continuing complaints of unfair competition in exports to market economies. Its best options would appear to be:

1.   Attempting to eliminate subsidies through a revaluation of steel assets.

2.   Seeking to enter joint ventures in the United States with U.S. integrated companies, perhaps supplying semifinished steel.

3.   Concentrating on the bar, rod, and small structural products that the U.S. integrated companies have largely abandoned to the mini-mills.

4.   Accepting quotas on flat-rolled and tubular products, assuring the Mexican companies a small share of the U.S. market at artificially high prices.

The last of these strategies may be forced upon the Mexican industry by the U.S. decisions.

INTRODUCTION

There is a widespread view that the current problems in the world steel industry will dissipate once demand growth is restored and capacity is rationalized to more closely approximate current and future demand. By this line of reasoning, there is no fundamental change in the economics of producing steel. Rather, the problem is simply one of overcapacity that can be cured only by rapid demand growth or plant closures.

This view of the plight of the world steel industry ignores some fundamental changes that are occurring in the industry. Even if world economic growth had not slowed in the turbulent 1970s, the developed world's steel industries would have begun to encounter serious difficulties. Steel production would have shifted to the less-developed world anyway. Production technologies would have continued to change and a number of investment decisions in the older, developed industries would have proven to be a mistake.

RECESSION, EXCESS CAPACITY, AND RATIONALIZATION

No one can doubt the importance of excess capacity in the post-1974 world steel industry. Steel companies throughout the world have suffered through a period of essentially zero growth for more than a decade. In 1973-74, noncommunist world production averaged 543 million net tons of crude steel (Table 7.1). At the time, many were predicting western world steel demand of 1,000 to 1,400 million tons by the mid- 1980s. Instead, demand stagnated badly in response to two oil shocks and sustained world recession. In 1979, demand finally returned to its 1974 level, but since then steel shipments have sagged badly. In 1982 and 1983, total western world steel production was approximately 100 million tons below its 1973-1974 peak.

At its next peak, it seems unlikely that world demand will be much above the 1979 or 1974 levels. The International Iron and Steel Institute (IISI) predicted that even by 1990, the non-communist world will not be back to its 1973-74 output level.[1] In short, we may well pass through more than 15 years of zero growth for this basic world industry.

Surprisingly, this period of no growth has been one of continuing concern about "shortages." Beginning in 1975, the American Iron and Steel Institute (AISI) projected shortages for the 1980s unless substantial capacity (30 million tons) were added in the United States.[2] Responding to optimistic growth forecasts, the OECD countries (the developed countries) expanded capacity by 13 percent between 1973 and 1979 despite operating rates that languished in the 80 percent range.[3]

By the late 1970s, it became apparent that the earlier forecasts of strong growth and future shortages had been off the mark. Despite occasional forecasts of shortages by 1986 or 1987, most industry participants began to look for methods of rationalizing capacity, often advocating cartel-like agreements. A succession of Davignon Plans resulted in the imposition of a formal cartel in the EEC countries. The U.S. producers began to talk of import quotas and to pursue trade cases against most steel exporting countries.[4] Only Japan seemed to hold to a steady course, but even the Japanese began to question the need for keeping so much capacity.

The newly-industrializing countries continued to expand production after 1974, although their expansion rate slowed in the late 1970s and early 1980s in the face of the world

160

TABLE 7.1
World Steel Production, 1973-82
(million net tons of raw steel)

Area or Country	1973	1974	1975	1976	1977	1978	1979	1980	1981	1982	1983
EEC	166.6	172.5	138.8	148.6	139.9	147.3	155.7	141.8	139.2	122.7	119.6
Other Western Europe	31.3	33.3	31.7	31.8	31.3	33.2	36.1	36.0	35.9	35.8	36.7
USA	150.8	145.7	116.6	128.0	125.3	137.0	136.3	111.8	120.8	74.5	83.3
Canada	14.8	15.0	14.4	14.6	15.0	16.4	17.7	17.5	16.3	13.1	14.1
Japan	131.5	129.1	112.8	118.4	112.9	112.6	123.2	122.8	112.1	109.7	107.1
Mexico	5.2	5.7	5.8	5.8	6.2	7.5	7.8	7.9	8.4	7.8	7.5
Latin America	18.4	19.6	20.5	21.4	24.2	26.8	30.3	32.0	30.2	29.8	30.1
Africa	7.3	7.4	8.6	9.3	9.6	10.5	11.4	11.8	11.7	11.8	n.a.
Asia (except Japan & PRC)	14.2	15.7	16.5	20.4	24.1	28.0	31.3	32.5	35.7	38.5	n.a.
Oceania	8.7	8.8	8.9	8.8	8.3	8.6	9.2	8.6	8.7	7.3	n.a.
Total (Non-Communist World)	541.1	544.7	466.6	499.1	488.8	516.9	548.1	511.0	507.2	438.7	405.0
Industrial Countries	509.8	510.7	430.5	457.9	440.5	463.6	487.7	448.3	442.1	372.2	341.0
Developing Countries	31.3	34.0	36.1	41.2	48.3	53.3	60.4	61.7	64.5	66.5	64.0

Source: International Iron and Steel Institute, Steel Statistical Yearbook 1983 and World Steel in Figures 1984.

n.a. - not available.

glut. From 1974 through 1982, these countries increased their steel production from 34 million to 67 million tons (Table 7.1). Had world demand increased in the last ten years, the newly-industrializing countries would certainly have expanded more rapidly, but weak prices due to excess supply obviously placed many of these enterprises under severe pressure. Equally important has been the external debt problem for many of these countries, which has severely curtailed domestic investment.

One might have expected developed countries to rationalize their steel capacity more rapidly than they have. The U.S. industry has shed about 30 million tons of its 160 million tons without the aid of a government rationalization plan.[5] Europe, on the other hand, has succeeded in closing some small plants, but its total capacity has shrunk by less than 20 million tons. Japan apparently retains most of its capacity, but it has operated at less than 70 percent of this capacity in recent years.

With much of their capacity built in the past ten years, the Japanese are less likely to retire assets permanently. The U.S. has been driven to reduce capacity more rapidly than its European rivals because of the play of market forces upon financially troubled producers. The Europeans have used government financing to slow this decline (with the exception of the British), but they too are facing difficult choices. Indeed, the French and Belgians face serious political difficulties in trying to shutter inefficient plants.

After years of extremely sluggish demand, the developed countries continue to hold perhaps as much as 100 million tons of unused capacity. This capacity will not be retired soon because of the prospects for an upturn in demand and because technological change in the industry has been very slow in recent years. If producers believed that these assets would be unprofitable to operate in three or four years, they would certainly move to scrap them now. Unfortunately, technological change has been so slow that the variable costs of operating many of these facilities is anticipated to be no higher than the average cost of new facilities. As a result, like the railroads, they hold on to dedicated plants in the hope of generating small positive cash flows in future years.

THE SHIFT OF STEEL PRODUCTION TO THE DEVELOPING COUNTRIES

It is not difficult to explain the movement of steel production away from the developed countries. While Europe, North America, and Japan continue to account for 80 percent of noncommunist world output, these countries' steel industries are in modest to steep decline. As we have seen, the developing countries in Latin America and Eastern Asia have been increasing their share of world output steadily. These countries doubled their steel capacity during the 1970s, and the IISI predicts that their capacity will increase by another 100 percent in the 1980s, despite a very low growth rate in world steel consumption.[6] Nevertheless, it is unlikely that these developing countries will account for more than 25 percent of (noncommunist) world steel production by the mid 1990s unless their economies grow very rapidly during the decade.

It is commonplace to ascribe the developing countries' interest in steel production to national pride, the follies of national planning, or a political drive to subsidize employment. Modestly sophisticated analyses focus on the desire of developing countries for import substitution regardless of comparative advantage. In fact, most of these explanations are incorrect, for steel production is an area of comparative advantage for many of the newly industrializing economies.

Modern steel production utilizes either the Linz-Donau basic-oxygen (BOF) process or the electric-arc furnace. BOF's are fed by molten pig iron from large blast furnaces with a supplement of scrap, while electric furnaces use either scrap or directly-reduced iron ore as their charge. Neither of these processes is very labor intensive. The BOF process requires large amounts of iron ore, metallurgical coal, and limestone, while the electric furnace requires substantial quantities of electric energy and either scrap or directly-reduced iron. If direct reduction is used, large quantities of cheap natural gas (priced at less than the market price of Btu equivalents from oil) must be available. For raw steel production, therefore, access to some combination of iron ore, coal, natural gas, and scrap is a necessity.

With the exception of natural gas, none of the above inputs to raw steel production is very valuable per unit weight. As a result, transportation costs loom large in the decision to build a steel plant. Access to a deep-water port allows a steel plant to obtain its raw materials from

competitive world markets for iron ore and coal. Inland
locations, on the other hand, suffer large inbound
transportation penalties unless they have access to water
transportation. It is for this reason that Japan, a nation
with virtually no raw materials for steel production, enjoys
a material cost advantage over landlocked integrated firms
in the United States.[7]

If steel production can be located anywhere where water
transportation to competitive world material markets is
available, it is obvious that there are numerous
possibilities in the developing countries. But why should
these countries have an advantage over more established,
developed industries? The answer lies mostly in the labor
costs of building plants and operating the rolling and
finishing facilities.

Steel production is a surprisingly labor-intensive
activity when all rolling and finishing stages are included.
Raw steel production requires little labor, especially in
modern plants. It is the rolling of the raw steel ingot,
slab, or billet into a variety of shapes that requires
substantial labor, particularly in older integrated plants.

The role of labor costs in steel production is
graphically exhibited in Table 7.2. In the United States
and Western Europe, labor costs are between 20 and 33
percent of total costs. Labor costs in the United States
are about $170 per net ton of carbon steel for the "average"
plant at 85 percent capacity utilization. While there is
considerable variance around this average, it is important
to note that these costs are more than 35 percent of the
current average price realized for carbon steel. Even with
the most modern technology, labor costs could not be reduced
to less than $100 per ton for an average mix of carbon steel
products from an integrated U.S. plant.

In developing countries, labor costs are substantially
lower. Even if integrated facilities require twice as much
labor as the average U.S. or European plant, total labor
costs are likely to be substantially less than in the
developed countries. With total compensation of no more
than $3 per hour in most cases (Table 7.3), labor costs are
likely to be less than $50 per ton as compared with $90 to
$170 per ton in Europe and the United States. Since
well-located plants on coastal sites can obtain raw
materials for less than U.S. or European producers, the
variable cost advantage to well-designed plants in
developing countries can easily range from $100 to $150 per
ton over U.S. or European plants. Obviously, this
substantial variable cost advantage must be offset by other

TABLE 7.2
Cost of Production in "Average" Integrated Carbon-Steel
Plant-Selected Industrialized Countries
(1983 $ per net ton)

Item	Japan	Germany	United States
Labor	64	88	168
Materials	275	300	310
Other	85	65	45
Total	424	455	523

Source: Author's calculations based upon standard (85 percent) operating rate and Peter Marcus, World Steel Dynamics.

TABLE 7.3
Total Compensation Per Hour for Production Workers in
Manufacturing and the Steel Industry in Selected Countries, 1983

Country	All Manufacturing	Iron and Steel
United States	12.31	21.73
Japan	6.24	10.72
Germany	10.39	11.25
Mexico	1.45	1.74*
Brazil	1.68	2.13**
Korea	1.29	1.90**
Taiwan	1.61	2.06**

*Author's estimate based upon 1982 relationship with average
manufacturing wage.

**Includes foundries.

Source: U.S. Bureau of Labor Statistics.

disadvantages or one would expect developing countries to have substantially more than 15 percent of the noncommunist world's output.

Integrated steel plants are enormous facilities, with minimum efficient scale in the 6 to 9 million ton range. A plant of this size requires a large work force and obviously a large market. Since it may cost as much as $10 billion to build, it is generally built in small stages. And with such enormous capital requirements, such projects are heavily encumbered by political considerations.

In the 1970s, a number of new steel projects were started all over the world. The British, French, Brazilians, Canadians, Koreans, Japanese, and Taiwanese began major new "greenfield" projects. Many of these projects have been delayed or "stretched out" as the result of the collapse in world demand. As a result, many of these plants are operating inefficiently or producing only a limited array of products. Any attempt to compare their current costs with the costs in other facilities is likely to be a biased indication of their future potential.

The political constraints on developing-country steel projects also contribute to their elevated costs. Location decisions, material supplies, employment policies, and engineering-management control are generally influenced by local political forces. If plants could be designed and built by consortia of Japanese, European, and North American engineers, using imported components, the cost of these facilities could well be substantially less than the cost of building them in Europe or the United States. As much as half the cost of an integrated steel works is site-specific labor and local building materials. In some countries, such as Korea and Taiwan, new-plant construction costs have been quite low due to the low cost of local construction labor.[8] However, infrastructure problems and political constraints can have substantial adverse effects on plant construction costs, offsetting some of the variable cost advantage that these developing countries enjoy.

INTEGRATED STEEL PRODUCTION IN THE UNITED STATES

Prior to 1960, the world steel industry was composed of essentially noncompeting national industries. Only one-eighth of the world's output was exported.[9] The United States exported about 3 percent of its output and imported 2 percent of its steel consumption in 1956-60.[10] Steel was and is a heavy product, and transportation costs provided a natural competitive barrier.

Beginning in the 1950s, however, shipping costs fell relative to steel production costs. Moreover, new sources of theretofore scarce iron ore opened up in Liberia, Venezuela, Australia, India, and China. The effect of these two developments was to facilitate the entry of new steel producing countries. The first such "new" industry was in Japan, which began to increase its capacity at a startling rate in the late 1950s. Subsequently, Brazil, Korea, and Mexico began to expand their capacity. Equally important, established producers in Europe, South Africa, and Australia became aggressive competitors in the world market.

At first, the United States industry responded to the change in world market conditions by taking an aggressive stance in labor relations. After allowing wages to escalate far more rapidly than the inflation rate throughout the 1950s, the industry took a long (four-month) strike in 1959. Thereafter, wage rates moderated until the 1968 negotiations (see Table 7.4). In 1968, the U.S. government negotiated voluntary import restraints with Japanese and European steel exporters, and in 1971 President Nixon devalued the dollar. Both of these events, combined with the effects of the Viet Nam War, strengthened the demand for steel produced in the United States. Prices for steel mill products rose sharply in 1970-1972. As a result, the industry was under less pressure to moderate wage increases. In the 1968, 1971, and 1974 wage negotiations, large increases in wages and benefits were granted. In 1973, the industry agreed to an "experimental negotiating agreement," guaranteeing the United Steel Workers at least 3 percent real annual wage increases in return for a guarantee of no strikes. Further increases in wages and benefits above this level were left to triennial negotiations.

The result of this new spiral in wages was to elevate U.S. steelworkers' total compensation from a level approximately 30 percent above the average for manufacturing in 1968 to nearly 90 percent above the manufacturing average by 1980. These labor costs have proven especially crippling during a period of dollar appreciation. After declining in value by 15 percent between 1978 and 1980, the dollar increased in value by 49 percent through the fourth quarter of 1983. Obviously, the combination of high wages, a high value of the dollar, and successive recessions have proved devastating to the industry.

The experience of the U.S. steel industry since World

TABLE 7.4
Total Compensation for Production Workers in Steel and all
Manufacturing in the United States, 1960-1980
($/hour)

Year	All Manufacturing*	Steel**
1960	2.87	3.82
61	2.99	3.99
62	3.06	4.16
63	3.16	4.25
64	3.29	4.36
65	3.35	4.48
66	3.50	4.63
67	3.68	4.76
68	3.94	5.03
69	4.20	4.38
1970	4.17	5.68
71	4.48	6.26
72	4.83	7.08
73	5.24	7.68
74	5.72	9.08
75	6.35	10.59
76	6.93	11.74
77	7.59	13.04
78	8.30	14.30
79	9.07	15.92
1980	9.89	18.45

Sources: *BLS

**American Iron and Steel Institute

War II is a graphic example of how labor can capture the rents from trade protection and how difficult it can be to squeeze those rents out of compensation packages when these trade restrictions are lifted. In the 1950s, the U.S. industry enjoyed natural protection due to high shipping costs and the absence of strong steel industries elsewhere in the world. In the late 1960s, informal quotas were imposed that were certainly binding by 1971 or 1972.[11] In 1978, "trigger prices," essentially minimum import prices, were imposed to deal with weak world export prices. These trigger prices had some effect in 1978 and 1979, but they became unenforceable after then. These bouts of trade protection were combined with dollar devaluations in 1971 and 1973, and the downward float of the dollar in 1978-1979. The result was to confer large potential rents on factors specific to the steel industry--specifically, labor.

Since 1980, there has been no effective protection for the U.S. industry despite a proliferation of complaints and trade suits. Import prices for most steel products have plummeted as the dollar has risen, placing downward pressure on domestic prices and increasing import penetration to 26 percent. The wage bargains struck in 1968-80 became a burden that the industry could barely withstand. In 1982, the major integrated producers lost more than $100 per ton of steel shipped.[12] Had wage rates been only 30 percent above the manufacturing average, the level in 1968, these losses would have been approximately halved.

With little hope of returning to 1973-74 production levels and the prospect of increasingly losing markets to domestic mini-mills and imports, the integrated firms face very difficult problems. They have been unable to build a new plant since the early 1960s and are therefore saddled with a large number of suboptimal scale plants built originally as much as half a century ago. Many of these plants have been kept in operation since the 1975 recession in the hope of a return to "shortage" conditions. Capital resources that could have been better spent on the more modern, larger plants on the Great Lakes were spent to keep plants in Alabama, Pennsylvania, Utah, and Texas in operation. With a more somber view of the future, the managements of these companies are beginning to close the most inefficient of these facilities. Since 1977, about 30 million tons of capacity have been closed, but much remains to be accomplished.

The integrated companies still enjoy substantial advantages in using Great Lakes ore and Appalachian coal to produce flat-rolled products (sheets) for appliance, automotive, and other uses in the lower Great Lakes. Plants along Lake Erie and Lake Michigan will survive, but integrated plants in areas closer to international competition and farther from midwestern markets and material supplies will continue to close unless the dollar depreciates drastically and mini-mills are slow to expand into new markets.

Were labor costs lower, the rate of decline might be slowed, but it would not stop. The United States simply cannot build and operate new integrated steel works in competition with foreign works with current U.S. construction costs and manufacturing wages. Even if the premium of steelworker compensation over the average manufacturing wage were to return to 30 percent, it would still be impossible to justify building new integrated steel works in the U.S.

THE NEWEST THREAT TO U.S. INTEGRATED PRODUCERS: MINI-MILLS

The decline in the competitiveness of U.S. integrated producers has thus far been attributed to soaring wage costs and the recent appreciation of the dollar. However, this analysis does not extend to another sector of the U.S. steel industry, the mini-mills. These companies do not have all of the inherited difficulties of their larger, integrated brethren, and they are continuing to grow despite recession and the high value of the dollar.

Mini-mills are essentially smaller steel companies, producing a limited array of products with electric furnaces. At present, they use virtually 100 percent scrap as their material charge, but they will undoubtedly turn to directly-reduced ore in future years for some of the input requirements. There are between 40 and 50 of these companies, with a total of about 20 million tons of raw steel capacity. Most produce small bar shapes, hot rolled bars, and reinforcing bars of carbon steel. Increasingly, they are moving into more sophisticated products and into products with larger cross sections. Some companies now produce drawing-quality wire rod, alloy bars, cold finished bars, plates, or larger structurals. With current technology, they are likely to make substantial inroads into all steel markets other than sheets, rails, and seamless tubes. In the future, however, even these markets are likely to be invaded by the mini-mill companies.

The mini-mill producers succeed in large part because they are entrepreneurial firms that are not organized by the United Steelworkers and have a much better productivity record. Their initial capital requirements are much smaller--only $250 to $300 per ton rather than $1,000 or more required for integrated production. And their raw materials costs are lower in all but boom conditions since they rely upon local scrap.

At the current price of scrap, mini-mills enjoy as much as $100 per ton cost advantage over the integrated companies for small carbon bar products. This obviously means that the larger companies are abandoning these markets to the small companies. Equally important is the fact that these mini-mill companies are spread over the entire country. Many are expanding in the southern and western areas of the country, whereas integrated producers are steadily withdrawing to the Great Lakes area.

The mini-mills enjoy such a large labor cost advantage over the larger companies that they will be able to dominate the smaller bar-product markets even in periods of high scrap prices. Moreover, given their efficiency and the low prices of bar products, imports will not be a major threat. Imports of hot-rolled bars, reinforcing rods, and small bar shapes have consistently been less than 10 percent of U.S. consumption. It is likely that the mini-mills will displace imports of wire rod and cold finished bars over the next few years, with other products to follow if some promising new technologies become commercially viable.

In the next few years, mini-mills will be venturing into the sheet markets if any one of a number of thin slab casting technologies under development proves successful. At present, steel slabs approximately six inches to one foot thick must be rolled on an enormous hot strip mill, requiring 3 to 4 million tons of throughput for efficient operation. If thin slabs are cast, much smaller rolling mills will be required, allowing mini-mills to venture into sheet markets with perhaps 500,000 ton plants. When this occurs, sheet production will proliferate around the United States, placing even the Great Lakes plants of the integrated companies under increased market pressure.

TABLE 7.5
Exports and Imports of Steel in Less-Developed Countries by Major
Area, 1973-1983
(millions of net tons)

Area		1973	1974	1975	1976	1977	1978	1979	1980	1981	1982
Latin America	Imports	7.8	11.0	9.7	6.6	7.7	7.2	6.7	8.3	8.8	5.9
	Exports	1.6	0.9	0.4	0.9	1.1	2.5	2.9	3.2	3.3	4.4
	Net Imports	6.2	10.1	9.3	5.7	6.6	4.7	3.8	5.1	5.5	1.5
Asia	Imports	15.2	16.1	14.3	16.0	18.1	25.4	26.8	23.8	21.8	23.6
(excluding Japan)	Exports	1.8	2.2	2.0	3.8	3.8	4.2	5.9	6.7	7.2	9.3
	Net Imports	13.4	13.9	12.3	12.2	14.3	21.2	20.9	17.1	14.6	14.3
Africa/Middle East	Imports	10.3	14.6	15.9	16.9	17.3	19.6	19.6	20.8	20.8	19.7
	Exports	0.7	0.7	0.4	1.4	2.5	2.6	2.9	2.4	2.3	2.8
	Net Imports	9.6	13.9	15.5	15.5	14.8	17.0	16.7	18.4	18.5	16.9
Mexico	Imports	0.4	0.8	0.8	0.5	0.5	1.4	1.7	3.0	3.5	1.6
	Exports	0.2	0.1	0.1	0.2	0.3	0.4	0.3	0.1	0.1	0.3
	Net Imports	0.2	0.7	0.7	0.3	0.2	1.0	1.4	2.9	3.4	1.3

Source: International Iron and Steel Institute, Steel Statistical Yearbook, 1983.

Note: Area Data include intra-area imports and exports.

THE MEXICAN INDUSTRY

Mexico is currently the second largest Latin American producer of steel and the fourth largest in the Western hemisphere. While it exports some steel, mostly to the United States, it is, on balance, a heavy importer of steel, importing as much as one-third of its domestic consumption in 1981 (Table 7.5). As a result, expansion of the Mexican steel industry is likely to rest on the attractiveness of displacing imports rather than emerging as a major exporter. This is not unusual among newly industrializing countries. In Latin America and Eastern Asia (excluding Japan), steel production is growing rapidly; nevertheless, both areas remain major net importers of steel. A few of the major new producers of steel, such as Brazil and Korea, are already net exporters, but in an early period of industrialization the demand for steel generally outruns the country's ability to produce it.

The Mexican industry is a mix of the three types of steel technologies in use in the world today: basic oxygen/blast furnace; electric furnace/scrap; and electric furnace/direct reduction. Some open hearths remain, but approximately 80 percent of annual output derives from electric or basic-oxygen furnaces. There are five major integrated companies, two using directly reduced ore produced by the HYL process (see essay by Bueno, Cortés, and Rubio), and the remainder using BOFs and open hearths. In addition, there are a number of smaller electric furnace companies that produce bar products and specialty steel. Raw steel capacity appears to be in the 8 to 9 million ton range.

The Mexican industry enjoys most of the advantages of a newly industrializing country in steel production. With lower wages than its more developed neighbors, it can construct and operate new integrated facilities more cheaply than U.S. or Canadian companies if it locates in coastal locations to obtain materials at competitive world prices (especially coking coal), or at inland locations near iron ore supplies when the direct-reduction process is used. Its growth is likely to depend mostly upon import substitution in the next few years. Consumption of steel grows much more rapidly in newly industrializing countries than in developed nations. Indeed, there are indications that steel consumption will continue to grow much less rapidly than GNP in all major western developed countries (Figure 7.1). With Brazil, Venezuela, and Argentina expanding their industries,

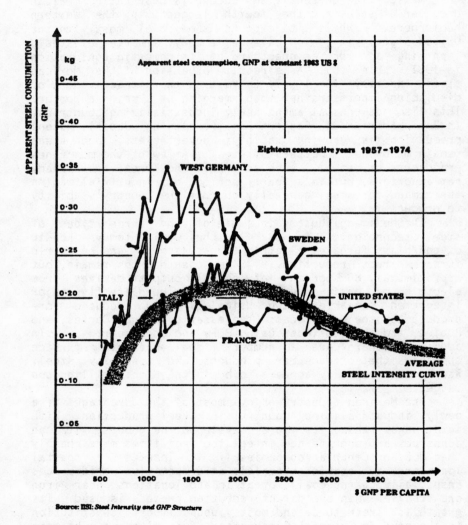

Source: IISI: *Steel Intensity and GNP Structure*

Figure 7.1
Industrialized Countries: Yearly Fluctuations in Steel
Intensity and the Average Steel Intensity Curve

it seems unlikely that Mexican steel exports to South
America will grow appreciably. Nor will the Pacific Basin
be an attractive market with the Koreans, Taiwanese,
Japanese, and eventually the Chinese competing actively in
that market. In short, growth in Mexican steel output is
likely to be focused primarily on internal Mexican demand
and some exports to the United States.

Apparent per capita steel consumption in Mexico has
been growing from 100 kg in the early 1970s, to 150 kg in
the early 1980s. In the wealthiest industrial countries,
per capita consumption is 600 kg, while in the more advanced
developing countries it is often 200 kg or more. As Mexico
solves its financial and macroeconomic problems, it can
expect its steel consumption to grow more rapidly than GNP
for some time. Indeed, expansion of automobile sector and
other fabricating industries may be expected to fuel this
growth and substitute for the recent diminution in energy-
related investment.

One must be cautious, however, in drawing quick
conclusions about the attractiveness of the U.S. market to
Mexican exporters. Obviously, the earlier high value of the
dollar made this market look uncommonly attractive, and the
disarray in the U.S. integrated industry augurs well for
opportunities to export to the United States. But the value
of the dollar and the Mexican-U.S. exchange rate are subject
to change. More important, however, is the role of the
mini-mill in the United States.

In 1983, Mexican exports of steel products to the
United States surged to 0.6 million tons, up sharply from
0.1 million tons in 1982. Much of this increase occurred in
wire rods and reinforcing bars, two product markets
dominated by mini-mills in the United States. One third of
all Mexican exports to the United States were in mini-mill-
dominated products, 25 percent in sheet products, 30 percent
in pipe and tubing, and the remainder in plate and large
structurals (Table 7.6).

Obviously, Mexico's market in the U.S. is in the
southern and western states. Exports from the Monterrey
area plants are likely to penetrate the Southwest, while
SICARTSA or TAMSA exports are likely to go either to the
West Coast or the Gulf ports. These areas are precisely the
ones where U.S. mini-mill investment is currently the
strongest. It is unlikely that, in the long run, Mexican
facilities can produce more cheaply than efficient, scrap-
based U.S. companies. This is not to say that Mexico will
not obtain some share of this market, but it will be neither
large nor extraordinarily profitable, particularly in a

TABLE 7.6
U.S. Imports of Steel from Mexico, 1983
(thousands of net tons)

COMPETITIVE WITH MINIMILLS		COMPETITIVE WITH INTEGRATED FIRMS	
Wire Rods	107	Hot Rolled Sheet & Strip	57
Reinforcing Bars	71	Cold Rolled Sheet & Strip	15
Bar Shapes	11	Galvanized Sheet	63
Hot Rolled Bars	10	Other Coated Sheet	13
Cold Finished Bars	1	Total Sheet	148
Total Bars & Rods	200		
		Plate	26
		Large Structurals	62
		Total Plate & Structurals	88

COMPETITIVE WITH INTEGRATED FIRMS AND MINIMILLS

PIPE & TUBING

Standard Pipe	95
Oil Country Goods	10
Line Pipe	54
Tubing (Mechanical & Pressure)	13
Total Pipe & Tube	172

Grand Total: 608

Source: U.S. Department of Commerce

regime of a weaker dollar.

Exports of sheet products to the U.S. will encounter stiff competition from the Brazilians, the Koreans, the Canadians, and the Japanese. Moreover, at the lower quality grades, the mini-mills are likely to become a factor in the next decade. Thus, even the U.S. market--one of the largest import markets in the world--will be a very difficult one in which to compete in the next decade. Mexico, enjoying all of the advantages of a newly industrializing country in steel production, will not find it easy to compete with its brethren to the south or east unless the direct-reduction technology it is developing proves extraordinarily successful.

Repeating the Japanese miracle, or even the modest successes of the Korean industry, will not be easy. Much will depend upon internal economic growth in Mexico. If macroeconomic policy can succeed in restoring substantial economic growth, steel consumption should grow much more rapidly than GNP. Given the role of steel in various infrastructure projects, oil and gas production, and private capital projects, the internal market should dominate exports in the growth of the Mexican steel industry for the next decade. Mexico enjoys many advantages in steel production that derive from its developing status, and its gas-fed direct reduction plants may add immeasurably to these advantages. Nevertheless, it would be naive to think that Mexico will find the world steel market easy to penetrate.

CONCLUSION

There are some observers who believe that the export market will be far more attractive when the developed countries work off their excess capacity that overhangs the market. They fail to recognize the potential for expansion of capacity in Korea, Brazil, Venezuela, Taiwan, and China when the world market begins to tighten. Absent an international agreement among all steel-producing nations to cartelize the world market, this market will remain very competitive even if demand strengthens and the French, Belgians, and Germans, Italians, and Americans retire substantial capacity. Mexico should reduce its net imports of steel as its industry expands, but most of its growth will be fueled by internal demand.

For the United States, the picture is mixed. The integrated producers are locked into a set of plants that they cannot sustain. Moreover, they have the heritage of extremely poor labor relations, despite offering their workers compensation which is almost double the U.S. manufacturing average. They cannot escape from this situation easily since workers are unlikely to grant major concessions in wages, benefits, or work rules unless their jobs are threatened. Employment in the integrated industry has been declining for nearly two decades, but at a rate that is not much greater than natural attrition. Workers in the Great Lakes plants understand the plight of their employers, but they also know that they are unlikely to lose their jobs before either retirement or early retirement under the very liberal provisions in their contract. As a result, they will continue to earn very high wages and watch their employers decline slowly.

The mini-mill sector will take up most of the market abandoned by the integrated firms over the next decade or two. Technological developments that will allow them to invade the sheet market are now very close to reality. With much better labor relations and, therefore, lower unit labor costs, these companies can and will compete with imports unless the dollar strengthens. It would not be surprising to see these smaller companies account for 25 to 30 percent of the U.S. market by the end of the decade and perhaps even surpass the import share of U.S. steel companies.

The appropriate industrial strategy in this situation is to avoid supporting U.S. integrated plants that have been obsolete for years. These plants should be closed and the integrated companies should be free to concentrate on their better plants. Trade protection should be avoided since it will only further reduce the vigor of steel-using industries in the United States. Lower wage costs for the integrated companies would allow them a more leisurely rate of retrenchment, but there is little reason to believe that the workers will be sufficiently concerned to grant such concessions. We are simply seeing a large, old industry gradually giving way to a dynamic new industry of smaller firms, a change which is quite in keeping with current trends in market economies.

NOTES

[1]Annual Address of Mr. Leonard Holschuh, Secretary General of the International Iron and Steel Institute, November 1983.

[2]For a discussion of this claim, see U.S. Council on Wage and Price Stability, A Study of Steel Prices, July 1975, Ch. 4.

[3]Eurostat, Iron and Steel Yearbook, 1983. OECD is the Organization for Economic Cooperation and Development, headquartered in Paris.

[4]See the petition of the United Steelworkers of America and Bethlehem Steel before the U.S. International Trade Commission, seeking Section 201 relief, January 24, 1984.

[5]American Iron and Steel Institute, Annual Statistical Reports. This is an estimate of gross retirements, excluding capacity additions at the mini-mills.

[6]See note 1.

[7]For a discussion of these issues, see Robert W. Crandall, The U.S. Steel Industry in Recurrent Crisis. Washington, D.C.: The Brookings Institution, 1981; and Donald F. Barnett and Louis Schorsch, Steel: Upheaval in a Basic Industry, Cambridge, Mass.: Ballinger, 1983.

[8]See Crandall, op. cit., Ch. 4, for a more complete discussion.

[9]International Iron and Steel Institute, Annual Statistical Reports.

[10]American Iron and Steel Institute, Annual Statistical Reports.

[11]Crandall, op. cit., Ch. 3.

[12]John Tumazos, Oppenheimer and Co., Metals Meetings Notes, February 1984.

8

The U.S. Motor Vehicle Industry: Emerging Trends and Impacts on Mexico

Neil D. Schuster

INTRODUCTION

The formation and development of a motor vehicle sector can be a significant contributing factor to the economic health of a country and make possible a role in world trade. This is true for nations with emerging economies as well as for those with mature markets. Often, the greater the role a country's motor vehicle sector plays in the national economy, the more numerous the government policies which directly or indirectly affect the industry. With increased globalization of the motor vehicle industry, government policies in any one country often have profound impacts on motor vehicle producers and consumers in other countries as well.

This paper addresses these issues in the context of the U.S. motor vehicle sector in general and with regard to developments in U.S.-Mexico automotive trade. An attempt is made to describe emerging U.S. industry trends and corporate strategies and to review relevant government policy developments in the United States. The paper also looks at the impact of industry strategies and U.S. government policies on the Mexican motor vehicle sector. The impact of overseas vehicle manufacturers, most notably in Japan, on the U.S.-Mexican motor vehicle market is also addressed. Conclusions are drawn with respect to the automotive issues facing the United States and Mexico.

THE U.S. MOTOR VEHICLE INDUSTRY

The past few years have brought dramatic change to the motor vehicle industry in the United States. Following four years of industry recession, marked by declining annual production (as high as 30 percent in one year), the U.S. market began to improve in 1983 with a 17 percent increase in overall sales (from 10.5 to 12.3 million units) and a 20 percent increase in sales of domestically-produced vehicles. Production in 1983 was nearly 32 percent higher than in 1982 (from 7.0 to 9.2 million units), while employment rose almost 10 percent to 772,000. The industry operated at 72 percent of capacity, compared to 56 percent in 1982.[1]

Many factors contributed to the industry's recovery. In 1978, as the recession began to develop, motor vehicle manufacturers embarked on a multi-billion dollar capital expenditure program which resulted in major improvements in vehicle design and quality, fuel economy, and productivity and costs, thus increasing responsiveness to import competition. Industry capital spending, which was no higher than $4.6 billion per year during the early and mid 1970s, jumped to an annual range of $8 to $12.6 billion between 1978 and 1982.[2] As a result, domestic manufacturers were able to realize significant improvements in their fleet, such as an 86 percent increase in fuel economy over a ten-year period,[3] as well as significant quality improvements. At the same time that manufacturers were building more competitive vehicles, they were also streamlining operations to achieve lower production costs. Robots are being relied on to a much greater extent. Employee involvement has been given greater emphasis as a result of the new focus on employee relations. The reduced inflation rate and lower interest rates in the United States, both of which have substantial impacts on vehicle sales, helped fuel the industry's recovery.

Specific forecasts of future vehicle sales differ, but there is general agreement that domestic sales will continue to rise in the next few years. Data Resources, Inc. projected rising auto production in 1990 of 7.88 million units. By 1990, DRI expects new truck registrations to reach 4.63 million units.[4]

Competition from vehicle manufacturers in Japan was a significant factor affecting vehicle sales in the United States during the industry's recession and continues to be a factor during its recovery. Import models today offer a wide range of the product mix. In 1978, when U.S.

manufacturers had their most profitable year, small cars accounted for about 45 percent of sales. By 1983, over half of all car sales were in the small car market, which is subject to considerable import competition.

Japanese imports captured 21 percent of the domestic car market in 1983, compared with 12 percent in 1978 and 4 percent in 1970. Largely as a result of these gains by Japanese importers, the total import share grew from 15 percent of U.S. sales in 1970 to 26 percent in 1983. The lion's share of that increase, both in total and for Japanese imports, took place since 1978.[5]

Import sales in the truck market exhibited a pattern similar to auto sales. In 1983, Japanese imports held 18.7 percent of truck sales, almost all of the 19.3 percent foreign market share.[6]

Small car competition in the domestic market is likely to remain intense. The demand for vehicles will most likely remain highly sensitive to interest rates, inflation, the unemployment rate, and fuel prices in the coming years.

Foreign vehicle producers are also expanding their participation in the large and luxury car segments. For example, Honda sells a luxury automobile in the United States and European producers such as Mercedes-Benz, Volvo, and Saab have significantly increased their sales in recent years.

Foreign competition for truck sales in the United States closely follows the patterns existing for automobiles. Considerable foreign competition exists for compact and medium-size trucks and several Japanese and European producers are now offering, or will shortly offer, medium and heavier trucks.

INDUSTRY TRENDS

DRI projections also deal with car and truck production in Western Europe, all of North America, and Japan.

Auto production is forecast to reach 11.98 million units by 1990 in Western Europe, up 8 percent from 11.1 million units in 1983, or less than the 15.5 percent increase forecast for the United States. Auto output in Japan is forecast to grow by 15 percent as well, reaching 8.24 million units in 1990.

Truck production is expected to rise 16 percent from 1983 levels in Western Europe, reaching 1.49 million units in 1990. By comparison, North American light truck production is forecast to grow by 53 percent, reaching 4.12 million units in 1990.

Projections of vehicle registrations show a slightly different picture. Auto registrations are forecast to grow 12.2 percent in Western Europe, 15.3 percent in Japan, and 28.7 percent in North America between 1983 and 1990.

New truck registrations are expected to grow by 11.1 percent in Western Europe and by 48 percent in the United States during that same time period.[7]

In comparison, a United Nations study in 1983 indicated that vehicle demand in developing countries could exhibit a three-fold-plus increase between 1979 and 1990.[8]

Possibly in anticipation of this trend, motor-vehicle production has exhibited a modest but noticeable shift away from mature markets since 1950. In that year, more than 95 percent of worldwide production was concentrated in developed market economies, dropping to 84 percent by 1981. Centrally-planned economies (the USSR, Czechoslovakia, German Democratic Republic, Hungary, and Poland) have more than doubled their share of vehicle output from 3.7 percent in 1970 to nearly 11 percent in 1981. Developing market economies, which include Mexico, Brazil, Argentina, India, and Yugoslavia for purposes of the U.N study, exhibited a 16-fold increase, from 0.3 percent in 1950 to more than 5 percent in 1981. Mexico's share of world vehicle production grew from 0.3 percent in 1960 to 1.6 percent in 1981.[9]

Recent trade statistics highlight the extent of Japanese vehicle imports and the trend to foreign sourcing. Motor vehicle trade in the United States has run a growing deficit in recent years, doubling from a $9 billion gap in 1979 to nearly $18 billion in 1982.[10]. This deficit is primarily the result of the dramatic increase in imports of built-up vehicles; parts and accessories trade has exhibited a surplus as high as $1.3 billion in 1981. The parts surplus dropped in 1982 to $69 million.[11] The U.S. auto trade deficit with Japan alone was $55 billion between 1978 and 1982.

Each manufacturer has followed a somewhat different strategy in responding to competitive and economic pressures, but a common element runs through the individual company responses to the changing marketplace. The following summary of individual company plans, compiled from published reports, highlights these responses.[12]

General Motors' strategy has been one of significant investment in foreign supply sources. The company has a one-third interest in Isuzu and a small interest in Suzuki, with plans to market small cars from both these Japanese producers in the United States.[13] In addition, GM and Isuzu plan to build trucks and buses together in Egypt.[14] Of more recent note, and what many consider a major industry development, is a 12-year joint venture between GM and Toyota to produce some 200,000 small front-wheel-drive cars annually in the United States.[15]

General Motors has also expanded capacity at its Mexican assembly plant and has invested in a plant to produce engines in Mexico. The company is reported to have invested some $300 million in Mexico, in part to supply components to the United States. Much of this foreign sourcing is expected to pertain to small car production, with Japan likely to become the company's principal source of vehicles in the coming few years and Mexico supplying a substantial percentage of GM foreign-sourced engines. Heavy-duty diesel engines are also assembled in Mexico.[16]

Ford has long incorporated an international focus into its corporate strategy. Ford has a 25 percent interest in Toyo Kogyo, manufacturer of Mazda vehicles. The company recently announced plans to produce vehicles in Mexico at a new plant, with production designed for the local market and export to the United States and Canada. Reports indicate that Toyo Kogyo may supply components.[17] [18]

Chrysler has sold many of its foreign interests over the past few years, but remains actively involved in Mexico. Chrysler has a 15 percent interest in Mitsubishi,[19] which provides engines for Chrysler vehicles as well as vehicles for sale in the United States under the Chrysler nameplate. The company has a 15 percent interest in Peugeot as well. Chrysler's engine production capacity in Mexico is under expansion, with plans to export a high percentage of output to the United States.[20]

American Motors has developed a close link with Renault, which has invested over $400 million into AMC over a three-year period.[21] The two companies are further involved in a major vehicle design program. AMC now produces the Renault Alliance and Encore and distributes other Renault models in the United States. AMC's most extensive foreign sourcing operation is located in Mexico. Further, Renault has built a new engine plant in Mexico, with output geared toward export.

Volkswagen produces vehicles in the United States and is heavily invested in Mexico as well. Recent reports indicate a significant shift is likely in sourcing engines and transmissions for U.S. manufacturing operations from existing West German sources to those in Mexico.

186

Truck manufacturers have established numerous international links, although many have been in operation for some time. PACCAR has a minority position in Kenworth Mexicana as well as an Australian operation. Mack is also involved in Mexico.[22] Harvester has retreated from direct manufacturing in Mexico, but remains involved in the Mexican market and maintains technical and licensing agreements with FAMSA, which assembles IH trucks, and a technical agreement with DINA. The company's principal foreign investments are now in Venezuela, Australia, and South Africa.

GOVERNMENT POLICIES

Approximately one job in six in the United States is in the motor vehicle and related industries, and for every one person employed in the motor vehicle and equipment industry directly, two jobs are created in support industries.[23] Motor vehicle manufacturers consume substantial amounts of steel, plastics, rubber, and glass, as one might suspect. But the industry is also a large consumer of fabrics, chemicals, machine tools, robotics, and electronics, and has a substantial impact on a variety of economic sectors, including the financial and insurance industries.

Because the motor vehicle industry has an impact on so many aspects of the domestic economy, government policies which affect vehicle production and sales are critical to the economy as a whole. At times, government policy provides the framework within which the industry evolves and can influence the direction the industry may take. Under different circumstances, industry strategies and the evolution of the marketplace affect the direction of government policies.

In the United States, the former is more often the case. The theoretical cornerstone of U.S. foreign economic policy is free trade, based on open markets at home and with our trading partners. The United States recognizes that international trade is becoming increasingly important to our economy and to those of our major trading partners. Domestic economic programs no longer deal exclusively with domestic issues, but are often designed to address international trade objectives as well.

The United States actively pursues reduction and elimination of tariff and nontariff trade barriers and distortions wherever possible. In addition, U.S. trade policy addresses investment issues that potentially distort trade flows, including trade-related investment incentives and performance requirements in other countries.

In practice, however, U.S. trade policy decisions do in fact allow for circumstances where industries or countries cannot compete on an equal footing, or where short-term exceptions to completely free trade are necessary in achieving long-term goals and objectives. The executive branch has taken some trade actions to limit imports, when perceived to be in the national interest.

U.S. policymakers are also faced with legislative and other initiatives which often run counter to established trade policy. For example, a bill to establish local-content levels for U.S.-built vehicles has been proposed in Congress. Passed by the House of Representatives in 1982 and again in 1983, the measure would represent a major departure from existing U.S. trade policy and is a reaction to concerns about the level of vehicle imports to the United States, increased foreign sourcing by domestic vehicle producers, and the decline in the level of motor vehicle industry employment in the United States.

Domestic-content legislation would impose certain constraints on U.S. vehicle producers and in all likelihood would affect the industry's growing reliance on Mexico as a source of vehicle components for U.S. motor vehicle production, a trend that is expected to continue in the future in the absence of government-imposed restraints.

Government policymakers, from Mexico as well as the United States, are faced with addressing the growing interdependence between the automotive sectors of both countries and whether the existing bilateral relationship is adequate to address the type and level of automotive trade which has developed between the two countries.

In the United States, some interests have expressed concern over the level of automotive trade with Mexico. Specifically, U.S. labor groups as well as component manufacturers, and certain government officials, have raised the issue of Mexican motor vehicle performance requirements and investment incentives as they affect the U.S. economy. Government officials are concerned with the potential negative effect of these foreign policies on bilateral trade and on the increased potential for protectionist legislation in response. Labor groups and parts manufacturers see export requirements and incentives as a direct cause of lost sales and reduced domestic employment.

IMPACTS ON MEXICO

The United States and Mexico represent a combined market of over 300 million people, substantially larger than the combined population of the 10 countries which comprise the European Community. Mexico ranks as our third largest trading partner, a level of importance which extends to motor-vehicle sector trade as well.

The U.S. trade surplus with Mexico reached $3.7 billion in 1981, then reversed to a $4.5 billion deficit in 1982, climbing to a $7.8 billion deficit in 1983.

U.S. imports of engines from Mexico have grown nearly four-fold in only four years, from $53 million in 1979 to $196 million in 1982, as vehicle manufacturers rely more heavily on foreign sourcing. Despite these growing imports, the United States still maintains a substantial automotive trade surplus with Mexico. In 1982, that surplus was $874 million.[24]

The strategies adopted by motor vehicle manufacturers have had a profound impact on the Mexican motor vehicle sector. Largely as a result of industry strategy and government policy, the motor-vehicle sector in Mexico, while increasing local content levels, is concurrently launching a major export drive to balance the auto trade account.

U.S. investment in the Mexican automotive sector is substantial and continues to grow. According to recent studies, total automotive investment in Mexico since 1980 reached $2 billion. The three largest U.S. manufacturers as well as Nissan and Volkswagen all have major investments and expansion programs in Mexico. The recent investments place a strong emphasis on achieving cost efficiencies and economies of scale, thus aiming at greater competitive potential in global markets.

One U.S. trade-policy issue which is likely to affect Mexican automotive and other exports to the United States is the Generalized System of Preferences (GSP). The GSP is a unilateral program which provides duty-free treatment for a variety of products imported from developing countries. U.S. imports of GSP automotive products grew from $159 million in 1976, when the program went into effect, to $787 million in 1982, representing nearly 11 percent of total U.S. automotive imports.[25]

Mexico ranks third in utilizing U.S. GSP benefits for automotive trade, exporting $88 million of duty-free automotive products to the United States in 1982, representing 15 percent of Mexico's total GSP trade. Of the major GSP beneficiary countries with respect to automotive trade, only Brazil has a greater concentration of GSP benefits in motor vehicle products at 41.5 percent.

THIRD COUNTRY IMPACTS

Industrial policies as well as company strategies in third countries have had a significant impact on the motor vehicle sectors in the United States and Mexico. As discussed above, the level of import penetration, particularly from Japan, has grown at a dramatic rate in the recent past. U.S. motor-vehicle manufacturers, and government officials have responded to growing imports in a variety of ways. Partly in response to legislative domestic-content initiative, the Japanese government, for four years, voluntarily limited its vehicle exports to the United States.

Some Japanese manufacturers are now building vehicles in the United States. In addition, Volkswagen maintains a significant presence in the U.S. market, not only selling imported vehicles, but producing as well. Renault, linked with American Motors, is also heavily involved in the U.S. market.

Volkswagen, Nissan, and Renault represent the major overseas producers in Mexico. Overseas investments have had a positive impact on the Mexican motor vehicle industry and on Mexico's balance of payments. According to a U.S. Department of Commerce study, some 2,000 Mexican firms supply Volkswagen de México with parts.

CONCLUSIONS

Competitive forces and emerging market potentials affecting the motor-vehicle industry worldwide have led U.S. vehicle manufacturers to adopt strategies necessary to insure their ability to compete in global and domestic markets. A variety of factors, including growing import competition, the effects of the sustained high value of the dollar, tax inequities, wage-rate differentials, and constraints imposed by government policies, have influenced U.S. motor vehicle manufacturers to seek a broad range of cooperative arrangements with other vehicle producers and to increase the internationalization of component and vehicle sourcing.

While most industry developments have occurred within the framework of existing government policies, particularly in the United States, the potential exists for government policies to increasingly influence the direction of industry strategy.

The motor vehicle industries in the United States and Mexico are becoming increasingly interdependent. Each country's automotive sector is becoming more reliant on developments in its counterpart and also on government policy decisions in both countries. These trends are likely to accelerate, possibly adding to existing tensions between the United States and Mexico with respect to automotive trade. The two countries, therefore, need to improve their existing bilateral trade relationship if they are to avoid future conflicts. They should adopt a framework for trade negotiation which can adequately address the variety of concerns associated with the level and type of automotive trade which is developing between them.

Unless these trade issues are resolved, the threat of adverse government policy decisions will escalate, with potentially serious negative consequences for the motor vehicle sectors and the economies of both countries, and possibly for U.S-Mexico relations in general.

NOTES

[1]*Economic Indicators*, Fourth Quarter 1983, p. 1.
[2]*The U.S. Automobile Industry* (Washington, D.C.: Department of Commerce, 1983), p. 20.
[3]Motor Vehicle Manufacturers Association of the U.S., *Facts and Figures '83* (Detroit: MVMA, 1983), p. 74.
[4]*Automotive News*, March 19, 1984, p. 77.
[5]*Economic Indicators*, Fourth Quarter 1983, p. 16.
[6]Ibid., p. 19.
[7]*Automotive News*, p. 77.
[8]*Transnational Corporations in the International Auto Industry*, Centre on Transnational Corporations 1983, p. 9.
[9]Ibid., p. 14.
[10]Scott Laing and Robert Rahn, *Foreign Outsourcing by U.S. Auto Manufacturers* (London: Economist Intelligence Unit, 1982), p. 9

[11]Ibid., p. 10-11.

[12]Company plans have been synthesized from published reports.

[13]United Nations Centre on Transnational Corporations, _Transnational Corporations in the International Auto Industry_ (New York: UN, 1983), pp. 80 ff.

[14]Automotive Industry Data Ltd., _Joint Ventures & Collaboration Agreements_ (London, 1983).

[15]Ibid.

[16]_Transnational Corporations_, p. 81.

[17]A.T. Lowry and Scott Laing, _Financial Assessment of the U.S. Automotive Industry_ (London: Economist Intelligence Unit: 1982) p. 26.

[18]_Transnational Corporations_, p. 83.

[19]Ibid, p. 84-85.

[20]_Foreign Outsourcing_, p. 83.

[21]Ibid., p. 27.

[22]Motor Vehicle Manufacturers Association of the United States, _Overseas Facilities_ (Detroit: MVMA, 1979).

[23]_Economic Indicators_.

[24]_Foreign Outsourcing_, p. 14.

[25]Office of the United States Trade Representative.

[26]Ibid.

Appendix 8.1

U.S. AUTOMOTIVE TRADE
(thousands of dollars)

	EXPORTS		IMPORTS	
Year	Vehicles	Parts and Accessories[1]	Vehicles	Parts and Accessories[1]
1982	5,509,057	10,249,082	25,236,606	7,580,359
1981	7,175,648	10,544,984	22,513,215	6,933,189
1980	6,909,287	8,768,617	20,608,335	6,283,613
1979	7,909,158	8,462,485	18,349,565	7,154,957
1978	6,375,128	8,001,102	17,508,998	7,216,101
1977	5,666,968	6,719,309	13,860,396	4,990,976
1976	5,365,023	6,514,521	11,594,251	4,759,801
1975	5,157,161	5,304,886	8,865,930	2,731,922
:	:	:	:	:
1970	1,458.034	2,372,635	4,299,850	1,352,310

[1]Includes used vehicles and motor vehicle bodies

Source: U.S. Department of Commerce, Bureau of the Census

Appendix 8.1 cont.

U.S. AUTOMOBILE REGISTRATIONS
(millions)

Year	Registrations
1983	125.4*
1982	123.7
1981	122.6
1980	120.9
1979	117.6
1978	115.8
1977	113.0
1976	109.5
1975	106.1

*MVMA estimate
NOTE: privately owned vehicles
Source: Facts and Figures '84, MVMA

U.S. SALES OF JAPANESE IMPORTS
(millions)

Year	Total Sales	From Japan	% Japan
1982	5.76	1.80	22.6
1981	6.21	1.86	21.8
1980	6.58	1.91	21.2
1979	8.34	1.77	16.6
1978	9.31	1.36	12.0
1977	9.11	1.39	12.4
1976	8.61	.94	9.3
1975	7.05	.81	9.4
:	:	:	:
1970	7.12	.31	3.7

Source: Facts and Figures '83, MVMA

Appendix 8.1 cont.

U.S. DOMESTIC VEHICLE PRODUCTION

(thousands)

Year	Passenger Cars	Trucks and Buses	Total Vehicles
1983	6,781	2,424	9,205
1982	5,073	1,912	6,985
1981	6,253	1,690	7,943
1980	6,376	1,634	8,010
1979	8,434	3,046	11,480
1978	9,177	3,723	12,900
1977	9,214	3,489	12,703
1976	8,498	3,000	11,498
1975	6,717	2,270	8,987

Source: Facts and Figures '84, MVMA

U.S. DOMESTIC VEHICLE FACTORY SALES

(thousands)

Year	Passenger Cars	Trucks and Buses	Total Vehicles
1983	6,739	2,414	9,153
1982	5,049	1,906	6,955
1981	6,255	1,701	7,956
1980	6,400	1,667	8,067
1979	8,419	3,037	11,456
1978	9,165	3,706	12,871
1977	9,201	3,442	12,643
1976	8,500	2,979	11,479
1975	6,713	2,272	8,985

Source: Facts and Figures '84, MVMA

PART THREE

The Border Region

9

Industry on the Northern Border of Mexico

José Luis Fernández
and Jesús Tamayo

INTRODUCTION

This essay explores the possibilities of complementarity between Mexican border industry and the national Mexican and U.S. productive structures.

The essay is organized in four sections. The first is a description of the relevant characteristics of border industrialization for making choices of industrial complementarity. In the second section, it is postulated that the connection between industry located on the northern border and other national productive systems is not an end in itself, but rather should be analyzed in terms of the contribution it makes to the economic recovery of the country by easing the balance-of-payments constraint. In the third section, a selection is made of areas of industrial complementarity starting from the contribution of each for achieving the objectives of import substitution and the promotion of exports. The conclusions are found in the last section.

THE BORDER INDUSTRY

Mexico's national industrialization process began toward the end of the last century, but the civil war kept it in a dormant state until the consolidation of the revolutionary governments. During the 1940s it appeared that the Mexican economic development model was finally becoming explicit and coherent, with modern industrial development playing a major role.

We will note here two characteristics of the country's process of industrialization: production is oriented principally toward the internal market; it is spatially

197

concentrated and no decisive attempt was made to incorporate Mexico's periphery. Economic activity is concentrated in the urban areas of the country--Mexico City, Monterrey, and Guadalajara.

The border industrialization effort is a more recent development. It arose in the mid-sixties because of various factors. First, the technological advances of the industrialized countries permitted the segmentation of production processes in some industries. This made possible the transfer of stages using unskilled labor intensively to countries where the low cost of labor compensated for increased costs associated with the spatial relocation of production. Second, the development of systems of communication and transportation following the Second World War made possible the transmission of work orders, the sending of materials, and the return of finished products between plants located in distant places at relatively low cost. Finally, various production free zones were created in border territories and endowed with the legal and physical infrastructure needed for the operation of the finishing (maquiladora) plants.

There are significant differences between the type of foreign direct investment (FDI) which the country's overall industrial development attracts and that which is stimulated by the Border Industrialization Program (BIP) after 1965. The former is generally oriented to taking advantage of a protected domestic market through the establishment of affiliated plants tied in a horizontal manner to the parent plant. The specialized literature indicates that in such a new market FDI has initial oligopolistic advantages over domestic industry which derive from technological and marketing superiority.

For its part, the BIP attracts capital to establish a filial enterprise with the goal of minimizing wage costs in order to maintain a role in some market, whether that is a national or an international one. This investment lends itself to a filial-parent production relationship of the vertical type, under which the former receives materials from abroad and is oriented fundamentally to export.

We next center our attention on the theme of industrial complementarity, which is the target of these essays. In this task, the identification of potential areas for the involvement of national and U.S. productive activities in borderlands industry has been carried out in two stages. In the first, we analyze what the role of such industry should be in the economic recuperation of Mexico; in the second, we seek to establish how industrial complementarity can contribute to fostering economic growth.

ROLE OF BORDER INDUSTRY IN ECONOMIC GROWTH

In the 1977-1981 period, net external indebtedness functioned as a variable for the adjustment of the imbalance in the trade account, which in turn was the result of the rate of economic growth selected ex ante by the Mexican government.[1] That is to say, the country grew at a higher rate than would have been possible on the basis of the trade (or current account) balance.

Nevertheless, starting in the second half of 1982, because of the curtailment of the supply of international credit, the external indebtedness ceased to be a variable of adjustment and became a constraint on growth. Under this new situation, the net flow of the external debt, in the best of cases, grows at a rate equal to the external interest cost and this will oblige the country to maintain the current balance in equilibrium.[2]

In an alternative scenario, the level of inflow of net external credit would be less than the cost of international interest payments, which would require the generation of a surplus in the current account in order to meet the financial service of the debt.

Until now it has been argued that the principal limitation on economic growth is the balance of payments. This view is based on two reasons: one is the structural nature of the trade deficit; and the other is the profile of payments reflecting the stock of debt.

With respect to the former, an economic recovery which does not base its dynamism on a change in the historic rates of growth of non-petroleum exports and in the income elasticity of the demand for imports would run the risk of generating new disequilibria in the trade account. This could not be financed with new debt and would lead to the adoption of political economy measures tending to decelerate the growth of the economy.

If this analysis is correct, it would be appropriate to implement a national industrial policy designed to reduce the foreign-exchange gap. This could be done in two ways, which are not mutually exclusive. One way is to establish measures which deepen import substitution; the other way is through the promotion of exports.

Consequently, the role of border industry in the

economic recovery of the country should be measured by its contribution to the achievement of those objectives.

BORDERLANDS INDUSTRIAL COMPLEMENTARITY AND NATIONAL ECONOMIC GROWTH

The potential contribution of border industry to the objectives of import substitution and promotion of exports can be analyzed by taking two scenarios as points of departure: the first assumes that the border industrial structure is maintained in the medium term; the second posits a policy of gradual changes in the structure of border industry.

It is precisely the combination of scenarios and objectives that permits us to identify potential areas of complementarity for the industry located along the northern border of the country.

A.   The first scenario analyzes the economic benefits of a policy that maintains the existing industrial structure on the country's northern border.

1) Substitute for imports used by the border industry by national production. The history of the BIP demonstrates that, despite governmental efforts, the coefficient of imported materials to total requirements is high (90 percent) and has been maintained practically without variation.   This situation, far from being attributable to shortcomings of the program, responds to restrictions of a technological character and of the scale of production in some industries and to U.S. tariff protection in others (e.g., clothing).

2) The substitution for imports of production by border industry for national industrial production. We are thinking here of components and parts assembled by the electrical, electronic and automotive industries on the northern border of Mexico. National production of these intermediary goods could serve to deepen the process of import substitution. The net gain for the country would be represented by the value added.

From the scenario considered (maintaining the existing industrial structure) and the objective of promoting exports, what emerges is a policy of:

3) promoting those branches with greater dynamism than the average.

From our point of view, this option is the most

favorable for the national interest because of the vulnerability of exports of border industry to fluctuations in the economic cycle in the United States. Border industry has extreme specialization and a high proportion of exports to production.

B. The second scenario analyzes an industrial policy which would introduce gradual changes in the composition of investment at the border, either for import substitution and/or export promotion.

1) The establishment of new industries on the northern border to provide materials required by national industry and which are now imported. Because of the lack of accessibility of urban locations at the border to the central national system and their relative closeness to some urban centers of the United States, it is difficult to think of new border industries that could be established with the goal of substituting for imports of materials for national industry. This may be feasible for industries already established at the border which eventually could increase their scale of production through sales in the national market that substitute for imports.

One is prompted, based on this conclusion, to favor investment designed to change the profile of industrial activity with the goal of promoting exports. On arriving at this point, two possibilities open up:

2) Attraction of industries oriented to taking advantage of labor. This option assumes the traditional arrangement of the assembly industry, although utilized by new industries. Even if that arrangement could contribute to the growth of exports, it has limitations. One constraint is competition of countries with more backward industrial structures and this would limit the export of products for which transportation cost is of little significance. Another danger is that the technological advances of the robotics industry pose a significant risk to employment in this sector.

3) The attraction of industries based on location because of the presence of a specific natural resource. Given the type of FDI which we think would be feasible to attract to Mexico's northern border zones, it is logical to think of industries designed to transform natural resources and oriented, from their inception, to exports. One can imagine industries dedicated to the transformation of mineral products (copper and coal, for example), and to processing products of the sea. The analysis of the viability of this option requires comparing the natural resources of the region with recent tendencies of U.S. FDI

generally.

CONCLUSIONS

We have identified two potential emphases in our review of options for industrial complementarity:

A.   To substitute national products for imported products used by industry located at the border.

B.   To attract industries oriented to exports based on the transformation of natural resources.

These conclusions have obvious implications for future border industrialization policy. Until now, the policy has consisted of the promotion of foreign investment in the form of assembly plants (maquilas) with the basic goal of generating foreign exchange. From our point of view, while it would continue to be appropriate to maintain a policy of promotion, this should be selective, based on the sectoral criteria which have been identified.

NOTES

[1]Net external indebtedness is equal to gross indebtedness less repayments.

[2]Current balance refers to the difference between exports of goods and non-factor services and the corresponding imports.

10

Industry on the Southern Border of the United States

Jerry R. Ladman

INTRODUCTION

This paper examines industrialization in the U.S.-Mexico border region, its history, and the strategies and policies that have affected it. The emphasis in this essay is on the U.S. side of the border.

The paper is organized as follows: (1) the border region is defined; (2) the economic growth of the border region and its importance to the United States are examined; (3) past border industrialization and border industrialization policies are described; (4) the current U.S. industrialization strategy is analyzed; and (5) projections for future industrialization are made. The roles of federal, state and local governments in the industrialization process are examined, using Arizona as a case study.

THE BORDER REGION

The U.S.-Mexico border region is defined in many ways, depending on the intent of the analysis or the availability of data. For purposes of this study, the region considered

*The author is grateful to Gonzalo J. Afcha and Jorge Gobitz for their assistance in data collection and tabulation.

is the geographic area contiguous to the international boundary that encompasses the economic activities directly derived from location along the nearly 2,000-mile border. This narrow definition of the border is employed because this paper deals with the economic activities of the border proper and not with those of larger "border" spaces, such as the border states, whose economies have a much larger economic base than that derived from their border location. Data for the border counties and border cities in the four U.S. and five Mexican states are presented.[1] [2]

THE GROWTH OF THE BORDER REGION ECONOMY

The economy of the U.S.-Mexico border region is heterogeneous; it is comprised of a number of contrasting binational subregions that derive their economic bases from different factors, including the border location, the availability of natural resources, government works or military installations, and transportation linkages with other parts of the two nations.[3] Most of the border region is arid and sparsely populated. Much smaller portions are highly urbanized and dense. Yet, beneath this heterogeneity there are a number of commonalities, the most salient being the unique blending of two national cultures. Another characteristic common to all subregions has been the development of economically interdependent twin cities, one located on each side of the border.

Historically, the subregional economies developed at different rates, depending on changes in their economic base brought about by migration, public policies, and linkages with the non-border economies. Since the mid-nineteenth century, when the international boundary was established, twin border towns grew up at points on the existing north-south transportation routes. Their economic base was the activity associated with flows of goods and visitors between the two countries. Later, at border sites with rich natural resources, twin towns developed in subregions specializing in mining or irrigated agriculture. Notwithstanding the changes taking place in this period, the geographically remote twin towns were relatively small and isolated from the mainstream of both U.S. and Mexican economic activity.

By the third decade of the twentieth century, changes began to occur. In the United States, migration to southern

California and south Texas increased the population base in those subregions. The expansion of military installations located at the border in World Wars I and II created important new economic activity. Simultaneously in Mexico, there was the beginning of significant migration to border cities as persons were attracted by higher incomes and growing opportunities, as well as the possibility of working in the United States. Tourism and border-crosser shopping expanded on both sides of the line. U.S. prohibition and the opportunities for gambling and vice promoted night life on the Mexican side. Public works in both countries expanded irrigated agriculture.

In the post-World War II period, the border area began to be recognized as a unique region that had a cultural and economic identity of its own and, moreover, was becoming increasingly important to both countries. There were two basic reasons for this: (1) the rapid population buildup in the region from in-migration, especially on the Mexican side; and (2) the ensuing economic development and the interdependence of the two nations' border economies.

POPULATION GROWTH

Extensive in-migration has been the principal factor contributing to the region's growing importance to the two neighboring countries. Comparison of population trends in the border region between 1950 and 1980 show the magnitude and patterns of change.

First, the population growth on the Mexican side has far exceeded growth on the U.S. side. As shown in Table 10.1, between 1950 and 1980, the population of Mexico's border counties increased 253.4 percent, mostly in the border cities, which grew by 355.1 percent. Population growth in the U.S. border region was impressive, but considerably less than in Mexico. In the thirty-year period, the populations of U.S. border counties and cities expanded at about the same rate, 178.3 and 174.4 percent, respectively.

Second, despite the more rapid population growth in the Mexican border region, the population of the U.S. region is considerably larger than its Mexican counterpart. In 1980, the U.S. region had more than 4 million inhabitants compared to Mexico's 2.9 million.[4]

Third, as shown in Table 10.2, in 1980, with the

TABLE 10.1
United States and Mexican Border Population, 1950-1980

Border State	Population 1950	Population 1980	Percent Change 1950-1980	Percent of State Total 1950	Percent of State Total 1980
United States					
Arizona	749.6	2,718.2	262.6	-	-
Border Counties	225.6	775.8	243.9	30.1	28.5
Border Cities	24.7	73.1	104.0	3.3	2.7
California	10,586.3	23,667.9	123.6	-	-
Border Counties	619.2	1,953.9	215.6	5.8	8.3
Border Cities	377.9	1,022.6	170.6	3.6	4.3
New Mexico	681.2	1,302.9	51.6	-	-
Border Counties	53.3	117.9	121.2	7.8	9.0
Border Cities	0.0	0.4	-	0.0	0.0
Texas	7,711.0	14,229.0	84.5	-	-
Border Counties	554.1	1,194.2	115.5	7.2	8.4
Border Cities	260.1	723.4	178.1	3.4	5.1
Border State Total	19,728.1	41,918.0	112.5	-	-
Border Counties	1,452.2	4,041.8	178.3	7.4	9.6
Border Cities	662.7	1,818.6	174.4	3.3	4.3
Mexico[a]					
Baja California Norte	227.0	1,177.9	418.9	-	-
Border Counties	195.9	1,002.5	411.7	86.3	85.1
Border Cities	124.6	771.1	518.9	54.9	65.5
Chihuahua	846.4	2,005.5	136.9	-	-
Border Counties	170.2	631.3	270.9	30.6	31.5
Border Cities	142.9	564.7	295.2	16.9	28.2
Coahuila	720.6	1,557.3	116.1	-	-
Border Counties	64.1	142.9	122.9	8.9	9.2
Border Cities	38.9	106.4	173.5	5.4	6.8
Sonora	510.6	1,513.7	196.5	-	-
Border Counties	88.3	312.1	253.4	17.3	20.6
Border Cities	39.0	171.1	338.8	7.6	11.3
Tamaulipas	718.2	1,924.5	168.0	-	-
Border Counties	299.2	801.1	167.7	29.2	41.6
Border Cities	137.6	585.2	325.3	13.4	30.4
Border State Total	3,022.8	8,178.8	170.6	-	-
Border Counties	817.7	2,889.9	253.4	27.0	35.3
Border Cities	483.0	2,198.5	355.1	16.0	26.9

Sources: U.S. Department of Commerce, Bureau of Census, Census of the Population, 1950, 1980.
México, Secretaría de Economía, Dirección General de Estadística, VII Censo General de Población, 1950.
México, Secretaría de Programación y Presupuesto, Instituto Nacional de Estadística, Geografía e Informática, X Censo General de Población y Vivienda, 1980.

[a]Excludes Nuevo León.

TABLE 10.2
Population of United States-Mexican Twin Border Cities, 1950-1980

U.S. City	Mexican City	Population 1950		Population 1980		Percent Change 1950-1980		Ratio U.S.City/Mex.City	
		U.S. City	Mexican City	U.S. City	Mexican City	U.S. City	Mexican City	1950	1980
San Diego, Chula Vista, and National City, Cal.	Tijuana, B.C.	371,513	59,952	1,008,237	429,500	171.4	616.4	6.19	2.35
Calexico, Cal.	Mexicali, B.C.	6,433	64,609	14,412	341,559	124.0	428.7	.10	.04
Yuma and San Luis, Ariz.	San Luis, R.C., Son.	9,145	4,079	43,379	76,684	374.3	1,780.0	2.24	.57
Nogales, Ariz	Nogales, Son.	6,153	24,478	15,683	65,603	154.9	168.0	.25	.24
Douglas, Ariz.	Agua Prieta, Son.	9,442	10,471	13,058	28,862	38.3	175.6	.90	.45
Columbus, N. Mex.	Palomas, Chih.	-	694	414	2,072	-	198.6	-	.20
El Paso, Tex.	Cd. Juárez, Chih.	130,485	137,624	425,259	544,496	225.9	295.6	.95	.78
Presidio, Tex.	Ojinaga, Chih.	-	4,568	1,723	18,162	-	297.6	-	.09
Del Río, Tex.	Cd. Acuña, Coah.	14,211	11,372	30,034	38,898	111.3	242.1	1.25	.77
Eagle Pass, Tex.	Piedras Negras, Coah.	7,276	27,581	21,407	67,455	194.2	144.6	.26	.32
Laredo, Tex.	Nuevo Laredo, Tam.	51,910	57,668	91,449	201,731	76.2	249.8	.90	.45
Hidalgo and McAllen, Tex.	Reynosa, Tam.	20,067	34,087	68,569	194,693	241.7	471.2	.59	.35
Brownsville, Tex.	Matamoros, Tam.	36,066	45,846	84,997	188,745	135.7	311.7	.79	.45
Total:		662,701	483,029	1,818,621	2,198,460	174.4	355.1	1.37	.83

Sources: U.S. Department of Commerce, Bureau of Census, Census of the Population, 1950 and 1980.

México, Secretaría de Economía, Dirección General de Estadística, VII Censo General de Población, 1950.

México, Secretaría de Programación y Presupuesto, Instituto Nacional de Estadística, Geografía e Informática, X Censo General de Población y Vivienda, 1980.

exception of the San Diego complex, all Mexican border
cities were considerably larger than their U.S. twins.[5]
Including San Diego, the total U.S. border city population
of 1.8 million was only 83 percent as large as the 2.2
million of Mexico. Indeed, there were only four U.S. cities
that were at least half as large as their Mexican twins.
This is in sharp contrast to 1950, when three U.S. cities
were larger and eight were more than half the size of their
Mexican counterparts.

These figures reflect both the strong growth of the
Mexican border cities and their relatively greater
importance in the border counties compared to the United
States. Several of these Mexican cities are among the most
populous in the nation. In 1980, three--Ciudad Juárez,
Tijuana, and Mexicali--were ranked among the ten largest
Mexican cities. In the United States only San Diego was
ranked as high.

Fourth, the heterogeneity in the size of the subregions
along the border is amply illustrated by Table 10.2. The
San Diego-Tijuana and the El Paso-Ciudad Juarez subregions
are considerably larger than the others. In sharp contrast,
subregions along the Arizona, New Mexico, and the rest of
the west Texas border are much smaller, and those of
Calexico-Mexicali and the Rio Grande Valley in Texas are
intermediate in size.

Fifth, the populations of the Mexican border counties
and cities are relatively more important to the Mexican
border states than are their U.S. counterparts. In 1980,
Mexican border counties and cities accounted for 35.3 and
26.9 percent of the combined Mexican border state
population. In stark contrast, the U.S. figures were only
9.6 and 4.3 percent. This illustrates that, contrary to the
Mexican experience, the in-migration to the U.S.
southwestern sunbelt has been primarily to urban areas in
non-border locations.

ECONOMIC INTERDEPENDENCE

Regional border economic activity is concentrated in
the subregional twin cities and their immediate environs.
The economic bases of these subregions, while varied,
include: international commerce; tourism; export-oriented
(to markets outside the region) mining, agriculture and
industry; and government activities, such as military

installations. The demand for goods and services produced by the economic base activities is largely determined by markets outside the region. Therefore, the border economy is highly subject to external developments, such as business cycles and government decisions about the location of military bases.

Income earned from economic base activities in the border region creates a demand for goods and services within the region and on both sides of the border. A portion of the income is spent on the side of the border where it is earned, but part is also spent on the other side. This spending pattern leads to an economic impact on both sides of the border, which through a twin-city multiplier effect, eventually is much greater than the original amount of additional income.[6] No matter the source, economic activity on one side of the border creates opportunities on the other side.

These conditions have led to the formation of highly-interdependent sets of twin border cities. A relatively open border and readily convertible currencies have fostered exchanges of goods, services and labor. This unique twin-city relationship means that changes in the economic base or level of economic activity in one border city will have important impacts on the other. When incomes rise in one city, the other city also benefits.

Changes in the exchange rate will also have impacts on both twin cities by altering the relative prices of goods and services on both sides of the boundary and changing the levels of real income and spending patterns. The city in the country whose currency has appreciated will lose, because its goods become higher priced for residents of the other city. Conversely, the city in the country whose currency has depreciated will gain.

Mexican cross-border shopping has been encouraged by several additional factors. First, Mexico has tended to maintain an overvalued peso relative to the dollar. This policy has the effect of making goods in the United States less expensive compared to those in Mexico. Second, the high cost of manufacturing in Mexico, plus the additional cost of transporting goods the long distances from the principal production sites located in central Mexico to the border, have contributed to higher Mexican prices. Third, the quality of many Mexican-made goods has not generally been up to the standard of comparable items in the United States, especially for clothing, processed foods, and appliances. Finally, there are some goods that are not produced in Mexico, or at least not in sufficient supply to satisfy local demand.

The extent of Mexican border residents shopping in the U.S. border cities is illustrated by a 1973 study undertaken in Mexicali and Calexico. Estimated per capita expenditures were 78 percent higher for Calexico than in a similar nearby, but non-border, town.[7] This clearly shows the dependence of this U.S. border city on the residents of Mexicali. Data collected in Mexicali also showed the strong propensity for its residents to regularly cross the border to shop for groceries, clothing, and appliances.[8]

The importance of Mexican shopping in U.S. border cities was dramatically shown with the devaluations of the Mexican peso in 1976 and 1982. The abrupt changes in relative prices caused sharp declines in sales by U.S. merchants, forcing them to lay off numerous employees and causing many establishments to go out of business. The impact was so severe that the federal government declared the U.S. border region an area of economic disaster. Conversely, Mexican sales to U.S. border residents picked up considerably. There was much press coverage, especially of the 1982 devaluations. Perhaps no other single development was as important in calling attention to the U.S. border region.

GOVERNMENT PROGRAMS FOR THE BORDER REGION

At the federal level, the border as a region has received more attention in Mexico than in the United States. There has been a series of border-specific programs established by the Mexican government.[9] Long concerned with developing a population along its northern boundary, Mexico, in the 1930s, encouraged migration by the development of irrigation districts along the Rio Grande and in the Mexicali Valley. In 1933, a free zone was established in Baja California, later extended to parts of Sonora, to allow residents and merchants to import duty-free goods from the United States and, thus, reduce the cost of living in this region that was so remote from Mexican suppliers.

With extensive migration to the border, the problems changed in character, i.e., how to accommodate the rapidly increasing numbers.   In 1961, the National Border Program (PRONAF) was instituted in Mexico to improve the border economy and its social and cultural development. There was concern about balance-of-payments leakages from the extensive Mexican shopping on the U.S. side. One PRONAF measure was designed to alleviate this by offering transportation subsidies for many products manufactured in the interior of Mexico and shipped to the border. Other measures were programs for developing social infrastructure and tourist and cultural sites. The program was discontinued in 1972.

In 1965, the Border Industrialization Program was established in an attempt to alleviate unemployment. It has been successful in attracting industry to the region. A discussion of this program is presented in a following section.

In the early 1970s, there was a concerted effort to deal with border problems. In 1970, the artículos gancho program was established to encourage Mexican border shoppers to buy in Mexico, by allowing quotas of duty-free imports to Mexican border merchants. In 1971, an Intersectoral Commission was organized by the federal government to deal with border problems. In 1972, a special program for the construction of shopping centers was implemented.

The United States has not matched the direct governmental effort of Mexico in programs for the border. An exception is U.S. support of the International Boundary and Water Commission that continues to actively work in matters dealing with water resources and boundary issues in the region. The first major regional initiative occurred in 1975 when, upon petition of the governors of the four U.S. border states, the federal government established the Southwest Border Regional Commission to deal with the unique problems of the U.S. border region. The Commission was never able to clearly define its goals or overcome the political obstacles of working with four regional states and was discontinued in 1981.

With the failure of the Commission, the United States government has reverted to treating border problems in an ad hoc manner or by using existing programs that are not border specific. The most recent example was that after the 1982 devaluation crisis when the four border states and twenty-three border counties petitioned the Reagan administration for assistance. In August 1983, the President formed the Inter-Agency Action Group headed by Vice-President Bush. Unfortunately, it was not very active and its formation smacked heavily of political motives to court Hispanics in the 1984 election.[10] Nevertheless, its formation suggests a recognition of the unique problems of the border region.

In comparison to federal activity in dealing with border problems, that at the state and local levels has been much more important. In the mid-1970s, the Organization of United States Border Cities and Counties was formed. Governors from the U.S. and Mexican border states have held conferences since 1980. Each of the U.S. border states has a commission that works with its Mexican counterpart. Local officials often work closely and informally to resolve mutual problems.

RECOGNITION OF THE BORDER'S IMPORTANCE

The fact that the Mexican government has developed more comprehensive programs for the border than the United States should not be surprising. There are a number of reasons for this.

First, the highly centralized role of the federal government in Mexico means that it must assume the initiative and responsibility for these programs. In contrast, in the United States much more authority is delegated to state and local governments.

Second, the relatively more rapid growth of the Mexican border region has placed many and serious strains on the economic and social infrastructure of Mexican border cities. The ensuing problems demanded the development of special programs.

Third, the isolation of the Mexican border region from the urban and industrial centers in the interior of the country in combination with the availability of less-expensive, higher-quality products on the U.S. side, has created a concern in Mexico about the loss of foreign exchange, jobs, and income in its northern border region. This led to a number of special policies to encourage production and consumption of Mexican-made goods in the region.

Finally, in comparison to national totals, the populations of Mexican border counties and cities are more important than those of the United States. In 1980, the inhabitants of Mexican border counties and cities accounted for 4.3 and 3.3 percent of the national total, respectively. The corresponding percentages for the United States were 1.8 and 0.8.

In summary, it is clear that the border region has been much more important to Mexico than to the United States. Yet, the border region is gaining increasing recognition in the United States. The underlying reason has been the growth on the Mexican side. The population trends in the border region do not imply that the growing imbalance favoring Mexico detracts from the importance of the border region to the United States. Indeed, the contrary is true, for several reasons. First, because of the border-crosser shopping, the large Mexican border population created an important market for commercial establishments in U.S. border cities and has become an important element in the economic base of the U.S. cities.

Second, the population centers have placed demands on common natural resources, such as surface and ground water, which must be shared. These problems have attracted considerable national attention. One example is the salinity problem of the Colorado River in the 1960s and early 1970s.

Third, the population has contributed to binational environmental problems, such as air and water pollution. Many twin cities share sewage disposal facilities, with treatment plants usually located on the U.S. side. The rapid population growth on the Mexican side has begun to overtax these facilities, endangering health in the U.S. border cities.

Fourth, the Mexican border cities are an important source of both legal (green card) and illegal (undocumented) workers. The latter, who mainly just pass through the border on their way from the interior of Mexico, are a matter of national concern. Although most undocumented migrants do not work in the border region, they are often considered to be a border-associated problem. Likewise, the increased presence of a Hispanic culture in the United States is often viewed as creeping north from the border.

Another reason for the increasing importance of the U.S. southwestern border states in the national picture is their increases in population. These states have stimulated national recognition of border problems. Examples were the petitions of the four states leading to the formation of the Southwest Border Regional Commission and the Inter-Agency Action Group. The growing congressional delegations and voter constituencies have been effective in bringing the federal government to pay more heed to the region. Particularly important is the concentration of Hispanic voters along the border. In 1980, there were 1.4 million persons of Hispanic origin residing in border counties, corresponding to 35.6 percent of the counties' population. President Reagan's interest in attracting Hispanic support was an important factor in establishing the Inter-Agency Action Group.

It is clear that the border, as a region, has gained increasing recognition in both countries. Not only have there been a series of new initiatives by federal, state, and local governments, but during the last decade the border region has been considered as an important and continuing element in U.S.-Mexico relations. The numerous research and academic programs that have been established in both countries are further evidence of this.

INDUSTRIALIZATION IN THE BORDER REGION

Historically, the natural resource base and the remoteness and isolation of the border region, in combination with its small population, did not generally provide incentives for manufacturing, much less industrialization, on either side of the boundary. An exception was the San Diego region, which was part of the southern California industrial complex and, with World War II, became closely tied to manufacturing military warships and airplanes. In other subregions, agricultural goods and minerals that were produced from the natural-resource bases did not require much processing and were shipped outside the region for consumption or for use as raw materials. The population bases were insufficient to create local markets of sufficient size to give rise to a derived demand that would encourage much local manufacturing. It was more economical to import both consumer and capital goods, in spite of the distances from manufacturing centers. In recent decades, as a result of the border population growth, the situation has changed, most importantly on the Mexican side where there has been both a growing border market and active government policy to promote industrialization.

MEXICAN INDUSTRIALIZATION STRATEGY

The first major initiative by Mexico that encouraged manufacturing in the border region was the previously mentioned Free Zone. Established in 1933 in Baja California to benefit local merchants and consumers, it proved to be a major stimulus to manufacturing. A 1973 survey of 28 Mexicali industrial firms that produced products for sale outside the region indicated that the Free Zone was the most important historical factor in causing them to establish their businesses. All but nine of the firms considered, it continued to be of great importance to their business in 1973.[11]

Another important Mexican initiative for industry was the Border Industrialization Program (BIP) that was established to create jobs in Mexican border assembly plants in order to reduce unemployment and promote economic growth in the Mexican border region. The program was designed to encourage U.S. firms to take advantage of items 807.00 and 806.30 of the U.S. tariff schedules to export components to affiliated in-bond plants on the Mexican side of the border. There, they would be assembled as final products, using relatively inexpensive Mexican labor, and then re-exported to the United States. U.S. customs duties would be assessed only on the value added in Mexico. The program got off to a rapid start. Many assembly plant industrial parks were established. By May of 1984, there were 559 plants located on the border that employed an estimated 159,000 workers.[12] The recent devaluations of the peso have given impetus to more firms to establish assembly operations. Between January of 1983, and May of 1984, employment in Mexican assembly plants rose 43 percent.[13]

The growth of employment in manufacturing in the Mexican border region is shown in Table 10.3. In 1980, there were nearly 155,000 workers in this sector, an increase of 1,076 percent over the 13,180 workers in 1950. Over the thirty-year period, employment in the manufacturing sector grew half again as rapidly as the growth of the total labor force; in 1980, manufacturing employment accounted for 15.8 percent of the work force, whereas in 1950 it was only 10.2 percent. Much of the increase is attributable to employment in BIP plants. In 1980, workers in the manufacturing sector at the border accounted for 6.2 percent of the national total.

Industry is concentrated in counties of three border states: in 1980, Baja California, Chihuahua, and Tamaulipas, states with large concentrations of both border population and BIP plants, accounted for 85.5 percent of all employees. Historically, these have been the most important states, but, since 1980, Baja California has gained considerably in relative importance.

The development of manufacturing in the Mexican border region has had indirect, but important, effects on the growth of the U.S. border economy through the twin-city economic linkages. Most important are the increased

TABLE 10.3
Employment in Manufacturing in Mexican Northern Border Counties, 1950-1980

Border State	Employment in Manufacturing				Percent of Total Workforce in Manufacturing		
	1950	%	1980	%	Percent Change 1950-1980		
					1950	1980	Percent Change 1950-1980
Baja California Norte	2,692	20.4	48,424	31.2	1,698.8	10.4	14.8	42.3
Chihuahua	3,908	29.7	45,528	29.4	1,065.0	14.6	20.3	39.0
Coahuila	1,733	13.1	7,061	4.6	307.4	8.5	15.0	76.5
Sonora	1,498	11.4	15,479	10.0	933.3	9.2	15.0	63.0
Tamaulipas	3,349	25.4	38,499	24.8	1,029.6	8.2	14.6	78.0
Border County Total	13,180	100.0	154,991	100.0	1,076.0	10.2	15.8	54.9

SOURCE: México, Secretaría de Economía, Dirección General de Estadística, Séptimo Censo de Población, 1950.

México, Secretaría de Programación y Presupuesto, Instituto Nacional de Estadística, Geografía e Informática, X Censo General de Población y Vivienda, 1980.

expenditures in the United States resulting from the larger incomes created. In addition, the BIP has created a need for U.S. activities related to export and import of components and finished products. Originally, BIP was conceived of as a "twin plant" program where manufacturing would be located on both sides of the border. This has not usually materialized. Most U.S. plants with a Mexican BIP affiliation are located in the interior of the country.

U.S. BORDER INDUSTRIALIZATION STRATEGY

Whereas the Mexican federal government has actively utilized specific policies to encourage industrialization in the border region, the U.S. government has not. Industrialization has occurred, however. As shown in Table 10.4, there were over 216,000 employees in the manufacturing sector in U.S. border counties, which represented a 391.4 percent increase over the 44,000 in 1950. The relative importance of manufacturing employment increased 47.9 percent over the 30-year period; in 1950, it accounted for 9.6 percent of the total work force, whereas in 1980 it was 14.2 percent.

The heterogeneity of the region is clear; in 1980, 58 percent of border county manufacturing employment was in California, almost entirely in San Diego County. Texas accounted for 27.4 percent, which was concentrated in El Paso County and Cameron and Hidalgo counties in the Rio Grande Valley. Arizona's share of 13 percent was largely in the non-border city of Tucson in Pima County, and Doña Ana County accounted for most of New Mexico's share. The 1977 U.S. Census of Manufactures reported 3,507 manufacturing establishments in the border counties. Most are quite small; only 24.9 percent had more than twenty employees. The total value added was $3.8 billion. A variety of goods was manufactured, but the largest number of firms was in food processing. The most common large-scale industries were apparel and textile products, electric and electronic equipment, printing and publishing, and stone, clay and glass products. San Diego was an important manufacturer of transportation equipment, mostly airplanes and ships.

In contrast with Mexico, the national importance of U.S. manufacturing in the border region is small. The number of workers, the number of firms, and the value added by manufacturers located in border counties were less than 1

TABLE 10.4
Employment in Manufacturing in U.S. Counties on the Mexican Border

Border State	Employment in Manufacturing			Percent of Total Workforce in Manufacturing		
	1950	%	1980	%	Percent Change 1950-1980	1950	1980	Percent Change 1950-1980
Arizona	3,553	8.1	28,079	13.0	690.3	5.4	9.8	81.5
California	25,331	57.5	125,534	58.0	395.6	13.2	15.9	20.5
New Mexico	354	0.8	3,572	1.6	909.0	2.2	8.6	290.9
Texas	14,830	33.7	59,342	27.4	300.2	8.0	14.7	83.7
Border County Total	44,068	100.0	216,527	100.0	391.4	9.6	14.2	47.9

SOURCE: United States Department of Commerce, Bureau of Census, County and City Data Book, 1952.

  United States Department of Commerce, Bureau of Census, Census of Population, 1980.

percent of the national total for each category. Manufacturing in U.S. border counties was even small in relation to border state manufacturing. For the above three categories, the percentages were 5.4, 5.2, and 4.2 percent, respectively.

THE EFFECT OF THE 1982 CRISIS

The formation of the 1983 Inter-Agency Action Group was the first directed federal effort for industrialization in the border region. As noted, the Group was formed in response to the economic depression that engulfed the U.S. border cities after the 1982 peso devaluations. The effect of the devaluations was so severe that the U.S. border cities determined not to allow their economies to remain so dependent on sales to Mexican residents.

This had not previously been an apparent problem. Between 1954 and 1976, Mexico maintained a constant exchange rate with the dollar and U.S. merchants were lulled into a false sense of security as their sales rose steadily because of the increased market that was developing on the other side of the border. Indeed, over time as the peso became increasingly overvalued, this encouraged even more purchases by Mexicans from U.S. border merchants. The 1976 devaluation sent shock waves through the border but, since the Mexican government again allowed the peso to become overvalued while Mexico experienced an economic boom, the crisis in the U.S. border region was short-lived. The devaluations of the 1982 crisis were much more severe. In less than a year's time, the free-market value of the peso depreciated 5.6 times. Recovery this time has not come so easily.

There are several reasons for this. First, the devaluation and the high Mexican inflation have severely reduced the levels of real income of many border residents. Second, since it is clear that Mexico must try to become more competitive as an exporter of manufactured goods, Mexican economic managers are less willing to maintain an overvalued peso. Therefore, one of the incentives for Mexican border residents to shop in the United States is diminishing. Third, Mexico's renewed drive to industrialize should make more and higher quality Mexican-made goods available to border residents at more competitive prices.

There are, however, several factors that will

contribute to a recovery of U.S. sales to cross-border shoppers. First, the population and economic activity in the Mexican border region should continue to grow. Second, there is certain to be a lag in Mexico in developing manufacturing capabilities to produce goods at competitive prices.

On balance and taking into account the threat of future devaluation crises, the communities of the U.S. border region should look to other sources of economic activity. The possibility for more industrialization is one option.

FEDERAL PROGRAMS TO PROMOTE INDUSTRIALIZATION IN THE U.S. BORDER REGION: THE CASE OF ARIZONA

Under the Inter-Agency Action Group, the federal government's approach to dealing with the economically depressed areas of the border was to draw upon existing federal programs and apply them to the border region, rather than to establish a special border program. The objective of the Group was to bring together federal agencies that have programs to offer and to urge them to give attention to the border. In most cases, the programs were undertaken in cooperation with the individual states, often with private sector participation.

A description follows of programs in Arizona.[14] This may not include all initiatives in all border subregions, but is illustrative of U.S. strategy.

Urban Development Action Grants (UDAG)

UDAG grants are administered by the Department of Housing and Urban Development (HUD). They are designed to provide flexible, incentive financing to developers and businesses that create jobs and a tax base by establishing a specific project (not necessarily industrial) in an economically distressed community. The grant is made to the community to finance the fixed assets of the project. The community then lends the money to the business or project. The final borrower repays the community. A major criterion in providing federal funds is the degree of commitment of the community, as measured by private sector participation.

A ratio of 6/1 for private sector and UDAG funds is the goal. Other major criteria include job creation and impact on low- and medium-income families. Projects are selected on a national basis, without quotas. Border cities must therefore compete with the rest of the nation. Between January 1983 and March 1984, the State of Arizona's Office of Economic Planning and Development (OEPD) has assisted in obtaining eight UDAGs, of which one is in Nogales for an industrial enterprise (creating 90 jobs with a total investment of nearly $600,000) and two are for non-industrial purposes in Bisbee, a town about five miles from the border (creating about 165 jobs with a total investment of $4.4 million).

Small Business Administration Economic
Revitalization Program (SBER)

The SBER program is a joint federal effort of the Department of HUD and the Small Business Administration (SBA). To participate in this program, the Arizona OEPD established a statewide, non-profit Arizona Certified Development Company (ACDC) to operate as an SBA section 503 loan administrator. ADEC loans are restricted to small businesses and companies. The SBA guarantees ADEC financing. Loans must be used to acquire fixed assets and the 503 portion of the total financing cannot exceed 50 percent; the rest must come from non-federal sources. The 503 portion of the loan carries subsidized interest rates. These loans can be combined with UDAG. Arizona began to participate in this program in the fall of 1982. Between then and February of 1984, eleven projects were approved, but none in the border region.

Department of Defense (DOD)

The DOD has an Office of Economic Adjustment that works with communities that are economically distressed because of closing of DOD facilities. The office also helps communities to become contractors to supply locally produced or purchased goods and services for DOD installations. This is considered to be a way to promote industrialization.

This office has been working in Arizona and other border states, with emphasis on the border region.

Small Business Administration Peso Pact Loans

In September 1982, loans were made available, as part of the SBA's Economic Injury Loan Program, for businesses located in the economically-distressed border region. The loans are designed to cover temporary shortfalls in revenues caused by an injurious economic event. As of March 1984, there had been little loan activity in Arizona, the number not exceeding ten. Of these, most went to retail establishments.

Job Training Partnership (JIPA)

In October 1982, the federal government established JIPA. Its primary emphasis is to train economically-disadvantaged individuals in high-demand occupations. Arizona established a pilot program in 1984 to work primarily in areas affected by the closing of the copper mines, including the border city of Douglas.

Summary

The federal government's approach to the border has been directed to economically-distressed communities, but there is no concerted federal effort for industrialization in the U.S.-Mexico border region. Several loan funds are available that could be used for industrialization, but none is border-specific. Projects financed must usually compete with proposals and initiatives from elsewhere in the border states and the United States as a whole.

The State of Arizona works with the federal government in identifying projects. Although there is considerable interest by the governor's office and the OEPD in the border region, the state has not established any specific policies or strategy for the border. Persons interviewed in that office believe that such an effort is warranted.

This does not mean that the OEPD does not stress the border. For example, the OEPD has worked with border communities on the UDAG grants, 503 loans, and JIPA. In April 1984, the office sponsored a large conference for national businesses to encourage them to take advantage of the BIP in Mexican twin cities across from Arizona sites in the belief that more plants would create significant linkages with Arizona firms.

A major problem identified by all persons interviewed was the inability of Arizona border cities to adequately come to grips with their economic problem and subject themselves to a detailed community development assessment. This may be due to the inertia that developed during the long period when the peso was stable and overvalued, or to the lack of cohesiveness among community leaders and institutions. The State of Arizona offers guidelines for and assistance in undertaking such assessments. Since the federal programs only respond to community interest, the initiative must begin at the level of the border community.

CONCLUSIONS AND PROJECTIONS

In contrast with Mexico, the United States has not had a government-sponsored comprehensive development strategy for the U.S. border region. Although the region's development has been affected by federal government programs for specific sectors, such as agriculture and defense, the development of the region has been left largely to market forces. This is certainly the case for industrialization. With the 1976 and 1982 Mexican economic crises, there has been considerable clamor for a regional development program, of which one proposed element is to expand manufacturing. It is unlikely, however, that any specific border regional program will be forthcoming in the near future. The Reagan administration, under the Inter-Agency Action Group arrangement, has shown its preference for treating the border as an adjunct to existing national programs. The case study of Arizona demonstrates that this approach has limits in its impact on the border region. It is a passive approach, responding with assistance where sound new projects are available or with emergency loans to small commercial establishments. It is not designed to restructure the region.

The future development of industry in the region will most likely continue to depend on market forces. It is useful to review the past. Industrialization in the region is concentrated in San Diego, Tucson, El Paso, and to some extent the Rio Grande Valley in Texas, and most of this development has not been determined fundamentally by the border location. The expansion of industrialization in the medium term can be expected only at these proven sites. Most of the other subregions do not have characteristics that readily lead to the development of industry. They are remote from suppliers and product markets, have small local markets, lack experience and entrepreneurship in industry, and have a shortage of skilled labor. Most cannot offer the amenities that are important to attract executives and professionals. There are other sites in the United States that do not suffer under these disadvantages and that have proven records in attracting industry.

It might be argued that the Mexican border cities could supply the labor force for a U.S.-based border industry, using green card workers. The argument, however, is faulty because firms basing their decision on this factor would likely prefer to locate on the Mexican side and operate within the BIP arrangement where wages are lower.

In the longer run, the outlook for industrialization may be more promising. As Clark Reynolds points out, if the disparity between Mexican and U.S. wages continues, U.S. firms will increasingly be attracted to establishing manufacturing or assembly operations in Mexico to produce goods for both Mexican and U.S. consumers.[15] If this binational manufacturing arrangement occurs, it should favor increased industrialization in both the U.S. and Mexican border regions under an arrangement very much like the BIP. Activity may be encouraged on the U.S. side if the U.S. firm's operations on the Mexico side of the border reach a scale sufficiently large to justify locating offices and related manufacturing at the U.S. border. If this were to occur, backward and forward linkages to other industries should encourage even more industrialization. This, in combination with growing nearby markets from the continued expansion of the Southwest, might serve to be the long-run impetus for industrialization in the region. Such a phenomenon would require close collaboration between the two countries to establish the structure and means to facilitate binational production. Furthermore, it would represent a commitment to the integration of the two economies as well as a further recognition of the complementary interdependence of the two-nation border economy. Political and nationalistic obstacles would certainly be encountered. Yet, the advantage to both countries might be sufficiently strong to overcome the resistance.

This assessment suggests that many U.S. border subregions should not look to significant advances in industrialization in the near or medium terms as means to restructure their economies and reduce their dependence on cross-border shopping. In the longer run, the outlook is more sanguine. Binational manufacturing arrangements appear to be a result of market forces blending the complementary economic factors in the two countries. Indeed, evidence of this is the recent decision to establish a Ford automobile manufacturing plant in Hermosillo, Sonora, to produce cars for export. Border sites may be desirable locations, especially those subregions that are adjacent to large Mexican border cities that can provide a sizeable labor force, sources of inputs and supplies, local product markets, and have good access to both Mexican an U.S. non-border markets. The power of the economic forces embodied in the evolution of the two national economies will hasten the process, but, given the binational nature of the structure, the arrangements will need to be undertaken within a framework that is acceptable to the businesses and governments of both nations. This will require a coordinated effort by Washington and Mexico City. Even though these arrangements will not be confined to the border region, they may have potential for the economic development for this unique part of both countries. They should therefore be strongly considered as elements in a strategy to diversify and enhance border region development through increased industrialization.

NOTES

[1]The Mexican state of Nuevo León actually fronts the border but is eliminated from the analysis because it only has one municipio (county) that touches the border. This county, located in an isolated region, does not contain a twin border city and has a small population.

[2]Unless otherwise stated, the U.S. data presented are taken from: United States Department of Commerce, Bureau of the Census, Census of Population 1980 and 1970; and United

States Department of Commerce, Bureau of the Census, County and City Data Book, 1952 and 1983. The Mexican data come from: Mexico, Secretaría de Economía, Dirección General de Estadística, Septimo Censo General de la Población, 1950; Mexico, Secretaría de Industria y Comercio, Dirección General de Estadistíca, VII Censo General de Población, 1960, IX Censo General de Población, 1970, and Mexico, Secretaría de Programación y Presupuesto, Instituto Nacional de Estadística, Geografía e Informática, X Censo General de Población y Vivienda, 1980.

[3]For a good analysis of the growth of the U.S. border area see Niles Hansen, The Border Economy, Regional Development in the Southwest (Austin: University of Texas Press, 1981).

[4]The fact that U.S. border counties continue to have a larger population than Mexico is largely attributable to the growth of Tucson, Arizona. While in a border county, Tucson is located some distance from the border and is not considered as a border city in this paper. In 1980, the population of Tucson was 330,537.

[5]Chula Vista is the city contiguous to the border in San Diego County. In 1980, it had 83,927 inhabitants. Were it not for the exceedingly large sizes of San Diego and National City, which in 1980 had 875,538 and 48,772 inhabitants, respectively, the balance for border city populations for Mexico would have been considerably larger.

[6]Jerry R. Ladman, "The Economic Interdependence of Contiguous Border Cities, The Twin-City Multiplier," The Annals of Regional Science, XII, No. 1 (March 1979), pp. 23-28.

[7]Jerry R. Ladman, The Development of the Mexicali Regional Economy: An Example of Export-Propelled Growth (Tempe: College of Business Administration, Bureau of Business and Economic Research, Arizona State University, 1975), p. 119.

[8]Comite Para el Desarrollo Económico de la Peninsula de Baja California y Parcial del Estado de Sonora, Importación Doméstica, Mexicali, June 1968, pp. 9-24.

[9]For a good summary of Mexican border programs in the 1960s and early 1970s see Victor Urquidi and Sofia Mendez Villarreal, "Economic Importance of Mexico's Northern Border Region," Views Across the Border: The United States and Mexico, ed. Stanley R. Ross (Albuquerque: University of New Mexico Press, 1978), pp. 157-162.

[10]Frances X. Cline, "Reagan Offers Plan for Help on Border and Draws Rebuke," New York Times, August 14, 1983, pp. 1, 17.

[11]Jerry R. Ladman, The Development of the Mexicali Regional Economy, op. cit., p. 110.

[12]American Chamber of Commerce, Mexico City, Maquiladora Newsletter, May 1984, p. 2.

[13]Ibid.

[14]The author is grateful to the State of Arizona Office for Economic Development and Planning for sharing information about these programs in interviews and documents.

[15]Clark W. Reynolds, "The Structure of the Economic Relationship," Mexico-United States Relations, Proceedings of the Academy of Political Science, ed. Susan Kaufman Purcell, Vol. 34, No. 1, 1981, pp. 125-135.

PART FOUR

Complementation and Conflict

11

A United States View

Clark Reynolds

DIFFERING POLICY PERSPECTIVES

Increasing interdependence between the United States and Mexico is only beginning to be taken into consideration as a guide to policy, at least on the northern side of the border. The most obvious instances are in agriculture, employment, energy, and finance. Mexico's performance in these areas is having an increasingly obvious impact on the U.S. through trade, migration, and debt relations. The industrial links between the two countries, on the other hand, have yet to be considered significant by most policy makers despite important effects on certain sectors (such as steel and autos) and regions (such as the Southwest).

In Mexico, on the other hand, U.S. investment has long been dominant in key sectors of the economy; two thirds of Mexico's trade is with the U.S. and American products, tastes, and advertising are ubiquitous. All these are viewed as a potential, if not an actual, threat to the uniqueness and autonomy of its system. Representatives from every branch of society recognize the importance of expanded exchange with the U.S. in trade, technology, and investment, yet most are uneasy about the potential cost to national sovereignty that might come with greater economic interdependence. Mexico's current economic crisis makes these ambiguities more relevant than ever, since limitations on further borrowing, fiscal austerity, and the undesirability of mortgaging future oil revenues make direct investment essential to recovery and growth. Mexico's private sector has yet to recover from the shock of devaluation, exchange control, nationalization of the banking system, and recession. In addition, a growing recognition of the close relationship between equity ownership, innovation, and market access implies an increasing role for foreign direct investment.

The U.S. is only beginning to awaken to the demand potential of its southern neighbor as Mexico's population becomes a full participant in the development process. The scope for productivity growth in Mexico, given its abundant labor and natural resources, is large. In Mexico, on the other hand, there is growing concern about the dangers of U.S. penetration of its economy and society. Given such differing perspectives, it is not surprising that until now we have heard little discussion of ways in which industrial development in the two countries might be better coordinated. Yet, my experiences while working with colleagues in a binational project on U.S.-Mexico relations illustrate that the less commonality there is between the two nations in terms of institutions, ideology, and cultural norms, the more important such coordination becomes. Thus, the need for policy coordination is particularly great at the present time. This conference is a pioneering effort to expand discussion along those lines, building on the unique history of The University of Texas as a center for research on Mexico and the foresight of its hosts in anticipating what is certain to become a major issue for both countries. This paper attempts to set in a general framework the detailed sectoral and thematic studies of the earlier sessions. It presents a range of options for the binational relationship with possible policy implications at the level of firm, industry, and government in both countries.

FUTURE UNCERTAINTIES

Neither country has a clear sense of its future industrial development potential, even though Mexico makes a major attempt at indicative planning while the U.S. relies primarily on market forces to determine the level and pattern of investment among sectors and regions of the economy. The two nations are in different stages of the business cycle. In the Mexican case, the recession produced the first absolute decline in GNP in decades after four years of eight percent growth fueled by oil and foreign borrowing. The U.S. appears to have passed through a structural recession, associated with declining competition in key industries, even as others take the lead in international product development. Important voices in the Mexican system argue that future recovery and growth may be hampered by serious structural problems associated with the historical pattern of import substituting industrialization. Mexican firms in both the private and public sector have in the past been sheltered from competition through a combination of external protection and the limitations of domestic market size. In the late 1970s, domestic demand, inflated by oil-boom riches, coupled with massive increases in government spending, made it unnecessary for Mexican firms to consider export markets or to actively compete internally in terms of price or quality. Now, however, this is no longer the case. The crisis makes it evident that business as usual cannot continue, since there is little prospect that the public sector can continue to subsidize the growth of inefficient enterprise and the imports needed to sustain the economy must be purchased by exports other than oil or additional foreign borrowing.

PRODUCTION SHARING

Given the structural problems faced by both countries, it might seem premature to talk about sharing industrial development, if such an approach did not offer some prospect for a joint solution. In fact, however, there is strong evidence that both countries' competitiveness could be considerably enhanced by taking advantage of the natural complementarities between the two systems. We have heard about production sharing that already exists between the U.S. and Mexico in particular industries such as automobiles. In this case, the decision to produce part of value added in Mexico and part in the U.S. was initially imposed by Mexican regulations designed to insure that dollars spent on imported intermediate goods would be offset by export sales. However, for a number of firms the measures appear to have been profitable, since the industry itself has become increasingly international in the production of components of value added. More recently the Mexican government has passed similar regulations for the establishment of personal computer production and technology sharing in high-tech areas. Notwithstanding the unilateral nature of such policy decisions to date, there may be reason for both countries to consider joint negotiations on an industry-by-industry basis to facilitate much wider production sharing (along the lines of the auto pact between the U.S. and Canada).

Production sharing could offer an important way out of the structural problems facing both countries. In the U.S., for example, industries which are well along in the product cycle may not be doomed to extinction if they can increasingly share in the stages of production with a neighbor such as Mexico, which is easily accessible in terms of transport costs and communications and which has abundant energy and human resources, a burgeoning market of its own, and access to markets in other developing countries. By the same token, Mexico's attempts to enhance the competitiveness of its own industries can take advantage of the potential for production sharing with the U.S., permitting the step-by-step development of high-quality and low-cost products at all stages of the production process.

For the United States, production sharing is already taking place on a wide international scale (e.g., in automobiles and semiconductors) in pursuit of more favorable wage/productivity relations than those which obtain domestically. What is argued here is that a concerted effort to expand production sharing between the U.S. and Mexico, if managed effectively, could offer additional social returns that could go well beyond the private return to capital, in terms of enhanced security, welfare, and social progress of both countries. Higher incomes and greater employment opportunities in Mexico would be combined with the preservation of complementary jobs on the U.S. side and scale economies plus opportunities for new investment in expanded plant and equipment would enhance productivity growth in both countries. The U.S. would not have to write off many of its "smokestack" or labor-intensive industries or lose the benefits of its managerial techniques and market access, while Mexico could progressively upgrade its technology and integrate its economy both vertically and horizontally as a new pole of North American growth.

RELATIONS BETWEEN GOVERNMENT AND BUSINESS

Taking advantage of structural complementarities would involve an important role for government in both countries, just as it would imply major decisions for business north and south of the border. Hence relations between the private and public sectors must be compatible with the need for a consistent and predictable set of rules governing such relationships, since they would involve a major commitment of funds over the medium and long run. Both the U.S. and Mexico have passed through a period of major expansion in government regulation and involvement in the economy, and both are now undergoing a fundamental reappraisal of that process from all political perspectives. Unfortunately, however, such counter-trends only increase the uncertainty of investors as well as the concerns of policymakers in each country about the stability of decisions in the other. This complicates the environment for agreement not only within each country but between them.

In addition to differing perspectives between the two countries, there is the critical problem of restoring relations between the private and public sectors in Mexico. Sudden nationalization of the banks in 1982, imposition of exchange controls, and collapse of the peso rocked the business community to its foundations. Subsequently, the incoming administration passed a number of measures to ease the difficulties, while at the same time enforcing an austerity program that cut sharply into profits and sales and restricted access to foreign exchange needed for imported inputs. A new ministry was established to audit public expenditures and investigate corruption.

For both business and government the old rules of the game are changing in directions that have yet to become clear to any of the major actors, much less to those involved in day-to-day transactions. The state, which had long tolerated the accumulation of wealth and privilege in high places in exchange for rapid growth and gradually rising incomes for the poor, suddenly revealed its populist foundations. The end of the boom reawakened the country to a fundamental dilemma. As in previous times of crisis, such as the mid-seventies (before oil offered an apparent panacea), Mexico was forced to renegotiate its social contract, namely, finding the appropriate means of sustaining accumulation and investment by middle- and upper-income groups, while at the same time drawing the mass of the population into increasing participation in the economy and society. Once the oil bonanza revealed its limitations, new answers were needed; the response on September 1, 1982, was quick and drastic expropriation of the financial system of the country. But this measure only bought time and, without resolving the basic dilemmas, created a whole new set of problems.

Without going into the basis for such a decision, taken without warning by a President who acted on his sole

authority in the final months of his administration, it made
two fundamental points: First, that in time of economic
emergency, Mexico could be ruled by decree, its economy
subjected to executive action that fundamentally alters the
structure of ownership and decision-making without prior
consultation with the parties involved or full consideration
of the possible consequences. Second, notwithstanding the
impressive austerity program and more favorable attitude
toward the private sector of the succeeding administration,
it is evident that the balance of power has changed in favor
of the state.

      From the viewpoint of possible production sharing, this
offers both advantages and disadvantages. It is likely that
a continuation of the present regime in Mexico will mean
that the social contract must be honored by the private
sector, imposing conditions on future investment   that
require the benefits of growth to be more fully shared with
the mass of the population. This could contribute to the
expansion of the market, economies of scale, and greater
social and political stability essential for the security of
investment decisions.   But, one disadvantage is that it
could also herald a return to the populist-nationalist
rhetoric of the 1970s, hindering serious U.S.-Mexican
economic linkages.

      One would have to go back a number of years in U.S.
history to recall similar periods in which its social
contract was revised to better accommodate all groups in the
development process. The presidencies of the two Roosevelts
offer certain parallels, although the two-party system was
vastly different from Mexico today. Teddy Roosevelt used
his charismatic appeal to take the Republican party at the
turn of the century into an era of moderate populism,
attacking the trusts and inveighing against corruption in
government. In the 1930s, Democrat Franklin Roosevelt faced
the financial crisis not by nationalizing the banks but by
closing them briefly and then passing major regulatory
legislation.   His administration acted to fundamentally
alter power relations between government and business in
ways that are still being debated.

      The differences between such periods in the U.S. and
Mexico today are enormous, however, and cannot be
overstated. Both Roosevelts operated within a pluralistic
political system and, although many accused them of
authoritarian designs, most of their measures were
scrutinized by a wide range of influential interest groups
with considerable influence before being acted upon by a
bipartisan Congress. Moreover, they were subject to review

by an independent judiciary. Despite its support of increased representation of minority parties in the Chamber of Deputies and opposition victories in some state and local elections, Mexico remains an essentially one-party system with a powerful executive who dominates the legislature. What is important from the viewpoint of investment potential in each country is that a strong stable government role in the expansion of the economy favoring wider social participation can be highly complementary to the expansion of industry and to private participation in the investment process. Even China is seen as a potential profit center by many firms in the West. What is most problematic is the element of uncertainty about policy actions which requires investors to apply a significant discount for risk, a discount which may preclude investing in what would otherwise be an excellent environment in which private and social benefits could coexist regardless of the structure of the political system.

STABLE RULES OF THE GAME

What is needed is some evidence that the power relations are adjusting to restore a balance between the private and public sectors capable of insuring investors against the risk of similar actions in the future. As we have seen, the present administration is continuing a "democratization" program begun by its predecessor in which a certain number of seats in the Chamber of Deputies is reserved for representatives of opposition parties of left and right, including the Unified Socialist Party of Mexico (PSUM) and the increasingly popular National Action Party (PAN). Ironically, some of the success of the conservative PAN movement is due to frustration with abuses by the ruling party which the Institutional Revolution Party (PRI) itself has revealed in its own attempts to purge the corruption of previous administrations. To some investors, however much they might prefer the conservative opposition, political pluralism cuts both ways, tending to undermine the stability and predictability of the one-party system which has governed Mexico since the Revolution. By the same token, the government's own anti-corruption program makes it difficult for the kind of deals to be made between agents of business and government which have been so much a part of the development process until now (just as they were in many

parts of the U.S. in its period of greatest growth).
Reprehensible as the system was, the mordida frequently
served to increase the efficiency of an encumbering
bureaucracy and prevented unwise regulation from producing
the opposite of its intended effect.

IS THERE A BASIS FOR BINATIONAL INDUSTRIAL POLICY?

We have seen that not only do the two countries differ
in terms of the degree of planning and the role of
government in the investment process, but within each there
are strong differences of opinion about the appropriateness
of industrial policy. In the U.S., the two main Democratic
candidates in 1984 had very different approaches, one
favoring the rehabilitation of "smokestack" industries
through subsidies and import protection, and the other
championing government encouragement of high-tech industries
with traditional sectors encouraged to phase into new lines
of production or decline. The position of the Republicans,
on the other hand, was and is to let the market forces work
and minimize government regulations and controls. The
obvious benefits of production sharing would seem to
transcend such differences, however. Decisions to work
together could be made on a case-by-case basis, once
potential participants made known their interest or one of
the governments proposed that specific sectors be considered
for negotiation. In view of the nature of binational
investment decision-making and the disparate state and local
regulations on each side of the border, both federal
governments would have to play a role in such activities
regardless of their particular philosophies about
"industrial policy." Indeed, the U.S. has had de facto
industrial policies during many periods of its history,
particularly in times of war or depression. It could be
argued that the southwestern industrial economy of the U.S.
was created for the most part during World War II, primarily
for strategic reasons, with massive credit subsidies,
government procurement, and federal and state support for
education and infrastructure.
While it is still somewhat premature to talk of a
"binational industrial policy," it would be worthwhile to
consider the establishment of policy guidelines that could
draw on existing institutions to facilitate the expansion of
both production and market sharing between the two

countries. This will prove essential simply because of the natural evolution of the North American economy, which is becoming daily more interdependent regardless of decisions by the governments involved. However, if and when national industrial policy begins to be taken seriously in the U.S., it will be essential to ask where the line should be drawn in terms of geographic boundaries for the architecture of infrastructure planning and to what extent Mexico (and Canada, Central America, and the Caribbean) should be taken into consideration, given their proximity, strategic importance, and future growth potential. Early thinking along such lines, from the perspective of one's own country and one's neighbors, may prove not only prophetic but valuable in setting the course for change well before such policies become either fashionable or inevitable.

MAQUILADORAS--CAN THEY GROW UP?

The maquilas are Mexico's in-bond or so-called "border industries," though they are now being established throughout the country. They involve assembly plants which employ Mexican labor to process intermediate goods which are imported duty-free for resale in the U.S. Such industries involve production sharing, since part of value added in the industrial process is produced in the U.S. and part in Mexico. The drawback from the viewpoint of full interdependence is that, unlike the auto industry, it does not involve market sharing, since the products are generally not sold in Mexico under the terms of the in-bond arrangement. The Mexican maquila program was created in the 1960s, after the model of Puerto Rico's assembly plants, which had helped to make "Operation Bootstrap" attractive to U.S. investors a decade earlier. The objective was to find substitute employment opportunities south of the border for Mexicans displaced by the abrupt termination of the bracero program. The results have been mixed, as a number of studies has shown. Over two hundred thousand jobs have been created by the program, many in the past couple of years, but most have gone to younger women rather than men, and there has been a high turnover. Value added has been gained for Mexico, though less per worker than in non-maquila manufacturing, and there has been little profit retained in Mexico or demand generated for domestic inputs other than low-cost labor. The consumption multiplier from _maquila_ wages has been felt as much on the north as the south side of the border (except during periods of sharp peso devaluation). And neither vertical nor horizontal integration has taken place for most of the industries, either in the border region or with the rest of Mexico. Finally, _maquilas_ tend by their very nature to be "footloose," with little in the way of permanent installations, capable of moving away on short notice from areas with union problems or rising labor costs.

The _maquila_ program offers one possible opportunity for experimentation with combined production and market sharing. By their very nature, operations in the _maquila_ sector must be productive, since they were moved outside of the U.S. because of favorable wage/productivity relations, and most of the industries involved are highly competitive. For the most part, they are denied access to the Mexican market because of their use of duty-free imports of raw materials and intermediate goods which would provide a competitive edge over those domestic firms which must acquire their inputs from national suppliers operating behind protective tariffs and quotas. This leads to a two-tier system in Mexico, with productive firms along the border and in-bond zones and less-productive firms in the rest of the economy. Unfortunately the system does not facilitate gradual improvements in productivity of domestic firms since they are not forced to compete with the _maquilas_, much less with imports. From the viewpoint of firms interested in entering the Mexican market, the opportunity to combine export production from the _maquila_ platform with staged access to the Mexican market would permit an equally staged transition from the use of imported inputs (at lower price and higher quality than are currently available inside Mexico) to the gradual acquisition of domestically produced inputs. The assumption is made here that opening the Mexican market to _maquila_ production in a graduated manner (perhaps assuring that increased sales in Mexico would be related to increased domestic procurement of inputs, though with a possible lag to permit suppliers to improve price and quality) would permit increased production sharing with the U.S., along with market sharing, but in a way which would encourage the expansion of production in both countries.

The result of such a graduation of _maquilas_ into full production and market sharing, probably through joint investment between Mexican and foreign firms (and in some cases with government participation), would help to overcome the problems inherent in the original _maquila_ program. The industries would have incentives to integrate both vertically and horizontally, providing dynamic linkages with both economies. They would also have incentives to upgrade labor skills as the sophistication of the operations (and supplier firms) improved and to hire additional local management, and they would become less transient owing to their expanded role in the domestic market as a source of both supply and demand. This would transform the maquilas in ways similar to the industries of Asia's newly industrializing countries, where rising income, productivity, wages, and labor skills have made it essential for their "border industries" to "grow up." The essence of industrialization is the ability of firms to adjust product lines, processes, and markets in response to changing conditions. Production and market sharing would favor such a process for Mexico just as it has for those more distant countries, and it would stimulate research and development in what are at present simple assembly plants.

CONVERGENCE IN PRODUCTIVITY AND INCOMES: THE ROLE OF BINATIONAL INDUSTRIAL POLICY

Underlying the arguments in favor of a specifically binational approach to industrial policy is the fact of powerful pressures for convergence in productivity and income between the U.S. and Mexico. While such forces are increasingly in evidence throughout the international economy, they are particularly acute for neighbors which share such a long border, with so many avenues of exchange of goods and services, labor, capital, and technology. There is a "gravity mechanism" at work in any regional economy to break down barriers because of the gains from exchange. In classical economic theory, Ricardo talked about the gains from trade through specialization in terms of comparative costs. More recently the Heckscher-Ohlin theories have been used to argue that in special circumstances trade alone could equalize returns to labor or capital even without migration or investment flows. There has been gradual convergence between the U.S. and Mexico in per capita income and wages over recent years, although the gap remains wide (about 6 to 1 for income and 8 to 1 for wages of unskilled labor). In terms of dollars at the market exchange rate, the gap narrowed and then widened perceptibly after 1982. But the long-run trend is toward convergence. It is being influenced by all four flows: labor, capital, technology, and trade. The implications of the narrowing process, however, can be positive or negative to the high-wage country, depending on the extent to which it saves and invests and experiences productivity growth.

While the U.S. was growing at three percent or more per annum, the convergence process was consistent with steady or rising real wages for its low-skilled workers, even as Mexico's productivity and real wages rose at a faster rate. But during the past decade, there is evidence that in a number of sectors and regions, and for a number of skills, real wages in the U.S. declined (especially after taxes). I showed in a paper at a 1982 conference at The University of Texas that shifts in employment in Mexico among regions and sectors was leading to higher average productivity of labor, whereas in the U.S. it was leading to lower average productivity than would have been obtained with constant labor shares among the three sectors, primary, secondary, and tertiary. This was particularly owing to the shift in employment shares from the highly productive manufacturing and commercial agricultural sectors to low-skilled service occupations in the U.S. In Mexico, on the other hand, labor was moving from low productivity traditional agriculture to commercial agriculture, modern manufacturing, and higher skilled services. However, convergence between the two countries will tend to lead to a lowering of average productivity and wages in low-skilled occupations in the U.S. (and rising productivity and wages in Mexico) if it is not accompanied by rapid increases in investment and productivity in both countries. This is extremely important to our argument about binational industrial policy. Convergence can take place through migration, trade, investment, or technology transfer. But if the latter three possibilities are constrained, then migration becomes the main channel through which pressures for convergence operate.

During a recession in Mexico, the convergence process is exacerbated through migration (undervaluation of the peso has greatly widened the wage and income gap between the two countries), with possibly negative consequences for wages of competing labor in the receiving country. If Mexico's economy does not quickly recover in terms of employment, productivity, and income for its rapidly expanding work force (which is doubling every twenty years), the effect of convergence on the U.S. will be exacerbated. But if both countries were to pursue complementary industrial development policies, their combined growth would provide an expanding market for labor, permitting wages to rise on both sides of the border. Under such circumstances, migration could continue to take place (though at a slower rate) consistent with both convergence and joint income growth. However, if U.S. production sharing were to occur independent of the Mexican economy, and the latter were to continue to stagnate, pressures for convergence would lead to an erosion of wages in the U.S. even though its total income would grow, favoring the profit share but at the cost of social and political instability.

In short, I have tried to present a comprehensive view of binational development as an economic and social process which places demands for equity on the political leadership of both countries. This has important implications for industrial policy. Both firms and industries can gain from production and market sharing, provided that the sharing is managed in ways that permit gradual adjustments to changing opportunities. The two nations can gain from a binational industrial policy at the level of firm, industry, or total economy. And in the absence of creative leadership, migrants vote with their feet.

12

A Mexican View

Francisco Javier Alejo

A PECULIAR INTERDEPENDENCE

Relations between Mexico and the United States can be characterized as a clear phenomenon of interdependence. There exists, nevertheless, a combination of peculiarities in the relationship that should be kept in mind and clarified to avoid confusion.

While it is true that the interdependence is real and is based not just on territorial contiguity, but also on a solid foundation of economic, cultural, and political factors, the perception of the phenomenon on either side of the border is dissimilar. On the Mexican side, there has always been a consciousness of the dependency of Mexico on the United States, especially in economic and technological areas. However, there is little consciousness of the impact that developments in Mexico can have on the United States. Mexicans would react with incredulity that this is a real issue since their perception is that the United States is a large, modern, technologically advanced, powerful, and even invulnerable, imperial country.

In the United States, only recently have informed groups of the country (business, banking, government, and academia) begun to realize that the economic, political, and demographic dynamics of Mexico can influence correlative events in the United States. The traditional North American perception of Mexico, even of persons in the leading circles, was roughly as follows: small, backward, weak, colorful, nationalistic, and strangely hesitant to adopt as its own the cultural values of the United States. The crises of the last ten years, first of oil and later of debt, have placed Mexico in a prominent position, not just

among leaders, but also among the public in general. There
is thus a gradual perception of interdependence. This
perception lacks balance. It takes into account only the
extent to which some change in Mexico will affect the U.S.
economy, its finances, job markets, culture, and even its
ethnic balance; that is, it takes into account only the
extent to which the United States is becoming dependent on
Mexico. Other U.S. perceptions of Mexico add to this
imbalance: oil rich, inefficient, unstable, and
demographically explosive.

These differences in perceptions are not
inconsequential. They provide an ample basis for conflict
but only a limited basis for potential complementarity.
There is only limited awareness of the high degree of
complementarity that already exists between the two
countries, especially in the economic sphere.

An elementary principle of international politics is
that good relations between nations and people depend
largely on a calm and objective acknowledgement of the
differences between them. This can serve as a foundation to
identify points of correspondence that can serve as the
basis for a stable, positive, and mutually beneficial
dynamic relationship. There are many differences between
Mexico and the United States—so many so that it can be said
that there are few pairs of neighboring countries as
different as Mexico and the United States. It is essential
to make the differences explicit as the basis for a rich and
complementary relationship based precisely on the
differences.

It goes almost without saying that there is asymmetry
between the two countries in size, history and culture.

RECOGNIZING THE DIFFERENCES

The relationship between Mexico and the United States
can be defined by saying that they are two nations with
substantial and essential differences but relatively common
objectives; as a result, the roads to reach these objectives
must necessarily be different. This, perhaps, is the clue
to understanding the essence of what is unclear in the
relations between the two countries. Size, history,
cultural philosophy, institutions, and popular perceptions
are elements that define the two different roads to be taken
in pursuit of similar objectives: freedom, democracy,

national sovereignty, cultural identity, the well-being of the majority, and finally, equality. This is the least clear component in the relationship, namely, the specificity of final objectives. Problems arise from the lack of definition of differences in starting points, which, in turn, define separate roads in the search for equivalent objectives.

We must place these differences—historical, philosophical, and material—in evidence. It is convenient to begin with the different perceptions of their origins.

It is proper to ask, as Luis Maira does: Do the Americas have a common history?[1] At one time in the United States—as in Mexico and other Latin American countries during the nineteenth century—an effort was made to understand the history of the entire Western Hemisphere. "The Epic of the Great America" was formulated to study the historical paths of both Americas, Latin and Anglo-Saxon.[2] The basic assumption of this study was that the two groups of societies went through common stages: the transplantation of European colonial cultures, mixture with indigenous cultures; revolutionary separation from Europe; population of unpopulated areas; and creation of "A Great American Nation" with a common history and destiny.

Maira argues that it is difficult to agree, from a Latin American perspective, with the thesis of a common path in the historical course of the United States and Latin America. The revolution for independence of the United States was essentially an affirmation of positions already achieved by the founders of the nation. In Latin America, however, the independence movement was associated with the rupture of hierarchies and the subordinate status which leaders of the movement could no longer tolerate. Independence in Latin America accentuated disparities. In the United States, the national state was quickly consolidated and dynamic capitalist development led to a high degree of class mobility. In Latin America, the constitution of the state was slow and painful, and in some cases still has not ended; political instability, difficulties of modernization, and rigidities of social stratification still lead frequently to political crises or revolutionary processes. It is essential, therefore, to take as a point of departure for analysis of the organic and structural relationship, the historical diversity of North American society and the multiple mosaic of the Latin American societies, and in particular of the Mexican society. This explains why economic and social asymmetry is reflected in relationships of subordination, dependency and conflict between most Latin American countries, especially Mexico, and the United States. It is necessary, therefore, to start any analysis from the recognition of the negative burden that Latin America has about the North American "center".

In the case of Mexico, the differences between it and the United States could not be more clear. The theory of the European transplant is totally false if intended as an historical identity between the two countries. The founding of North American society was the result of the immigration of groups of Englishmen who were fleeing British theocratic and patrimonial absolutism but found a territory open to the possibility of founding a libertarian society based on the philosophical concepts of seventeenth century European reform. The European transplant in Mexico was diametrically different. The Mexican territory was not colonized but conquered by an absolutist monarchic state that derived its geopolitical philosophy from the Holy Roman-Germanic Empire. The difference between the relationship of England and its American colonies and between Spain and its American colonies is akin to the difference between the reformation and the counter-reformation, modernism and traditionalism, a theocratic state and a lay state, and mercantile society in transition to an industrial society as contrasted with a feudal society in transition to a mercantilist, patrimonial state.

The founding of the United States, from the very beginning, tended toward the creation of an open society. The founding of Mexico, on the other hand, constituted the conquest by an absolutist and traditionalist nation of another society with the same character.

From this, a liberty-fulfillment phenomenon took place in what is now the United States. On the other hand, in New Spain, a dependent, patrimonial, pluralist, and markedly mercantilist kingdom developed, in whose economic and political structures the large landed estates and communal land holdings (ejidos) coexisted, as did the corporations and seeds of capitalism. At its peak, the aristocratic and patrimonial court defined a philosophical universe that, ultimately, was a closed one, in contrast with the open world that English immigrants found in what is today of the United States.[3]

Octavio Paz describes the evolution of modernity as taking two parallel roads, one for countries whose modern era began with the triumph of the Reformation and one for those (for example, France) which adopted modernity without Protestantism. In one, modernity was expressed not only in criticisms of absolute monarchy, the court, and the old regime, but also in attacks on the Catholic church. There was an anti-Catholic phenomenon taking place in French democracy similar to that in the Nordic countries; this was Jansenism, as the basis for a modern moral conscience. However, this element never appeared in Spain or its American dominions, so that there never was an authentic movement in them toward modernization prior to independence.

In the case of Mexico, the theocratic, military, absolutist-patrimonial, conservative state, pretender to the succession of the Holy Roman Germanic-Spanish Empire, was superimposed on the Aztec theocratic-military state. This was contrary to movement toward modernization or toward a creative civil or modern democratic society.

As a result, Paz points out that during the seventeenth century, New Spain was a stronger, more prosperous, and more civilized society than New England, but it was a closed society, not only to the outside but to the future as well. Paz argues that while religious democracy in New England was transformed into political democracy, New Spain was unable to solve its internal contradictions. In short, the European transplant in what is now the United States was the transfer of the European search for modernity to an open territory populated by nomadic tribes situated in the upper Neolithic period, which, as a consequence, did not offer any resistance that could not be overcome by superior extermination technology. On the other hand, the European transplant that took place in Mexico was that of a theocratic-patrimonial-absolutist state in a territory populated and occupied by a highly developed culture of the lower Neolithic period, which had to be destroyed, but with which it also coincided. That is to say, a conservative culture dominated another conservative culture and the result was a society and culture resistant to modernization. There were no ingredients of modernism in the Mexican independence revolution (with the exception of the abolition of slavery); it was the middle of the nineteenth century before these elements became manifest under the influence of the new phenomenon which North American society signified for the world. However, three centuries of transplantation of the monarchic-absolutist-patrimonial society model that Spain provided for Mexico represented a great obstacle which remains to this day. In fact, we could say that the true transition to modernism in Mexico began with the 1910-1917 evolution and the agrarian reform (1915-1940).

The historical differences in the founding of the U.S. and Mexican states continue to exert influence to this day.

The Mexican state followed a development pattern similar to that of the French; the Tuxtepec Revolution (which brought Porfirio Díaz to power) produced the defeat of the premise of the Juarist liberal state and the emergence of a Bonapartist development pattern which ceased to be effective less than twenty years ago.

Fundamental issues of a philosophical nature are implicit in what has been said. The philosophic core of the Reformation is individualist and bourgeois. The philosophic core of the counter-reformation is absolutist, monarchical, and courtly. The former requires change to consolidate and grow; the latter denies it. In the same order of ideas, the legal-economic philosophy of North America is the common law and, therefore, it adapts itself in the legal-positive aspect to the objective necessities of its social environment. By contrast, the legal-economic philosophy of Mexico is doctrinaire and is derived from Roman law, through the transplantation of the Napoleonic Codes in the nineteenth century.

The U.S. Constitution is based on the definition of the rights of the people, of the citizens. The Constitution is the juridical expression of the revolution for independence of the United States. Once the ties with England were broken, the collective project of the country could be none other than the sum total of the individual projects. This is the source of the present day U.S. paradox; an imperial presence requires a single collective order as opposed to a diversity of individual orders that ignores or denies the existence of, or need for, an imperial order.

By contrast, the Mexican revolution for independence was based on the rupture of ties between a traditionalist society and a monarchical state, but the society reproduced almost the same absolutist relations that existed in the center of the empire. The history of the nineteenth century would confirm the need for a constitutional agreement that would be a collective project for the development of a diversified civil society, which, once mature, would rule the state, but which had to be developed by the state. That is why the constitutional concept of 1917 differs radically from the constitutional concept of the United States. Where the state represents civil society, it protects the society and projects it to the exterior; in Mexico, the state's mission is to develop civil society so as, finally, to be dominated by it.

Even at such abstract levels as the philosophy of the state and of law, it is easy to perceive the paradoxical parallelism between the Mexican and U.S. societies; these

are the identity of objectives (freedom, equality and
sovereignty) and disparity in paths and procedures. It is
evident that some of the recent conflicts have come about as
a result of the lack of understanding that the disparity of
procedures is an inevitable product of the difference in
historical experiences.

If we position ourselves in the present, it is evident
that there remains an ample set of objective differences
between the two countries. The United States has a
territory with the second largest endowment of natural
resources on earth. Its gross national product represents a
fifth of the world's, approximately ten times greater than
that of Mexico, and the per capita income of its population
is approximately five to six times greater than that of
Mexico. While the U.S. economy depends basically on its
internal dynamics, the Mexican economy is largely determined
by external events. The U.S. economy is entering a stage
that could be called post-modernism, while the Mexican
economy is barely starting to consolidate itself as a modern
economy. The population of the United States is at the
final phase of its demographic transition, while the Mexican
population is barely beginning to go through the second of
five phases in this transition, that is, the phase in which
the labor force growth rate reaches its historical peak and,
as a consequence, capital formation must also reach its peak
to sustain an appropriate rhythm of development.

To put this simply, the United States and Mexico, apart
from the fact that they are neighbors, are two nations, two
economies, two societies, essentially and fundamentally
asymmetrical. Since the relationship between them is
inevitable, it is necessary to understand the phenomenology
and the laws of asymmetry. When there is an inevitable
relationship between two asymmetric phenomena, that
relationship can be stable only if there are mechanisms to
compensate for the asymmetry. However, as we saw earlier,
the sources of asymmetry are varied: historic, demographic,
cultural, geographic, economic, technological, and
political. For this reason, the compensation mechanisms
have to be varied in their characteristics and in their
duration. The first compensation mechanism that must exist
is an effort in cultural communication between the two
peoples. This has not yet taken place with the required
amplitude, depth, and persistence.

The second element is compensation for differences in
constitutional regimes, which imply fundamental differences
in the role of the state in the economy. In one case, the
state withdraws from domestic affairs to play an active role

in foreign affairs; in the other, the state plays an active role internally and a defensive one abroad.

The dramatic difference in economic size between the two countries forces Mexico to put into effect defensive policies which are not always suitable when judged from a medium- and long-term perspective. This is an area in which agreements can be reached that define concrete compensation mechanisms for the asymmetry, in accordance with which Mexico could follow rational development policies with the certainty that impacts felt because of U.S. economic fluctuations would be absorbed or neutralized by the agreed compensation mechanisms. This deals not only with Mexico's need to adapt, with U.S. cooperation, to short-term cyclical fluctuations in the U.S. economy, but also with the need to adjust U.S. institutional reactions to development policies that Mexico must follow to reduce its historical differences in modernity compared with those of the U.S. economy.

With respect to trade and capital movements, the compensation of asymmetry requires that the U.S. economy must continue to move toward openness, while at the same time accepting that the Mexican economy still needs a certain degree of defensive closure in trade and capital movements; the relative degree of closure must be conceived in dynamic rather than static terms. This means that the structure of Mexican protection, in trade and in investment, must not be fixed, but rather change over time.

One specific aspect merits special attention; this refers to the need to create a compensation mechanism for external shocks which from time to time the Mexican economy receives from the United States. These can come from abrupt fluctuations in U.S. economic activity, significant variations in U.S. inflation or interest rates, or from stabilization or stimulative policies taken by the U.S. Government. In addition to the needed communication between the two governments regarding such events, and the indispensable adaptive flexibility of Mexican economic policy, the establishment of a sort of permanent (monetary) "swap" would be required, one larger and more flexible than what has been in effect until now.

We could also focus on structural pressures that force the Mexican economy to operate at an inflationary level higher than the U.S. economy, such as the different long-term demographic inertias in the two countries and the necessity for Mexico to overcome the social lags of the past.

THE ROUTE TO COMPLEMENTATION

The adoption and implementation of a complementation policy between the Mexican and U.S. economies, and more specifically a complementation policy for industrial development in both countries, requires an understanding of the different phases of industrial development in which the two countries find themselves, as well as of the different focuses followed by each country for the promotion of structural change of their industries.

The disparity in the degree of industrial development between the two countries is evident, as is the fact that the two economies are at different phases of development. U.S. productive structures are highly integrated. There is relatively small participation of farming, animal husbandry, and mining in total employment, high though decreasing participation of industry in production and employment, and high and growing participation of modern services in these aggregates. At the same time, the U.S. economy is facing problems of international competitiveness because of its recent slow pace of structural change and the rapid productive development during the 1960s and 1970s of some Western European countries and newly industrializing countries, particularly those from Southeast Asia, Korea, Brazil, and Mexico.

The Mexican economy, on the other hand, is only now entering an intermediate phase of development. Agriculture, cattle raising, and mining still contribute more than one-third of employment but a smaller and decreasing portion of production. Industrial activities grew rapidly during the last quarter of a century and contribute more than one-fourth of total employment and one-third of production, but they still lack sufficient internal integration, are too dependent on imports of capital goods, and lack sufficient capacity for their own technological development and international competitiveness. The service sector contributes an important portion of employment and production, but as a whole is still far behind its U.S. equivalent.

Such differences in degrees of development of the economic structures of the two countries constitute in themselves a vital basis for complementation. This has been demonstrated in recent decades, although in a manner too spontaneous, somewhat chaotic, and at times even pathological. The result of this complementation behavior between the two economies is twofold: on the one hand, an important proportion of the possibilities for complementation are wasted; and on the other hand, frequent frictions arise between the two countries which could be easily avoided in a more "administered" complementation environment in which the two governments would put in practice cooperation plans and policies that would allow for the exploitation of all the potential for their independent but coordinated development.

The United States is entering what is being called the post-industrial era, which we understand as the move from an industry based on the "smokestack factories" to one based essentially on high technology, electronics applied to industrial processes, the discovery and incorporation of new materials, the conquest of extra-terrestrial space, access to a service society, and sophisticated consumption, i.e., less massive and more individualized.

The present moment can be categorized as transitional in that a high proportion of smokestack industries exist in the industrial structure of the United States, but new high-technology industries are making their appearance. The international problem that arises in this transitional phase is that the emerging industries, notwithstanding their vitality, do not generate sufficient employment to provide jobs for those displaced from "traditional" industries if pressures of the interest groups are resisted and the latter types of industries are shifted to countries such as Mexico, which could operate them with higher international levels of efficiency. The U.S. Government cannot apply the same policy to high-technology industry that is applied to medium- or low-technology industry, or to those with limited technological requirements.

This does not mean that the United States must dismantle all of its traditional industry from one day to the next; it implies only the need to allow for the dynamics of comparative advantage to operate in a normal manner, with few obstacles. There are numerous traditional industries in the United States that have and will continue to have such comparative advantages, such as those linked to abundant U.S. natural resources and the exploitation of the large, mass-consumption U.S. market. These are precisely the industries that generate the largest amount of employment.

There are, however, numerous industries in which dynamic competitiveness depends on the specific efficiency of labor utilization, the cost of labor, the transportation of raw-material inputs, and the combination of these elements with a large domestic market, such as that of Mexico. In these cases, it is evident that the international mobility of capital and technology, especially the latter, and the elimination of barriers to access to the U.S. market, would allow the Mexican economy to make considerable progress. Taking these steps would foster substantial intensification of dynamic complementation between the two countries, with great benefits for the population on both sides of the border.

There are numerous Mexican industries that fit, or could fit, the circumstances described above: glass, cement, basic petrochemicals, food packing, steel, basic metals, textiles, clothing, shoes, tool and die-making, home electrical appliances, automotive components, machinery components, and others. There are also industries that have ceased to be efficient in the United States, but which can be efficient in Mexico and which, if placed in the location of greater efficiency, will result in a dynamic of shared production with benefit for the two sides. These benefits are more employment and higher wages and income on the Mexican side; and preservation of important portions of some industries in the United States, with corresponding benefits in productivity, efficiency, wages, employment, consumer satisfaction, and international competitiveness.

Affected interest groups from industries whose competitive position has deteriorated pressure Congress and the executive branch with such force that protection frequently becomes irresistible. The result is slower growth in productivity and real wages in the United States and a loss of employment opportunities, income, and the acquisition of foreign exchange for countries such as Mexico.

Some people in the United States are worried about the tendency in the U.S. economic structure to move away from the basic industries (smokestack industries) and to depend more on modern services. One reason may be that the former represents what, for more than two centuries, has been the basis of industrial power. These industries also have close ties with the security position of the United States. Questions arise about how the geopolitical order would be affected if the United States became dependent on other countries or regions (Mexico, Brazil, Latin America, South Korea, Japan, Southeast Asia) for supplies of products of these industries. The issue is not trivial. It is related to East-West relations and the degree of trust between the United States and Latin America. Much of this trust has been lost in the last few years.

Another economic change is the result of the evolution of the U.S. consumption market stemming from preferences of consumers. Growing incomes have led to sophisticated and individualized consumption habits, creating some departure from mass consumption of large-scale production goods characteristic of the past. Parallel with this, regional consumption characteristics have developed (for example, in the use of automobiles in California). The U.S. population is also consuming more goods and services with a large cultural content. This opens new possibilities for small and medium business and for industry and service providers from other countries, including Mexico. The U.S. economy is moving toward post-industrialism and society toward post-modernism.

Mexico's phase of industrial development is different. In the post-war years, Mexico followed a model of import substituting industrialization. This strategy worked well when international markets were expanding and the international monetary system created at Bretton Woods prevailed. When the latter broke down--starting in August, 1971--Mexico began to experience problems with its immature industrialization model. Pressures developed on the current account of the balance of payments. During the second half of the 1970s, the oil boom permitted continuation of the model and progress in some lagging activities, such as basic industry and capital goods. The decade of the seventies, however, synthesized the difficulties Mexico must face in modifying its industrialization model.

Mexico entered the 1980s with a financial and balance-of-payments crisis, which made evident the exhaustion of the previous industrialization policy. The seriousness of the crisis led to the adoption of a new strategy embodied in the 1984 National Program for Industrial and Foreign Trade Development (or the Spanish acronym PRONAFICE).

At the beginning of the eighties, the country's industry had seven negative characteristics that had to be overcome:

1. The industrial structure lacked an adequate degree of internal integration. There were large gaps in the production of capital goods and in the supply of widely used basic goods. The economy demonstrated a high income-elasticity of imports.

2. Industrial growth did not generate sufficient employment.

3. The extreme reliance of Mexican industry on a protected domestic market led to a growing foreign-exchange deficit because of the lack of capacity to export.

4. There was acute distortion of relative prices.

5. Industrial growth depended on a high and growing

level of subsidization.

6. The lack of competitive pressures inhibited technological development and led to growing relative backwardness.

7. The high concentration of wealth and the oligopolistic organization of production led to inequitable distribution of income.

Mexico must change this panorama. First, it is necessary to change the structure and logic of industrial protection, without destroying industry (as occurred in some countries in South America during the 1970s). The development of missing industrial branches (capital goods, widely used industrial supplies, and bases for high technology development) must be encouraged.

Second, exports must be increased by maintaining an appropriate structure of relative prices (rate of exchange, factor costs of capital and labor, among others). This is complicated by restrictions in the United States on imports from Mexico. The U.S. negotiating position is based on the concept of a quid pro quo. In exchange for access to the U.S. market, Mexico is expected to provide comparable immediate access to its market for U.S. products, a suspension of subsidies for Mexico's exports, and greater receptiveness to direct investments from the United States. The first two elements seriously limit attainment of the Mexican objectives stated earlier. The third does not pose the same difficulty, but it is obvious that it cannot be satisfied to the extent desired by the U.S. interests that have created the pressure.

Based on the priorities in PRONAFICE (which are discussed in the Villarreal essay of this volume), and the structural changes taking place in U.S. industry, we can find an ample spectrum of possibilities for mutually beneficial cooperation between the two countries. The main obstacles to cooperation are the radical differences in procedures to reach desired objectives and the lack of understanding of the disparity of the development stages of the two countries.

A central problem is the lack of adequate evaluation and understanding of the time needed for the Mexican economy and industry to mature. The determination of that period is highly controversial and subject to value judgments. There is, however, an objective factor which, while it does not refer directly to Mexico's economic maturity, does indicate the nature and intensity of internal pressures, namely, the dynamics of demographic transition. The U.S. population of European origin is in the final phase of its demographic transition; Mexico's is barely in the second and most problematic phase--one in which the labor force growth rate reaches its historical peak with continued high fertility levels. These circumstances impose tremendous demands on the economy's resources and create acute tensions in the country's political system. According to authoritative projections--which do not depend on subjective hypotheses-- it will take Mexico from six to ten years to pass through this second phase of its demographic transition.[4] It will then enter its third phase, with decreasing rates of growth of the labor force and low birth and mortality rates.

At the beginning of the third phase of its demographic transition, Mexico will have a little over 100 million inhabitants and, if the international environment is favorable for the country, a per capita income of about $5,000 in 1985 dollars. Thus, by 1995, the United States will have as a neighbor a business partner with an economy the size of France's in 1983; Mexico would be between the sixth and eighth largest economy in the world and a full member of the world trading system.

Mexico, therefore, will require from six to ten years of favorable treatment--of compensation for asymmetry--from the international economic community and especially from its principal trading partners. Failure to do this runs the risk of wasting the effort Mexico and the international community have made for forty years and bring the danger of political instability in a country that has been able to avoid this for more than half a century.

Finally, it is essential to consider an important source of resistance to industrial cooperation and complementation between Mexico and the United States. This is the profound difference in focus and method in the two countries in managing their industrial development.

In two of the U.S. contributions to this volume (Diebold and Weintraub), it is clearly shown that the federal government of the United States has always had an industrial policy, even if it is not explicit or organic, but which is implicitly contained in commercial, fiscal, and financial policies. There have been important variations over time in the protective measures granted to U.S. industry, even if these have been limited to specific sectors. We cannot deny that the U.S. Government has been the champion in the reduction of barriers to international trade since the creation of the General Agreement on Tariffs and Trade (GATT). In recent years there has been a protectionist resurgence which, while it fortunately does not stem from a general philosophical attitude, does endanger the progress made in the past and constitutes an element of serious concern for developing countries. The opposition of the executive branch to increased protection has been encouraging.

Many U.S. Government measures are development oriented, such as fiscal, export, and insurance credits, and financing for infrastructure, industrial parks, and other facilities. An important element in U.S. development policy is that half of the more than 2.5 percent of GNP that the United States devotes each year for research and development is channeled through the military budget. There are large programs of purchases associated with the military budget which are essential for many industries. While these purchases are tied to U.S. national security, they demonstrate the inconsistency of the unceasing U.S. opposition to purchases by the state in developing countries as an instrument of industrial promotion.

Despite the foregoing, the United States has generally relied on market forces as the determining factor in its industrial development in the postwar period. This is consistent with the size of the U.S. economy and its high degree of development. It could even be said that, precisely for these reasons, the logical path for the United States to follow in the future will be to seek decentralization of resource-allocation decisions, that is, decisions of a microeconomic nature. It would be strange if that were not to take place. However, it is not acceptable for the United States to try to have every country act in the same manner. No other country has the economic strength of the United States and few have reached the level of maturity of the U.S. economy. For newly industrializing countries, the U.S. demand for full reciprocity leads to excessive pressure in relation to the time required by those nations to conclude their process of industrial maturation. This is particularly true in the case of Mexico.

The evolution in the United States toward greater decentralization of economic decision-making will make even more complex the conclusion of agreements and cooperative projects between the United States and developing countries; this evolution may require the adoption of new forms of cooperation that respond to the new situation.

Mexico's post-war experience has been different from that of the United States. Mexico's industrial development has been based on an important role of the state as protector and promoter of the economy and as an important direct participant as investor.

Mexico arrived at industrialization relatively late.

At the end of World War II, it found itself with a fast-growing population and accelerated urbanization which required urban jobs in growing numbers. It was essential to have time to overcome the lag. Mexico's managerial class was limited in number; it consisted of a few businessmen (who concentrated on the domestic market and imports) and a small number of industrialists of the traditional type. At the same time, Mexico was neighbor to the leading industrial power in the world.

The only possible road to follow--within the framework of a market economy--was that of a mixed economy in which the state, in addition to establishing the basic economic and social infrastructure conducive to development, set out an appropriate structure of protection against imports of goods and services and capital. The state encouraged national private investment, orienting it toward new activities; the state also directed foreign investment into areas of national priority and regulated the degree of control of foreigners in activities of national interest. Finally, the state rectified deficiencies of private investment in strategic and priority activities. The direct investment of the state, in light of its essentially complementary character, was directed mainly at industrial branches important to national sovereignty (oil, electricity, railroads, communications), activities that required large volumes of investment that were difficult to obtain from the private sector. The state also guaranteed the supply of strategic materials for industry.

The success of this strategy is well known. Contrary to the image that has been spread recently--of a state that tends to annul the private sector--the main success of the policy was precisely to encourage the development of a modern and vigorous Mexican entrepreneurial class which did not exist at the beginning of the process.

The change in international circumstances during the 1970s and the economic crisis of the 1980s made clear the need to introduce important changes. The first change was a more precise outline of sectoral boundaries between the public and private sectors, for which a constitutional reform was enacted (Articles 25, 26, and 28) in December, 1982. This reform, far from posing any threat of subsequent increases in property controlled directly by the state, outlined precisely the limits of the state. The nationalization of commercial banks (September, 1982) was necessary for a reason totally different from the ones given at the time; it was needed to correct structures of power and property that had become deformed. As was to be expected, it caused confusion and anxiety for many. This has begun to dissipate with the return to the private sector of all non-banking activities (which made up a significant proportion of the country's modern economy) accumulated by the nationalized banking corporations. The later granting of franchises to private investors to act in non-banking financing activity will finally dissipate these anxieties.

The second important change consists in the acceptance, once and for all, of the fact that the protectionist policy followed until now is no longer appropriate, but, rather, counter-productive. The change has begun, but it must be gradual to avoid the risk of destroying what the country has built until now with so much effort. A change of great dimensions had to be put into effect in the structure of the country's relative prices, in the relationships between farming, cattle raising, and industrial activity, between tradable and non-tradable goods, and between labor and capital. Finally, as already stated, the industrial development program is designed to fill gaps in the country's industrial structure and promote the incorporation of new high-technology activities that will set the norm for international competition during the next decade.

Mexico's industrial policy will evolve during the next few years toward a structure based primarily on market indicators, but also involving a vigorous promotional and regulatory presence of the state. The state will continue to invest in strategic sectors of the economy. The industrial development program is based on consensus with the private sector. Each sector of our mixed economy must play a role based on the modification of relative prices. The other indispensable element for this strategy to succeed is to have a favorable international environment over at least the next six to ten years. This is where cooperation and complementation with the U.S. economy becomes crucial.

It is evident that procedures to be used by Mexico and the United States during the next few years will be different. Practices in each country are the result of their diverse experiences during recent decades and the circumstances each will face in coming years.

The elements that Mexico would have to contribute to make cooperation and complementation possible are:

1. As it matures, to gradually increase the openness of its economy to foreign goods;

2. To accept that Mexico will not be able to remain forever out of the GATT, a point which will become more evident as the country gains weight in the international economy;

3. To make its foreign-investment policy more flexible while guaranteeing the constitutional exceptions permitted in this field. This flexibility is particularly necessary in high-technology areas, because much technology can be provided by small and medium enterprises that cannot be subjected to cumbersome and complex procedures. In such cases--and not necessarily limited to high-technology activities--approvals for investment would have to be automatic, based exclusively on registration requirements;

4. To maintain realistic national policy regarding relative prices;

5. To intensify communication with the U.S. Government in order to have information on economic policy and be able thereby to flexibly shape national economic policy to deal in a timely fashion with external shocks; and

6. To diversify international economic relations in order to become less dependent on the United States.

The elements the United States must contribute are:

1. To be aware that Mexico still needs six to ten years to reach economic maturity and obtain significant relief from demographic pressure. During that time, Mexico will not be able to follow the same rules as the United States and will not be able to offer full reciprocity for concessions or cooperation received from the United States;

2. To be aware that the migration of workers to the United States is essentially the result of a persistent and ample U.S. market for these workers and that the only sure way of significantly reducing the flow is to accelerate structural change in both economies;

3. To adopt mechanisms of cooperation with Mexico that will help overcome the absence of a unified voice on the U.S. side. These mechanisms would have the purposes of coordinating, putting in contact, and promoting projects between enterprises of the two countries;

4. To continue to open its economy and to maintain existing preference schemes for the time required for Mexico to reach maturity;

5. To intensify communication with the Mexican Government to permit prompt U.S. reaction to events in Mexico and to take into account the repercussions of U.S. policies on the Mexican economy;

6. Enlarge and give greater flexibility to the monetary swap agreement between the two countries; and

7. To reduce real interest rates.

NOTES

[1]Luis Maira, "Los Estados Unidos y La América Latina," in Luis Maira, ed., Historia y Percepciones Mutuas Estados Unidos, Una Visión Latino-Americana (Mexico: Fondo de Cultura Económica, Colección Lecturas, No. 53, 1984), pp. 491-509.

[2]H.E. Bolton, "The Big Epic of the Great America," American Historical Review, 38 (1983), pp. 448-479.

[3]Octavio Paz, Sor Juana Ines de la Cruz: Las Trampas de la Fe. (Mexico: Fondo de Cultura Económica, 1982.) Subsequent references to Octavio Paz are from this same source.

[4]Francisco Javier Alejo, "Demographic Patterns and Labor Market Trends in Mexico" in D. L. Wyman, ed., Mexico's Economic Crisis: Challenges and Opportunities (University of California, San Diego: Center for U.S.-Mexican Studies, Monograph Series, No. 12, 1983), pp. 78-79.

List of Contributors

Lic. Francisco Javier Alejo is currently serving as vice-president of the International Financial Corporation of the World Bank. He received a bachelor's degree and a master's degree in British economics from Universidad Nacional Autónoma de México (UNAM). Among his previous positions were Minister for National Patrimony, adviser to the Minister of Finance, and Ambassador of Mexico to Japan.

Francisco José Barnés is currently serving as Director General of the Chemical and Petrochemical Industry, SENIP. He received a degree in chemical engineering from Universidad Nacional Autónoma de México in 1967, and a master's degree and a doctorate degree in chemical engineering (1973) from the University of California at Berkeley. He has been the coordinator of the chemical engineering department and secretary general of the chemistry department at UNAM. Among his published works are *Ingeniería de Procesos* (1979). He is a member of the American Institute of Chemical Engineers, the Federación de Profesionales de la Industria Quimica, and the Mexican Institute of Chemical Engineers. He has received the Premio Banamex de Ciencia y Tecnología and Premio Celanese de Tecnología y Quimica.

Gerardo Bueno received a master's degree in economics from Yale University. He has an extensive publications record. He is currently consultant to the Inter-American Development Bank and a research associate at El Colegio de México. He served in senior positions in both the Mexican government and international institutions.

Ing. Gustavo Cortés is currently serving as Director General of the steel company Hojalata y Lámina, S.A. (HYLSA), President of the National Board for the Iron and Steel Industry, and adviser to several mining companies.

He received engineering and business administration degrees
(an MBA) from the Technological Institute of Monterrey.

Prof. José Luis Fernández Santisteban is now an
economic researcher at the Centro de Investigación y
Docencia Económicas (CIDE) and adviser to the Ministry of
Health. He received a bachelor's degree in economics from
the Universidad Complutense of Madrid, Spain, and a master's
degree in economics from Cambridge University, England. He
worked previously with the Ministry of National Patrimony,
and served as coordinator of Mexico's Northern Border
Research Program, a CIDE project.

Dr. Rafael Rubio is the assistant director for economic
studies of the private industrial *Grupo Alfa* and the planning manager of HYLSA, the *Grupo's* steel plant. He is also
the director of budget and planning for the Fishing Commission of Baja California Norte. He received a bachelor's
degree in economics from El Tecnológico de Monterrey, 1972,
and a master's and doctorate degrees in economics from
Cornell University. He worked previously with the Presi-
dential Commission for Economic and Social Planning.

Prof. Jesús Tamayo received a degree in architecture
from Universidad Nacional Autónoma de México and a master's
degree in urban development from El Colegio de México.
From 1964 to 1976 he worked as an architect and was also a
visiting professor at UNAM. He joined CIDE in 1978, where
he is currently Coordinator of Regional Studies. He is
author of many articles and books dealing with Mexico's
northern border.

Dr. René Villarreal Arrambide is a former Undersecretary for Planning for SECOFI. He received his bachelor's
degree in economics from Universidad de Nuevo León (1969),
and his master's in economics from El Colegio de México
(1971), and his Ph.D. in economics from Yale University
(1975). He has held several positions in government:
assistant to the Undersecretary of Finance; Director
General and Technical Secretary of the Coordinating Commission, Industrial Policy for the Public Sector; and Director
of International Finance and Deputy Director of General
Planning of the Ministry of Finance.

Dr. Robert Crandall is a Senior Fellow at the Brookings
Institution, specializing in industrial organization,
antitrust policy and regulation. He taught economics at
George Washington University, the Massachusetts Institute of
Technology, and Northwestern University. Dr. Crandall has
served as a consultant or advisor to the Council on Wage and
Price Stability, the Environmental Protection Agency, the
Federal Trade Commission, the Urban Institute, and the

Department of Justice. Dr. Crandall has published a volume
on *Controlling Industrial Pollution: The Economics and
Politics of Clean Air* and another on *The U.S. Steel Industry
in Recurrent Crisis*. He also has co-edited a study at
Brookings entitled *The Scientific Basis of Health and Safety
Regulation*.

Dr. William H. Diebold, a graduate of Swarthmore College, did graduate work at Yale University and the London
School of Economics. He joined the Council on Foreign
Relations in 1939, working until 1943 in the Council's War
and Peace Studies on problems of the postwar order. From
1943 to 1945 he was in the Office of Strategic Services,
followed by a stay of comparable length in the Commercial
Policy Division of the Department of State. He returned to
the Council on Foreign Relations where he stayed until his
retirement in 1983. His work at the Council covered a wide
range of international economic issues and American foreign
economic policy, about which he published several books and
pamphlets and a number of articles. A reassessment of U.S.
foreign economic policy, *The United States and the Industrial World*, led to an interest in industrial policy which
he has pursued ever since. He published a book, *Industrial
Policy as an International Issue* (McGraw Hill, 1980) and was
the North American author of a study of industrial policy
for the Trilateral Commission.

Dr. Jerry Ladman, an economist, is director of the
Center for Latin American Studies at Arizona State Univer-
sity. He has undertaken research on Mexican topics for
twenty years. He worked at the Mexico City Office of the
Ford Foundation and was visiting professor at the Graduate
College of the National Agricultural University in Chapingo.
He is the author of many books and articles on U.S.-Mexican
relations.

Dr. Clark W. Reynolds is Professor of Economics at the
Food Research Institute at Stanford University. He has
served as visiting professor and research scholar at El
Colegio de México, the International Institute for Applied
Systems Analysis (IIASA, Laxenburg, Austria), the Brookings
Institution, the Wilson Center for Latin American Studies
(Washington, D.C.), St. Antony's College, Oxford, and the
National Autonomous University of Mexico (UNAM). At
Stanford, Dr. Reynolds coordinates the U.S.-Mexico Project.
He is the author of many books and articles, including *The
Mexican Economy Twentieth Century Structure and Growth*.

Dr. Stanley R. Ross was an historian who specialized in
the twentieth-century history of Mexico, emphasizing the
Mexican Revolution and its aftermath. He also devoted

considerable time to the analysis of the Mexican political
system. Dr. Ross was elected a Corresponding Member of the
Mexican National Academy of History and was the recipient of
the Mexican Order of the Aztec Eagle from the Mexican
government. His extensive publications include a biography
of Francisco I. Madero, co-editor of the two-volume *Historia
Documental de México,* and coordinator for the five volumes:
*Fuentes de la Historia Contemporánea de Mexico: Periódicos
y Revistas.* More recently he edited *Ecology and Development
of the Border Region.* He was the first holder of the C.B.
Smith Sr. Centennial Chair in U.S.-Mexico Relations at The
University of Texas at Austin.

Neil D. Schuster joined the International Affairs
Department of the Motor Vehicle Manufacturer's Association
in 1983 and currently serves as Senior Analyst. He is
responsible for association activities with respect to
international trade and investment issues. He also serves
on a Department of Commerce private sector advisory group
on U.S.-Mexico automotive trade issues under the auspices of
the U.S.-Mexico Joint Commission on Commerce and Trade. He
has an undergraduate degree in economics and an MBA degree
from the University of Colorado.

Dr. Sidney Weintraub is Dean Rusk Professor at the
Lyndon Baines Johnson School of Public Affairs at The
University of Texas at Austin. Before entering academe,
Dr. Weintraub served as a career diplomat for more than a
quarter of a century. Among his seven books and more than
fifty monographs and articles, Dr. Weintraub is the author
of *Free Trade Between Mexico and the United States?,* and
co-author of *Temporary Alien Workers in the United States*
and *Economic Stabilization in Developing Countries.* His
responsibilities during his governmental career included
monetary, trade, development and political-military issues.
Dr. Weintraub serves as a consultant to private companies
and various U.S. government agencies and commissions.

Index